Winning Airlines:

Productivity and Cost Competitiveness of the World's Major Airlines

Transportation Research, Economics and Policy

VOLUME 6

The titles published in this series are listed at the end of this volume.

Winning Airlines:

Productivity and Cost Competitiveness of the World's Major Airlines

By

TAE HOON OUM
University of British Columbia

and

CHUNYAN YU
University of British Columbia

KLUWER ACADEMIC PUBLISHERS
Boston / Dordrecht / London

Distributors for North America:
Kluwer Academic Publishers
101 Philip Drive
Assinippi Park
Norwell, Massachusetts 02061 USA

Distributors for all other countries:
Kluwer Academic Publishers Group
Distribution Centre
Post Office Box 322
3300 AH Dordrecht, THE NETHERLANDS

Library of Congress Cataloging-in-Publication Data

Oum, Tae Hoon.
    Winning airlines : productivity and cost competitiveness of the
world's major airlines / by Tae Hoon Oum and Chunyan Yu.
        p.   cm. -- (Transportation research, economics and policy ; v. 6)
    Includes bibliographical references and index.
    ISBN 0-7923-8010-X
    1. Airlines--Cost of operation. 2. Aeronautics, Commercial--
Management. 3. Competition, International.   I. Yu, Chunyan.
II. Title. III. Series.
HE9782.O58   1997
387.7'1--dc21   97-41219
                                                                                CIP

Printed on acid-free paper

Printed in the United States of America

Contents

Figures

Tables

Preface

Major institutional, regulatory, and structural changes have occurred in international air transport during the past two decades. Many countries have deregulated their domestic airline industries and open skies continental blocs have formed in Europe and North America. A movement is now underway to create a liberalized continental bloc in Australasia. International air transport has been substantially liberalized due to the diminishing role of IATA as an industry cartel, and via a series of liberalized bilateral agreements signed between many countries, including the U.S. and U.K. Increased liberalization and continentalization have induced major airlines to create global service networks through inter-carrier alliances. And all these changes are intensifying competition between major carriers in both domestic and international markets.

The increased competition and economic recession in the early 1990s led many airlines to massive financial losses, forcing them to undertake major restructuring to improve efficiency and reduce costs. Although it is important for an airline to map out proper strategies in the globalizing airline industry, the ultimate ability of a carrier to survive and prosper in increasingly competitive markets greatly depends on its productivity and cost competitiveness.

There are many books available on the airline industry. Most of these books deal with deregulation, public policy issues, and airline strategies. But as far as is known to us, there is no book which provides a systematic analysis of airline cost competitiveness. Yet, cost competitiveness is, perhaps, the most important determinant for a firm's success. This is an important reason why we decided to write this book, which focuses on fundamental issues related to airline productivity, input prices, exchange rate dynamics, and unit cost competitiveness. It also examines underlying trends in the airline industry and regulatory policies involving international air services, utilizing the latest information available. This book can be viewed as an important milestone in airline research by Tae Oum and his colleagues. A majority of their research outputs are on various issues related to productivity and costs. Tae Oum and ChunyanYu conducted research together over four years to build up a comprehensive data base to analyze the airline industry. This book is a keystone output from their efforts.

We hope to target this book to airline managers, government policy makers and regulators, academics, industry researchers, university students studying air transport, cost, and productivity management, international organizations such as ICAO, IATA, WTO, the European Commission, AEA, consultants, and others interested in airlines or airline industry. Although this book limits its investigation to the issues facing the airline industry, it is noted that issues addressed and methodologies used in this study could be fruitfully used for investigation of productivity and competitiveness problems facing many other industries or firms engaged in international business or any other service industry.

We gratefully acknowledge that during the course of writing this book we benefited significantly from past and on-going studies Tae Oum conducted with his colleagues, including Shelby Brumelle, Hong-Min Chen, Martin Dresner, David W. Gillen, Richard Harris, Jong Hur, Micheal Z.F. Li, Jeff McGill, Yoon-Keun Pang, Jong-Hun Park, Hamish Taylor, Michael W. Tretheway, Bill Waters, JongSay Yong,

Anming Zhang, Yimin Zhang. The authors are also thankful for comments and suggestions received from executives of Asiana Airlines, British Airways, Japan Airlines, Korean Air, Lufthansa, Singapore Airlines, Boeing Commerical Aircraft Co., and from participants of seminars given at the seventh triennial World Conference on Transportation Research (Sydney, Australia: July 1995), Osaka University (1995), University of Victoria (1995), University of California -Berkeley (1995), Canadian Transportation Research Forum (1996), Korea Transport Institute (1996), American Economic Association's Transportation and Public Utility Group Conference (New Orleans, January 1997), Inha University (Korea, May 1997), University of Hong Kong (May 1997), and City University of Hong Kong (May 1997), and Air Transport Research Group Conference (June 1997). And the authors would also like to acknowledge competent research assistance of Danny Chan, Jason Chuang, Terence Fan, Paolo Federico, Andy Fok, Anne Park, and Angelica Sparolin.

The authors would like to thank all of the airlines who kindly supplied additional data for this research upon our requests, and also, to the airlines who supplied annual reports and other publications to us every year. Special thanks go to Avmark Aviation who supplied data on aircraft leasing prices for our study. Both of us thank our families for the unending support they provided us during our countless long days of work.

During the last fifteen years, Tae Oum and his associates' airline research have been financially supported by three strategic research grant programs of the Social Science and Humanities Research Council (SSHRC) of Canada. The authors gratefully acknowledge the SSHRC research grants' support.

The views expressed in this book are those of the authors and should not be ascribed to those persons or organizations whose assistance is acknowledged.

Tae Hoon Oum and Chunyan Yu
Vancouver, Canada

Chapter 1
Introduction

The airline industry is a vital part of the world economy. In 1996, the world had approximately 1,200 scheduled airlines, of which 300 served international markets. In 1996, International Air Transport Association's (IATA) 255 member airlines collectively earned US$134.3 billion from international scheduled services. Also, the mere existence of the commercial airline industry is an important reason why the world has airports, air traffic control and navigation systems, and commercial aircraft industries. The airline industry is perhaps far more important than the amount of total revenues earned by all these industries. That is, it plays a key role in development of the world economy, tourism and related activities, by facilitating international trade and economic relations between countries and by stimulating exchange of people and ideas.

Since US deregulation of its domestic airline markets, many countries, including the United Kingdom, New Zealand, Chile, Canada, and Australia, have deregulated or substantially liberalized their domestic markets. International skies have also been substantially liberalized since the early 1980s. Liberalization of the international airline industry, to a large extent, mirrors development in trade liberalization. For example, open skies continental blocs closely follow formation of trading blocs in North America and Europe. As of April 1, 1997, 15-nation EU member countries, Norway, and Iceland formed a single aviation market. The United States and Canada signed an open skies agreement in February of 1995. And Australia and New Zealand have also formed a nearly open skies air transport bloc. As a result, international airlines face similar problems as firms in other globalizing industries. Like many other industries, the international airline industry is becoming increasingly exposed to the pressures of the market-place as deregulation and liberalization processes advance. Increased liberalization and continentalization have induced major airlines to create global service networks through inter-carrier alliances.

Increased competition and the recent recession led to severe and widespread losses in the international airline industry, forcing many airlines to undertake major restructuring to improve productivity and reduce costs. Although it is important for an airline to map out proper strategies in the globalizing airline industry, the ultimate ability of a carrier to survive and prosper in increasingly competitive markets greatly depends on its productivity and cost competitiveness.

What constitutes cost competitiveness of an airline? In simple terms, an airline is cost competitive if its unit costs are consistently lower than that of competitors. An airline may have lower unit costs than its competitors because it is more efficient, pays less for inputs, or both. That is, airline cost differentials are determined by differences in input prices and productive efficiency. Knowledge about existing levels and sources of cost differentials are essential for analysing public policies and strategies designed to enhance airline competitive positions.

Despite the importance of factors determining cost competitiveness, few studies in international business have systematically investigated this issue. Some studies examined competitiveness of a nation (see for example Porter, 1990) and some compared international competitiveness of specific industries in different countries. The latter studies, such as Toyne, Arpan, Barnett, Ricks, and Shimp (1984) and Doyle, Saunders and

Wong (1992), have generally focused on organizational strategies and comparative management. One exception is Mefford (1986), who attempted to explain the labor productivity differences between plants in a multinational consumer goods firm. However, he did not attempt to relate productivity differences to plant competitive positions. Few studies have examined contribution of various factors to the intensity and dynamics of international competitiveness, particularly to cost competitiveness. Such factors include input price differences, productivity differentials, corporate strategies, differences in market conditions, etc. In a recent survey article, Wright and Ricks (1994) acknowledged lack of research in this area by listing "comparative cost factors" as a major area for future research recommended by a committee of experts in international business.

In the transportation and applied economics areas, a number of studies have focused on airline productivity and efficiency. These include Caves, Christensen, Tretheway and Windle (1987), Gillen, Oum and Tretheway (1985, 1990), Bauer (1990), Encaoua (1991), Good, Nadiri, Röller, and Sickles (1993), Ray and Hu (1993), Distexhe and Perelman (1993), and Good, Röller, and Sickles (1995). Few studies, however, have examined the issue of airline cost competitiveness. Windle (1991) attempted to attribute unit cost differences between carriers to various sources. His study was based mainly on 1983 annual data for 14 US and 27 non-US airlines. Good and Rhodes (1991) examined three aspects of competitiveness and profitability of airlines in the Pacific region, using a panel of 37 airlines over the 1976-86 period. A recent study by Baltagi, Griffin and Rich (1995) used panel data from 24 US airlines over 1971-86. They analysed cost changes in the pre- and post-deregulation US airline industry and identified cost changes due to technical change, economies of scale and density, and input prices. Since the industry structure and regulations have changed considerably since the mid-1980s, these previous studies have become outdated.

There are many books available on the airline industry. Some deal with government policy toward industry or carrier network and globalization strategies, and some are basically descriptive about the industry. To our knowledge, no previous book has focused on measuring and comparing cost competitiveness of the world's major airlines using the latest data available. *This book will focus on fundamental issues related to productivity, input prices, exchange rate dynamics, global sourcing of airline labour, maintenance, and other services, and unit cost competitiveness of the airlines.* That is, this book mainly examines the supply side of air transport services, where airline management has considerable control. It will also examine underlying trends in the airline industry and provide systematic analysis of airline productivity and cost competitiveness using the latest available data.

This book aims to accomplish four major goals. First, it will provide a review of trends in international air transport's regulatory and business environments. Second, it will provide practical insights on various determinants of airline cost and productivity performance. Third, it will attempt to improve and apply existing methodologies to compare productivity and unit costs across airlines having different route network, serving different markets, and headquartered in different countries. And fourth, it will identify aspects of airline strategy, planning, and operations in which airline management and public policy makers should focus efforts to enhance cost competitiveness in increasingly competitive and globalizing airline markets.

The book is organized in the following manner. Chapter 2 sets out to describe the relationship between world economic growth and air traffic growth by geographic region. It also reviews long term industry trends including yields (revenue per unit of output), financial performance, globalization trends, and inter-airline alliances.

Chapter 3 reviews developments and the current status of regulatory environments in the international air transport industry. This includes development of the European Union single aviation market, the U.S.-Canada open skies agreement, and liberalization initiatives in Asia. Chapter 4 provides preliminary analysis of operating and network characteristics, and input factor prices for airlines included in our study. It also examines the relationship between exchange rates and input prices, and growing global sourcing of input factors.

Chapter 5 examines the efficiency of airlines' use of inputs for production. This is done after removing the effects of variables beyond airline managerial control. It includes efficiencies of using labor, fuel, capital (aircraft fleet and ground properties and equipment), and other purchased materials and services. In Chapter 6, the overall productive efficiency is measured and compared across airlines and over time within an airline, using two alternative approaches: the so-called total factor productivity (TFP) approach and the stochastic frontier production function approach. Major airlines in North America, Europe, and Asia are rated in terms of their overall productive efficiencies.

Chapter 7 provides a preliminary analysis of airline cost structures and effects of exogenous factors on airline costs. It includes a review of shares of labor, fuel, capital, and purchased materials and services input as part of total airline costs, input prices, and exchange rate impacts on input prices. Chapter 8 measures and compares airline cost competitiveness, which depends on input prices and efficiency. Observed unit cost differentials across airlines and over time within an airline are decomposed based on the effects of input price differences, productive efficiency, and variables beyond managerial control. Unit cost differentials attributable to differences in input price and productive efficiency are used as cost competitiveness (CC) indicators. Major airlines in North America, Europe, and Asia are rated in terms of their cost competitiveness. Exchange rate impacts on cost competitiveness are also analysed.

In Chapter 9, trends in average yield, unit cost, and financial performance are reviewed for each airline individually and as a group for each geographic region. The results are used to make comments on what each airline must do to improve profitability. And Chapter 10 provides a summary of findings, conclusions, and further research needed.

Chapter 2
The International Air Transport Industry

The international air transport plays a key role in the development of the world economy, stimulating exchanges between countries and facilitating international economic relations. At the same time, its economic well-being depends on the state of the world economy. Increasing demand for mobility, further globalization of society, and changing consumer behaviour lead to growth in traffic flow and segmentation of the air transport industry. Economic downturns, on the other hand, bring financial difficulties to the airlines - difficulties which at times have been financially disastrous.

This chapter examines major historical trends in the international air transport industry over the past decade in relation to development of the world economy as well as technological developments and innovations. It also reviews recent development in international airline alliances.

2.1 Air Traffic Growth and Economic Growth

The international air transport market experienced particularly rapid growth in the 1960s because of widespread economic expansion and the development of faster and more productive aircraft. In the 15 years between 1955 and 1969, annual growths in the world scheduled air passenger traffic averaged about 14 percent. Then, the first oil shock in 1973 slowed down world economic growth. World GDP growth fell to almost zero in 1975 from 6 percent in 1972, and this undoubtedly also slowed air traffic growth. However, the world economy quickly recovered from the recession. Consequently, air traffic experienced significant growth between 1977 and 1979, at an average rate of 11.5 percent per year. Part of this growth was due to the emergence of cheaper services provided by charter carriers (mostly in Europe, and to a lesser extent, in North America and Asia). In the 10 years from 1970 to 1979, the average annual growth rate of world air traffic was just below 10 percent, while the average annual world GDP growth rate was about 4.2 percent. This observation supports the proposition that air traffic growth has an income elasticity of approximate two (Tretheway and Oum, 1992 p.115). That is, for a one percent increase in world economy, air traffic level would increase by about two percent.

The economic cycle repeated its course during the early 1980s. World economic recession, reinforced by a second oil shock, led to low traffic growth and unprecedented losses for the international airline industry. By 1985, the world economy had recovered, and so had air traffic growth. Thus, between 1986 and 1990, the world economy, and consequently the airline industry, had a few years of "good fortune". Rapid economic growths helped bring about dramatic improvements in airline profitability worldwide. However, this "good fortune" vanished in 1991 as a result of the Gulf War and another economic recession.

Figure 2.1a shows changes in the level of world GDP during the period 1980-1994. Note that world GDP level is measured in constant prices and normalized at 1990 level. Figure 2.1b plots the annual growth rate of world GDP during the same period. The figures clearly indicate that the world economy was in recession between 1980 and 1982, with GDP growth rate being less than half a percent in 1982. Following the recession, world GDP growth improved substantially between 1982 and 1984, experiencing approximately a 4 percent growth. The world economy then experienced a slight downturn in 1985 and 1986, but was able to quickly recover before it started to slow down again, moving towards the 1991 economic recession. The GDP growth rate made a considerable recovery in 1992, and bounced back to the 1988 level in 1994, after slight staggering in 1993.

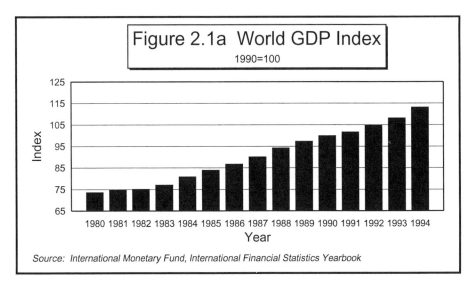

Figure 2.1a World GDP Index
1990=100

Source: International Monetary Fund, International Financial Statistics Yearbook

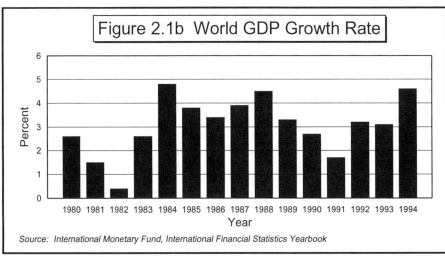

Figure 2.1b World GDP Growth Rate

Source: International Monetary Fund, International Financial Statistics Yearbook

Air traffic level is closely related to the overall level of economic activity. For example, the relatively prosperous countries of North America and Europe generally have higher levels of air transport activity compared to less developed countries (IATA, 1991). Figure 2.2a shows changes in the world's total number of scheduled air passengers during the 1980-1995 period, while figure 2.2b shows corresponding revenue passenger kilometres (RPK). It can be seen that the world's air traffic consistently increased until 1991. In fact, the demand for air travel increased through the 1980s at an average rate of six percent per year, while the world GDP growth averaged at about 3 percent during the same period. The economic recession and Gulf War caused a dip in air traffic in 1991, the first time in over forty years. The lower traffic level in 1991 occurred despite deep discounting of fares by many airlines. However, there was a strong recovery in the following year, consistent with the general economic recovery. International passenger traffic increased by over 11 percent in 1992, the first double-digit growth since 1988, one of the industry's best years. Of course, this is growth measured against a very bad year in 1991. Domestic traffic, however, did not grow as much. Domestic traffic level were actually 1.9 percent below those for 1990. As a result, total world air traffic (both domestic and international) increased by about 5 percent in 1992. 1993 saw a modest increase in revenue passenger kilometres (RPK), but a slight decline in the total number of passengers carried. 1994 was marked by the strongest traffic performance of the "Nervous 90s". According to *Air Transport World*, the world's airlines achieved an 11 percent increase in passengers carried, a 12 percent increase in RPKs, and a 14.2 percent jump in freight traffic. World air traffic continues its upward trend into the second half of the 1990s. The latest industry forecasts (Boeing, 1997) suggest that the demand for air travel will continue to grow between 1997 and 2006, at an average rate of 5.5 percent each year - twice the projected rate of world economic growth, indicating a doubling in the volume of traffic every twelve years.

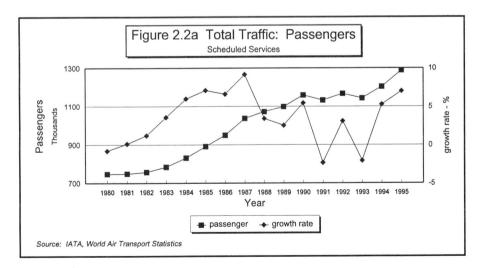

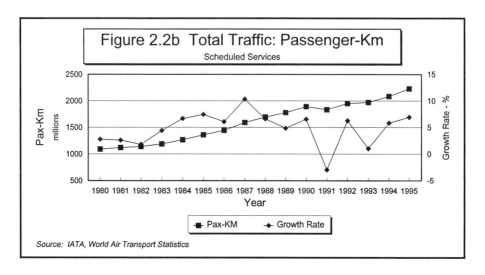

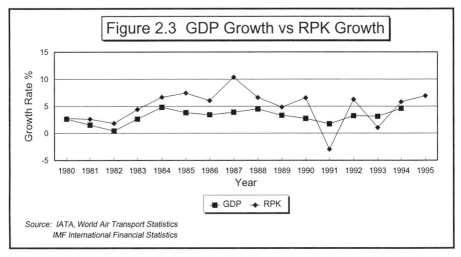

Figure 2.3 compares world GDP growth and RPK growth. It shows that there is a strong pro-cyclical relationship between the air transport industry and the world economy. That is, air traffic growth generally expands (or contracts) with increased (or reduced) economic growth, but at a much faster rate. For example, GDP growth rate decreased by about 3 percent between 1988 and 1991 due to economic recession. At the same time, the RPK growth rate decreased by more than 9 percent, which was three times the change of world GDP. Following the recession, the world GDP growth rate increased

by about 3 percent between 1991 and 1994, while the RPK growth rate increased by 8.8 percent during the same period. Therefore, the cyclical nature of economic growth indicates that future air traffic growth will occur in cycles within the industry with marked peaks and troughs.

Air traffic growth varies among different regions of the world. The Asia-Pacific market has enjoyed rapid growth in commercial air traffic during the past two decades, due mostly to dynamic economic development in the region. During 1989-1996, the region recorded an average annual growth rate of 7.9 percent, contrasted with the United States market, which grew at an average of 4.0 percent per year (see Figure 2.4a). The predicted annual RPK growth rate between 1997 and 2006 is about 7 percent for Asia, and 5.2 percent and 4.2 percent for Europe and North America, respectively (Boeing, 1997). The rapid growth in Asia-Pacific is changing the structure of the international airline industry. Twenty years ago, the Asia-Pacific region contributed less than 10 percent to the world's air traffic, but in 1996 it accounted for 24 percent. Its share in international scheduled passenger traffic is even larger: 26.5 percent in 1985, 35.3 percent in 1993, and is predicted to increase to 41 percent in 2000, and 51 percent in 2010 (see Figure 2.4b). According to Boeing (1997), air traffic growth in Asia-Pacific will account for 32.4 percent of the world's total air traffic growth over the next decade, while North America and Europe will account for 27.2 percent and 23.3 percent of the growth, respectively.

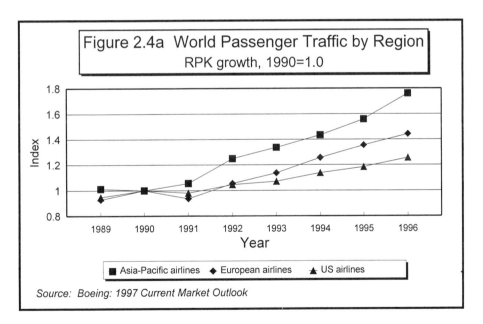

Figure 2.4a World Passenger Traffic by Region
RPK growth, 1990=1.0

Source: Boeing: 1997 Current Market Outlook

Figure 2.4b Asia-Pacific Share of World
International Scheduled Passengers

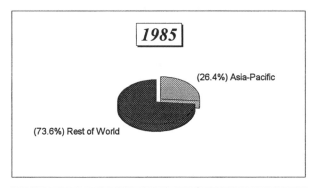

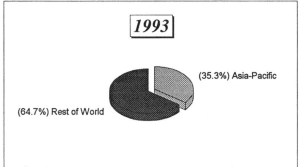

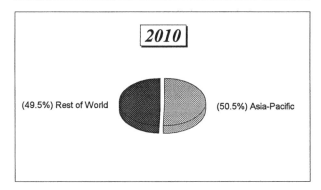

Source: Asia-Pacific Air Transport Forecast 1980-2010. Geneva: IATA, 1995.

2.2 Financial Performance

Despite years of unbroken traffic growth, the industry has not been able to produce healthy profit margins[1]. The main reason is that yields have not been high enough to cover costs. During the 1960-90 period, yields in real terms declined by 2.2 percent per annum for passengers and by 3.4 percent per annum for freight (Figure 2.5a). During the same period, unit costs (operating costs per available kilometre) declined in real terms at an average rate of only 1.9 percent per annum (Figure 2.5b).

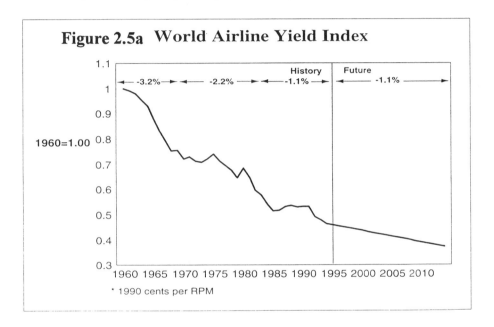

Figure 2.5a   World Airline Yield Index

Source: Boeing, *Current Market Outlook 1996*, page 27

Technological development, increasing globalization of the world economy, and increase in personal disposal income are among the factors which have increased demand for air travel worldwide. These factors, however, are beyond the airlines' control. Airlines' main lever to stimulate traffic growth is to reduce fares, and at the same time, to enhance quality of service. Fare reduction means reduced revenue yields for the airlines. Thus, airlines must be able to cut costs accordingly in order to remain financially viable. During most of the 1960s, unit costs declined steadily because of improved aircraft productivity, made possible by new technology, and because of the absence of significant factor price increases. As a result, there was a dramatic improvement in airlines' profit margins. During the 1970s, world prices began to rise rapidly because of wide-spread

---

[1] Of course, some individual airlines have managed to perform very well and have been able to obtain substantial profits.

inflation, especially fuel prices, following the fuel crisis of 1973 and 1978. The airlines tried to counteract the upwards pressure on costs by introducing new technology and by exerting more effective cost control. As a result of their efforts, airlines' costs did not rise as rapidly as world prices. In fact, during the 1970s, airline costs remained stable or moved slowly downward (Figure 2.5b) in real (constant) terms. However, a world-wide recession increases pressure on passenger and freight yields. The combined effects of upward pressure on costs and downward pressure on revenue yields pushed many airlines to a struggle for financial survival. With maturing technology, cost reduction was hence becoming more and more difficult. Consequently, airlines have been, and are still, increasingly under financial pressure.

Figure 2.5b World Airline Unit Cost Index

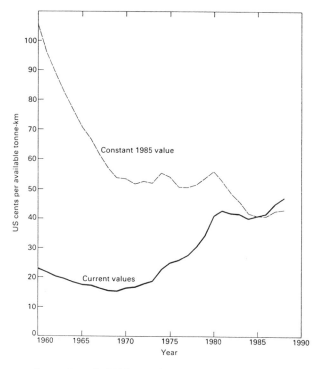

Source: Doganis (1991), page 4

In 1980, the world's airlines collectively suffered from an operating loss for the first time since 1961. Further operating losses occurred in 1981 and 1982[2]. Several airlines went bankrupt during this period, including Braniff and Laker Airways, while many others relied on financial support from their national governments. Note that despite all these negative pressures, some airlines, particularly rapidly growing Asian carriers such

---

[2] After paying interests, IATA member airlines collectively lost US$1.85 billion in 1980, US$1.9 billion in 1981, and US$1.8 billion in 1982.

as Singapore Airlines, were able to benefit from their low labour costs and high growth rates in their markets and thus operate profitably. Airlines that were able to achieve higher load factors, or reduce costs in real terms, or both, also continued to operate profitably.

Strong growth in demand in the late 1980s, and a significant fall in the real price of aviation fuel translated into improved profit margins for the industry. Figure 2.6 shows changes in aircraft fuel prices since 1980. Figure 2.7 shows airline nominal yields (measured by operating revenue per tonne-kilometre performed) and unit costs (measured by operating expenses per available tonne-kilometre) for IATA member airlines' scheduled services. Figure 2.8 then shows the corresponding operating and net results. Fuel prices remained relatively low during the second half of the 1980s, and airlines were able to make some improvements in their revenue yields (even in real terms as shown in Figure 2.5a) prior to 1989[3]. As a result, the airlines that had been making losses for years suddenly found themselves in profit, especially during 1987 and 1988.

True to the cyclical nature of the airline industry, this period of well-being was bound to be disrupted. A world-wide economic recession, aggravated by the Gulf War, pushed the industry back to a deep slump in 1990. The slow growth in demand was greeted, in 1990, by the delivery of a record number of aeroplanes ordered during the boom years of the 1980s[4]. Disruption in demand, excess capacity, coupled with the inability to raise fares due to pressure from fierce competition, led to record losses in the industry. The financial losses were widespread and severe (Figure 2.8). This sudden turnaround from the "good fortune" presented a particularly difficult situation for many airlines. Some 70 carriers went out of business as a result, including three large US carriers (Pan Am, Eastern, and Midway). Robert Crandall, chairman of American Airlines, stated that the two years, 1990 and 1991, wiped out all profits US airlines had made since the commencement of air travel (Hendersen, 1992). According to IATA estimates, IATA member airlines collectively incurred a net loss of US$15.6 billion from their international scheduled services during the four years 1990-1993.

Many airlines experienced painful restructuring to reduce cost, and build up market strength. By the mid-1990s, airlines had restrained capacity growth, increased load factor, and aggressively reduced costs. Worldwide economic recovery and stable fuel prices also benefited the airlines. These combined effects led to improved operating profits. In 1994, IATA member airlines were back in the black with a collective surplus of US$1.8 billion from international scheduled services. Airline financial results were further improved in 1995, with a 7.9 percent increase in international passenger traffic. IATA members' collective operating profits from international scheduled services was US$8.9 billion (US$14.3 billion from all services) in 1995, which resulted in a US$5.2 billion (US$4.1 billion from all services) net income. However, according to IATA, only 70 percent of its members reported profits in 1995, which means that the other 30% were still in the red. Overall, the industry is getting back into shape, but there are still winners and losers.

---

[3]Since the 1980s, all airlines in the United States and many major airlines in the rest of the world have adopted a more rational pricing practice, called "yield (revenue) management". This may have contributed to the increased average yield in the late 1980s.

[4] Orders for commercial jet peaked in 1989, with a total worth of US$96 billion (in 1991 dollars).

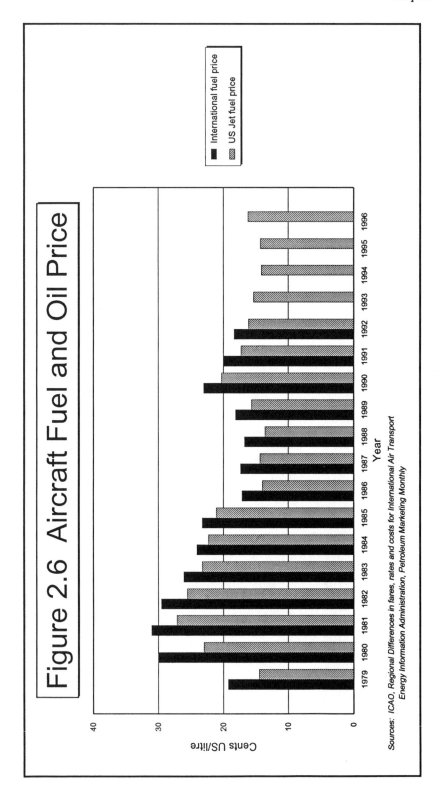

Figure 2.6 Aircraft Fuel and Oil Price

Sources: ICAO, Regional Differences in fares, rates and costs for International Air Transport
Energy Information Administration, Petroleum Marketing Monthly

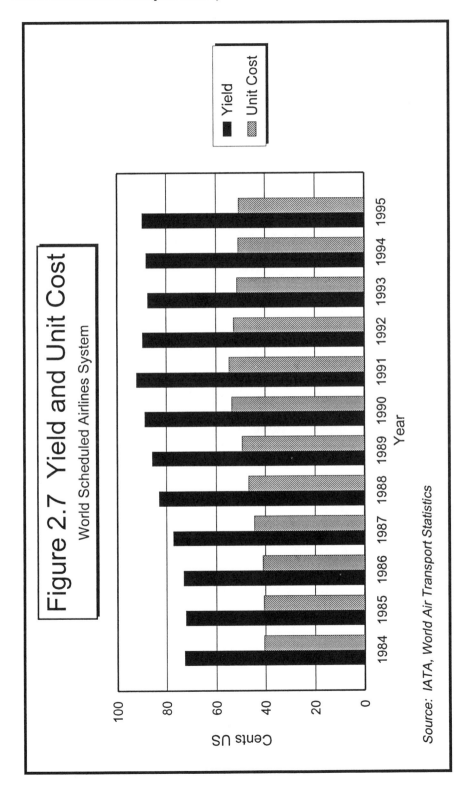

Figure 2.7 Yield and Unit Cost

World Scheduled Airlines System

Source: IATA, World Air Transport Statistics

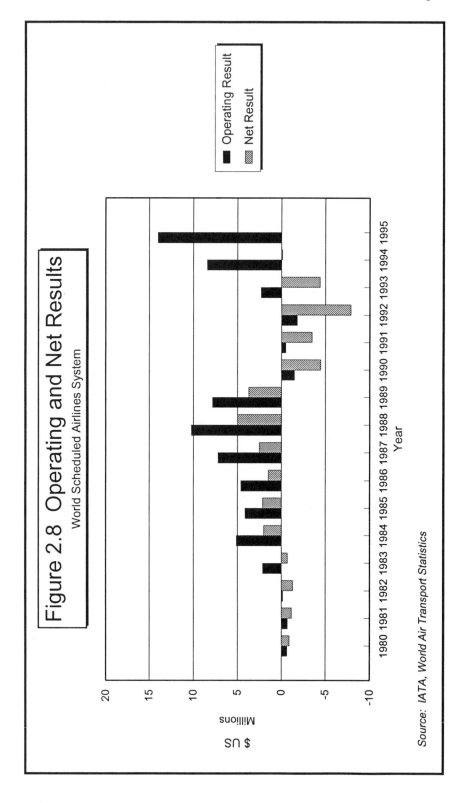

Figure 2.8 Operating and Net Results

World Scheduled Airlines System

Source: IATA, World Air Transport Statistics

2.3 Alliance and Globalization

Over the years, airlines have been constantly revising their growth and competitive strategies to survive and prosper. Airline growth and competitive strategies not only include cost cutting measures and better revenue management tools, but also strategic alliances with other airlines. Airlines construct alliances to gain access to global networks within the constraints of the current bilateral air services agreement (ASA) system. In many cases, they have entered into code-share agreements to maintain or expand network coverage. International codesharing has now become part of bilateral negotiations.

Alliances are formed as a means of forming global service networks. They allow airlines to access and establish identity in new markets without providing aircrafts and/or having full traffic rights, and to provide services which would be unprofitable if operated alone. Alliances also create a marketing advantage for the alliance partners. Consumers have demonstrated a preference for dealing with airlines with large service networks to minimize their own cost of travel, to get better services, and to take advantage of more attractive frequent flyer programs. Alliances can also lead to better access at congested airports, where landing restrictions, lack of landing and take-off slots, and other constraints would otherwise exist. Moreover, alliances can reduce costs through economies of scale associated with joint marketing, maintenance, ground facilities, training, CRS, purchasing of aircraft and fuel, and through elimination of duplication and redundancy in operation. The overall aim of alliances is to enhance partner airlines' competitive position, and to achieve higher profits for each of the partners.

The first international alliance in aviation was between Air Florida and British Island in 1986. Air Florida fed US originating traffic to British Island's flights on the London-Amsterdam route, where both airlines codeshared. Since then there has been a frenzy of alliance formations in the industry. According to *Airline Business* (1996), there were a total of 389 airline alliances by mid-1996 involving 171 carriers, a 19 percent increase over 1995 and a 39 percent increase over 1994.

Airline alliances cover a variety of areas, and have proliferated in type. Based on the extent of coordination, alliances can be classified into three general categories: (1) simple route-by-route alliance (interline), (2) broad commercial alliance, and (3) equity alliance. The simple route-by-route alliance is the simplest form of an alliance, involving low level of coordination on few routes. Potential areas of coordination include ground handling, joint use of ground facilities, code sharing and joint operations, block space sale, and coordination of flight schedules for directly related flights. One example of the simple route-by-route alliance is the KLM-Japan Airlines (JAL) alliance signed in 1993, which involves a codesharing agreement on Tokyo-Amsterdam-Madrid and Tokyo-Amsterdam-Zurich routes. JAL operates the Tokyo-Amsterdam leg and KLM operates the Amsterdam-Madrid and Amsterdam-Zurich legs of the routes.

The broad commercial alliance extends the areas of coordination to joint development of systems and joint marketing activities through codesharing and sharing frequent flyer programs. It involves collaboration between two airlines on more than a few routes, including feeding traffic to each other at hub airports. The alliance between United Airlines and Lufthansa is an example of the broad commercial alliance. Recently, this alliance network has been extended to include Air Canada, SAS, and Thai Airways in the alliance family.

With equity alliance, airlines either invest in their partners or exchange equity with their partners. Partners generally cooperate in almost all areas of joint activities. It involves codesharing on a large number of routes so as to strategically link partners' flight networks. An example is the alliance between American Airlines (AA) and Canadian Airlines International (CAI). In 1994, AA invested US$190 million into CAI in exchange for 25 percent voting shares and 8.33 percent convertible preferred shares. AA also provides a wide range of services to CAI including revenue accounting, data processing and communications, operations planning, and pricing and yield management. The equity alliance is the most advanced and durable form of alliance, but the proportion of alliances with equity investments has declined, with most carriers concentrating on purely commercial arrangements.

Most alliances tend to be between two airlines, but the emergence of several major groupings or "galaxies" is becoming indisputable. A recent survey conducted by IATA found that the consortium, if approved, of AA and British Airways[5], US Air, Qantas, CAI, TAT European Airlines, would account for 14 percent of world markets; After that, Lufthansa - United - SAS - Thai Airways International accounts for 13.8 percent; Delta - Swissair - Sabena - Austrian - Crossair - Singapore Airlines, 10 percent; KLM - Northwest - Kenya Airways - Air UK- Transavia has 8 percent; and Iberia - Viasa - LanChile - Aviaco - Viva Air, 2.2 percent (Reed, 1996). As shown in Figure 2.9, in 1995, the four largest alliance networks accounted for 51% of the world's scheduled RPKs (Julius, 1996).

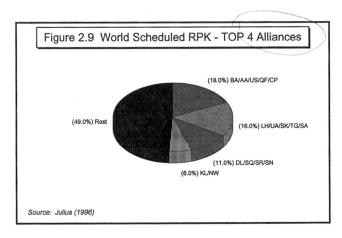

Figure 2.9 World Scheduled RPK - TOP 4 Alliances

(18.0%) BA/AA/US/QF/CP

(49.0%) Rest

(16.0%) LH/UA/SK/TG/SA

(11.0%) DL/SQ/SR/SN

(6.0%) KL/NW

Source: Julius (1996)

---

[5] The European Commission has concluded that the proposed alliance between British Airways and American Airlines would harm fair competition unless changed (CNN May 20, 1997).

Alliances are not an end in themselves. Rather, they are strategies for other outcomes. International air transport is a dynamic industry, changes can occur in any area of an alliance. Alliance groupings mentioned in the previous paragraph will most likely undergo many changes in the years, even the months, to come. However, the building of global alliances will certainly result in the emergence of truly global airlines. Globalization of airline systems and networks is inevitable, it is simply a matter of time.

2.4 Summary

Through examining historical trends, this chapter points out that there is a strong pro-cyclical relationship between the air transport industry and the world economy. That is, air traffic growth generally expands (or contracts) with increased (or reduced) economic growth, but at a much faster rate. For example, air passenger traffic (measured in RPK) increased at an average rate of six percent per year through the 1980s, while the world GDP growth averaged at about 3 percent during the same period. The strong correlation between economic growth and air traffic growth implies that air traffic growth varies among regions of the world with varying degrees of economic growth. Air traffic in the buoyant Asia-Pacific economies has grown, and will continue to grow, faster than in any other regions of the world. Given the forecasted growth of 7.2 percent per year, Asia-Pacific carriers, on average, will double their size in the next 10 years, whereas North American carriers, on average, will grow by 50% in the next 10 years.

Average airline yield in real terms has decreased faster than unit costs, which has led to financial difficulties for many airlines. Also, in view of the very cyclical nature of air transport demand, many airlines tend to over-expand their capacities during favorable economic times. As a result, the air transport industry has not been able to produce healthy profit margins despite years of unbroken traffic growth.

To gain access to global networks within the constraint of the current air bilateral system, and to strengthen domestic (or continental) feeder networks, airlines have constructed alliances, such as codeshare alliances. The ultimate aim of alliances is to enhance partner airlines' competitive positions, and to achieve higher profits for each of the partners. Although most alliances have been formed between two airlines, recently several major alliance groupings (alliance families among several carriers) have emerged, including the "star" alliance group (United- Air Canada-Thai-Lufthansa-SAS) and the American-British Airways alliance group (AA-BA-Canadian-Qantas-TAT European-Deutsche BA). Although the memberships in alliance families are likely to undergo many changes in the future, it is expected that alliance families are likely to form successful global service networks.

Chapter 3
International Regulatory Environment

International air transport has been and is still closely regulated. Thus, the regulatory environment in which international airlines operate will continue to have major impacts on airline network structures, management strategies, and consequently, airline productivities and efficiencies. Therefore, it is important to review developments in international regulatory structure in order to have a better understanding of airline competitive positions.

International air transport operates within the framework of the 1944 Chicago Convention[6], and is traditionally regulated by a complex network of bilateral and multilateral government agreements and International Air Transport Association (IATA) rules. Based on the principle that "every state has complete and exclusive sovereignty over the airspace above its territory", the Convention established multilateral agreements in some areas, mainly regarding overfly and technical stops in foreign territory, but not in areas of commercial rights. Commercial rights were left to bilateral agreements to be negotiated between the two countries involved. The Convention also set up the International Civil Aviation Organization (ICAO), an inter-governmental agency which provides a forum for discussion of key aviation issues and the basis for world-wide coordination of technical and operational standards and practices. Acting as a counterweight to ICAO, IATA was established in 1945 to represent the interest of airlines, and is involved in technical and commercial aspects of aviation. IATA was effectively a suppliers' cartel. Its most important functions have been to set air fares and cargo rates and to operate as a Clearing House for settling inter-airline accounts. However, since the mid-1970s, IATA's price setting ability has been seriously eroded due to competitive pressures from charter carriers and non-IATA carriers, and the move toward pro-competitive aviation policies.

Bilateral agreements are based on the principle of reciprocity, an equal and fair exchange of rights between countries very different in size and with airlines of varied strength. Bilateral agreements vary in form, but they generally specify services and routes to be operated between the two countries, designate airlines and capacity to be provided by each airline, and specify conditions under which passengers may be taken or picked up in each country and flown to third countries (so-called fifth freedom rights). There is, at present, an extensive network of bilateral agreements. Each international airline faces a complex web of bilateral air services agreements signed by its home state. The existence of these bilateral agreements has greatly constrained the freedom of individual scheduled airlines, and limited competition in the international air transport industry. However, the accelerating trend towards more liberal bilaterals, globalization of the industry, and a more multilateral approach to air transportation negotiations are introducing more and more competition into the industry.

In its early days as an infant industry, air transport depended on state support. It developed as a highly protected area of national economies, an integral part of government policy. Today, technological progress and economic developments have

---

[6] Convention on International Civil Aviation.

profoundly changed the air transport market. The air transport industry is gradually losing its status as an industry requiring special treatment. Governments are disengaging themselves from direct involvement in the provision of air services, and there are tremendous efforts for further liberalization of the industry. More weight is given to broad economic considerations, including the interests of consumers, in forming public policies. The move taken by many governments towards less economic control of airlines and greater reliance on market forces has resulted in privatization of government-owned airlines. Also, liberalization of the international air transport industry has resulted in a growing number of carriers which have acquired equity participation in foreign airlines.

This chapter sets the regulatory scene in which international airlines operate, and reflects on changes and developments in the regulatory structure of the international air transport industry by geographical region.

3.1 North America

The United States

The movement in the United States towards liberalizing international air service regulations was initiated by the Carter Administration in 1977. The White House produced guidelines on a new international aviation policy in late 1977, and President Carter signed a Presidential Statement on International Air Transport Negotiations on 21August 1978 following public hearings in the summer of 1978. Under this policy the United States' aim was "to provide the greatest possible benefit to travelers and shippers", and "maximum consumer benefits can best be achieved through the preservation and extension of competition between airlines in a fair market place". This broad aim was to be achieved through the negotiation or renegotiation of bilateral agreements. A series of crucial bilateral negotiations or renegotiations were thus conducted over the period 1977-80, resulting in the first round liberal bilaterals between the United States and the Netherlands, Germany, Belgium, Israel, Singapore, Thailand[7], Korea, and the Philippines[8]. The immediate effect of renegotiation of these U.S. bilaterals was a dramatic expansion in the number of airlines operating in deregulated markets and in total scheduled capacity offered in those markets. As a result, the number of US gateway points with direct services to European or Asian destinations increased dramatically. In addition, in 1981, several Asian airlines, such as Singapore Airlines and Thai International, started services to the United States for the first time.

The new US aviation policy also directly affected IATA's price-setting activities. In June 1978, the US Civil Aeronautics Board (CAB) issued an order requiring IATA and associated parties to show cause why CAB should not withdraw its approval of, and consequently anti-trust exemption for, IATA's Traffic Conferences and other related agreements. Without exemption from anti-trust legislation, airlines participating in pricing agreements would risk being taken to U.S. court when flying to the United States. The

---

[7] Thailand renounced its air service agreement (ASA) with the U.S. in 1990, claiming the agreement favored US airlines. A new agreement was signed in May 1996 to open their aviation markets to each other's carriers.

[8] Between 1978 and 1982, the United States government signed "liberal" or partially "liberal" air service bilaterals with 23 countries (Haanappel, 1983).

immediate short-term effect of the Show Cause Order was the withdrawal of all US airlines from IATA membership. Over 40 percent of IATA member airlines' international traffic was to and from the United States, so the potential threat to IATA was considerable. Although the Show Cause Order was subsequently abandoned amidst protests from governments worldwide, it undoubtedly seriously undermined IATA's influence in the industry.

Deregulation brought strong downward pressure on fares and yields along with rapid traffic growth. As a result, passenger load factors rose by about 10 percentage points. Consumers benefited from lower fares and better services, but many airlines faced spiraling operating losses as they tried to retain or increase their market shares.

As deregulation and liberalization in international aviation continues, and as the internationalization of production and marketing activities advances, such as creation of the World Trade Organization (WTO) and formation of continental trading blocs, the concept of "open skies" has been raised as a way to further liberalize air service agreements (ASA) between countries. In March 1992, the United States offered to negotiate "open skies" agreements with all European countries. The US' criteria for "Open Skies" will not create unrestricted open skies for air transport to, from, and over a country for any carrier. It does not allow foreign airlines having cabotage in the U.S., nor does it remove or reduce US foreign ownership provisions. The first US "open skies" deal under the new agreement was signed on 4 September 1992 between the U.S. and the Netherlands. In February 1995, US and Canada signed an open skies agreement with a three year phase-in provision. In May 1995, open skies agreements were signed between the United States and 9 European countries including Switzerland, Sweden, Norway, Luxembourg, Iceland, Finland, Denmark, Belgium, and Austria[9]. One year later, an open skies agreement was signed between the U.S. and Germany. The U.S. also signed a phased open skies agreement with the Czech Republic in December 1995, the first such pact with a former Eastern bloc country[10]. Talks between the US and UK over an "open skies" accord are underway as a prerequisite for approval of the proposed BA-AA alliance[11].

The U.S. started to shift the focus of its international aviation policy to Asia at the end of 1995 following successes in Europe. In the final months of 1995, the U.S. reached new agreements with Hong Kong, the Phillippines, Macau, India and China, and began talks with Thailand (McKenna, 1996). Furthermore, the U.S. Open Skies initiative in Asia was announced in summer 1996. In April 1997, Singapore became the first country in Asia to sign an open skies agreement with the United States[12]. An open skies aviation

---

[9] According to Air Transport Association of America (1995), the United States signed new liberal agreements or amendments with 16 countries in 1995.

[10] It offered a similar agreement to Poland too, but still needs to work it out.

[11] The United States has made open skies a condition for approving alliances.

[12] The U.S. also reached agreements on open skies with Taiwan and Brunei in early 1997 (US DOT News 48-97).

accord was also reached in May 1997 between the United States and New Zealand[13].

Canada

In Canada, the regulation of civil aviation is under the exclusive jurisdiction of the federal government. Since the mid-1970s, various pressures have been directed towards the government to liberalize its regulatory practices. The government gradually started to relax its regulatory grip, and in 1984, the government announced the "New Canadian Air Transport Policy" in the form of a ministerial policy statement. The new air policy divided the country into North and South regions. It set an aim for deregulation in the South, whereas many of the old rules would still apply to the North. In 1985, the government issued the policy paper "Freedom to Move" which proposed virtually complete deregulation of the airline industry. The National Transportation Act of 1987 came into effect on January 1, 1988[14]. Under this Act, Canadian carriers are subject to two distinct regulatory regimes based on the location of the points they serve. In the North, carriers are subject to controls over entry, fares, and other terms and conditions of service, although with reverse onus for the burden of proof. In the South however, which contains 95 percent of Canada's population, there is almost complete deregulation. To ensure that gains from a deregulated airline industry were fully realized, Air Canada was privatized in 1989. Approximately the same time, CP Air, the second largest Canadian carrier, four small regional carriers, and Wardair, primarily a charter carrier, were combined to form Canadian Airlines International (CAI). The result was a duopoly in Canada's scheduled air services, with Air Canada having a slightly larger market share.

Prior to 1994, Canadian international air policy was based on the "Division of the World" (DOW) principle which divided the international markets between Canada's two major international carriers, Air Canada and Canadian Airlines International. Each carrier thus had exclusive jurisdiction over respective regions of the world (Oum, 1992). This policy attempted to promote growth in the industry without the destructive impact of competition (Mitchell, 1991). But, the DOW policy was replaced in 1994 by a new "use-it-or-lose-it" policy. This policy allows for replacement of a designated carrier if it is not using, or is "under-utilizing" its route rights granted by a bilateral agreement (Transport Canada, 1994), and allocates a second carrier to serve an international market if that market is in a country with at least 300,000 scheduled one-way passengers, or equivalently 150,000 round-trip passengers, per year (Transport Canada, 1995). This new policy also grants operating rights to a foreign carrier if no Canadian carrier has an interest in a particular route.

Contrary to the U.S. government's pro-competitive approach to international air policy, the Canadian government has been rather cautious in its approach to promoting competition. Although Canada's bilateral agreements are more liberal than a decade ago, these bilaterals tend to restrict, rather than facilitate, international competition. Besides the 1995 open skies agreement with the United States, the most important "liberalized"

---

[13] Similar agreements were signed with six Central American Countries during the same month (US DOT News 82-97).

[14] The National Transportation Act (NTA) was slightly revised and renamed as the Canadian Transportation Act (CTA) in 1996.

Canadian bilaterals are those signed with Germany in 1983, the U.K. in 1988, and the Netherlands in 1990. These agreements are regarded as substantially more liberal than Canadian agreements with other countries, but they still contain clauses limiting pricing freedom of carriers operating to and from Canada, and are more restrictive than the U.S. "liberal" bilaterals (Mitchell, 1991, and Dresner and Oum, 1997).

The February 1995 open skies agreement between the United States and Canada is based on the same fundamental open market principles as the North American Free Trade Agreement (NAFTA), effectively increasing integration between the two countries' domestic air services network. The agreement covers all aspects of the two countries' aviation relationship, in contrast to the prior situation in which five separate treaties were signed from 1966 to 1984 covering scheduled, local, charter, cargo, specialty services, and preclearance. The new agreement allows Canadian carriers immediate unlimited route rights from any point in Canada to any point in the U.S., and gives US carriers unlimited routes rights from any US point to any point in Canada except Toronto, Vancouver, and Montreal. The US carriers are subject to a three year phase-in period on routes between these three (the largest) Canadian cities and U.S. points. Carriers of both countries are free to set their own prices for transborder services according to market forces. No cabotage is permitted under the new agreement. Since signing of this new open skies agreement, carriers from both sides have increased service frequency and capacity, and average fares have dropped significantly. However, the jump in traffic has not kept pace with the increase in new flights[15]. As a result, some airlines are facing a declining profit margin.

3.2 Europe

There are more than 22 independent countries in Europe, each with their own language, culture, and administrative procedures. As a result, some 80 percent of all airline journeys within Europe are international, with most flights being under two hours in duration. Traditionally, air services within Europe have been subject to highly restrictive bilateral agreements between countries concerned. In fact, each route was served by two coordinated duopoly carriers who jointly set a single price and pooled the revenue. That is, the intra-European air transport market was essentially characterized by heavily regulated bilateral cartels, dominated by government owned carriers. For nearly 40 years after the Second World War, the structure of the European air transport industry and its operating practices remained largely unchanged, except for the surge[16] of non-scheduled charter services during the 1960s and 1970s. Increased competitive pressures from charter carriers, which were not subject to regulations, exacerbated the need for changes within the regulatory framework.

Changes started to take place during the eighties. As the United States implemented its new international air transport policy, gradual liberalization was introduced in North Atlantic market through a series of liberal bilateral agreements

---

[15] *The Vancouver Sun*, September 14, 1996, B7.

[16] By the mid-1970s over half of the international passenger kilometers within Western Europe were generated by charter carriers (Doganis, 1991).

between the U.S. and a number of European countries including the Netherlands, Germany, and Belgium. Furthermore, US carriers succeeded in building their intra-European networks by extensively using their fifth freedom rights. Accordingly, some pro-competitive governments, in particular the U.K. and the Netherlands, started to renegotiate their intra-European bilateral agreements. The first major breakthrough was made in June 1984 when the U.K. and Netherlands signed the first liberal bilateral agreement. The agreement was complemented with further deregulatory measures in 1985. As a result, air services between the two countries were effectively deregulated. This new agreement is very similar to the renegotiated US bilaterals. It allows free entry of new carriers, open route access by designated airlines to any point in either country, is free of capacity control, and includes a "double disapproval" regime for fares. By allowing open route access, this agreement went a step further than US bilaterals, offering a more equal balance of opportunities to both countries' airlines.

The UK-Netherlands agreement set the pattern for renegotiation of other European bilaterals. Subsequently, similar liberal bilateral agreements were signed: UK-Germany in 1984, then in 1985 UK-Belgium, UK-Luxembourg, UK-Switzerland, and UK-Ireland. However, not all of these agreements are of the same format nor allow the same degree of freedom. Some maintained certain capacity and fare controls, such as the UK-France agreement. Some went through a two-stage process, such as the UK-Ireland agreement, where initial partial liberalization was followed by a more radical second agreement.

In addition to the intra-Europe liberal bilaterals, 12 European countries have forged open-skies pacts with the United States since 1992 (Kayal , 1997a), including Netherlands, Switzerland, Sweden, Norway, Luxembourg, Iceland, Finland, Denmark, Belgium, Austria, and Germany. In all, about 40% of Europe-US traffic flies under open skies (Hill, 1997). Italy has recently promised to work out a phased-in "open skies" aviation pact with the U.S. in the fall of 1997 (Kayal, 1997c). However, France[17], Spain and other countries with vulnerable airlines have so far refused to join Washington's open-skies club. Negotiations with the U.K. are under way.

Parallel to the bilateral liberalization process, the European Commission also started to take initiatives in introducing broader deregulation in order to achieve a common European aviation market. After a failed attempt to adopt a multilateral policy in 1979 (European Commission, 1979), the European Commission outlined its own air transport objectives in the March 1984 *Civil Aviation Memorandum No 2* (European Commission, 1984). This advocated harmonization and liberalization of intra-European bilaterals, and introduced the Treaty of Rome's competition rules into the aviation sector. The Memorandum proposed to reduce capacity controls within Europe and to introduce the concept of zones of non-intervention or approval for greater pricing flexibility. Although the Council of Ministers established working parties to consider how the recommendations could be implemented, they were not able to reach formal agreement until 1987.

Meanwhile, applicability of the Rome Treaty's competition rules was examined at the judiciary level. The European Court of Justice's decision regarding the "Nouvelles Frontiers Case" was that competition rules did apply to the air transport sector, and

---

[17] France renounced his ASA with the U.S. in 1991.

exemptions could be given if the Commission or Member states deemed appropriate. In a wider political context, the heads of member states had, after a series of meetings in the early 1980s, set 1 January 1993 as the date for a single European market to come into existence. It was evident that air transport deregulation within the European community was imminent. Finally, at the end of 1987, the Council of Ministers ratified the so-called "first package" of liberalization measures, marking the first step towards air transport liberalization within the Community. This first package included measures implementing the Rome Treaty's competition rules and measures aimed at relaxing the restrictions on fares, capacity and entry. To facilitate the reaching of agreement, a number of block exemptions were included in the package, providing immunity of many collusive practices (then used by the airlines) for a three year period. As limited as this first package was, France and Italy still showed reluctance to fully implement the agreements.

The second stage in the liberalization process was marked by ratification of the "second package" in 1990. The new package provided complete phasing out of revenue and capacity sharing agreements by 1 January 1993, and gave greater freedom and flexibility in the zonal fare system. Multiple designation was further liberalized with a reduction in thresholds. It introduced, in stages, double disapproval of fares and prevented governments from discriminating against airlines, provided that technical and safety standards were conformed with.

The "third package" of liberalization measures came into effect in January 1993. It initiated a phased move that, by 1997, would result in an European Community (EC) regulatory framework similar to that prevailing in the US domestic air transport industry. Starting April 1, 1997, any EU-registered carrier has the right to run domestic services within any of the EU's 15 member countries, as well as Norway and Iceland. The single European aviation market thus became the world's largest single aviation market with more than 370 million potential passengers. National ownership rules have been replaced by EC ownership criteria. That is, foreign ownership among EC carriers is permitted and carriers have, within the single European aviation market, become "European" airlines. Airlines have been given freedom to set fares, with safeguards against predatory pricing through competition rules. Furthermore, the European Commission is making proposals for creating a free market in airport landing and takeoff rights so that the airlines can truly enjoy freedom to fly wherever they want within the single European market. However, provisions included in the third package limit access and capacity under operational or traffic distribution rules of the EC, country or region. Such rules may relate to safety, environmental protection or traffic distribution, including congestion and allocation of slots. Both the Commission and member states have also been given power to withdraw fares considered excessively high on the basis of long term fully allocated costs, and to prevent downward spirals on air fares.

So far, these changes do not apply to extra-EC agreements. Negotiation of access by foreign carriers to EC member states presently remains with individual members of the community, as a proposal for conduct of such negotiations by the EC is excluded from the package. However, the European commission opposes independent negotiation by individual states, and is making efforts to negotiate air treaties on behalf of member states as a bloc[18]. Actions have been taken in negotiating an "open skies" accord with the United States, and the Commission is promoting a deal with the United States as a model for EC-wide accords with third countries.

3.3 Asia-Pacific

The Asia-Pacific region is the fastest growing air market in the world. However, air transport deregulation process in the region has been much slower than that in North America and Europe. Many countries in the region have not allowed their bilateral air services agreements to keep pace with their economies, and changes are usually reactive rather than pro-active. Protectionist attitudes still prevail among governments in their policies towards aviation regulation. Bilateral agreements are generally restrictive except for liberal bilaterals signed between the United States and a number of countries in the region, including Singapore, New Zealand, Taiwan, Brunei, Thailand, Philippines, Macau, and Korea.

The Asia-Pacific international air service market is traditionally dominated by monopolistic flag carriers. However, since late 1980s, some countries have started to allow second tier airlines to enter the market, although many of these smaller airlines are confined to relatively few points and are frequently excluded from long-haul high density markets. For example, Japan Airlines (JAL)'s monopoly was broken in 1986 by designation of All Nippon Airways (ANA) and Japan Air Systems (JAS) as alternative Japanese carriers on some international routes. Entry to a specific route, however, is still subject to regulatory control. The Ministry of Transport also retained control over fares by requiring the airlines to notify it of any proposed changes, and it has exercised its right to impose fare reductions on some routes (Hooper, 1997). South Korea had a monopolistic regime until 1988 when Asiana Airlines came into existence. Since then, the Korean government has allowed Asiana to expand into many inter-continental routes as well as intra-Asia routes. Second tier intra-Asia regional carriers are growing rapidly (Knibb, 1993), and are becoming a permanent and boisterous part of Asia's aviation industry.

The aviation reform/liberalization process has been progressing at varying paces among countries in the region. Singapore has the most liberal aviation policies in Asia with many liberal bilateral agreements, and is linked to 119 cities in 53 countries by 64 airlines. In April 1997, it became the first country in the region to sign an open skies accord with the United States under the US' Asian Open Skies Initiative[19].

Australia and New Zealand have both made major changes to their aviation regulatory framework. The Australian government completely deregulated its domestic air services, and fully privatized its national airline, Qantas. The New Zealand government divested itself of ownership of its flag airline, Air New Zealand. It has also opened domestic aviation to foreign competition. New Zealand has bilateral air service agreements with 30 countries/territories, and signed an open skies accord with the United States in

---

[18] The European Union's transport ministers recently decided to authorize the Commission to begin negotiation of a multilateral aviation agreement with the United States (Barnard, 1996).

[19] US DOT News 48-97.

May 1997[20]. Airports and air traffic control in New Zealand hav
well. Furthermore, under the Closer Economic Relations (CER)
and New Zealand's governments have taken measures to creat
with multiple designation.

    China restructured its civil aviation into five regional can
carrier (Air China) in 1988. The Civil Aviation Administra
regulates the industry, but no longer plays a direct role in operatin
its uncompetitive carriers, China has adopted a very restrictive a   ... international
air transport, allowing only a select group of foreign carriers to overfly its air space.
However, China is beginning to gradually move towards liberalizing foreign carrier access
to China. An agreement signed with the US in January 1996 allows the first non-stop
direct service from the U.S. to Beijing, including possible code-sharing between US and
Chinese carriers. In fact, American Airlines and China Eastern Airlines signed a
memorandum of understanding in February 1997 for a cooperative services agreement for
reciprocal code sharing programs between cities American serves in the U.S. and China
Eastern's gateways of Beijing and Shanghai in China[21] (*World Airline News*, February 21,
1997).

    Malaysia used to have a rather restrictive air policy. However, since 1993, the
government has allowed smaller airlines to seriously compete in the market, and in 1994,
privatized the national carrier, Malaysia Airlines (MAS). It also adopted a rather liberal
policy towards foreign carriers, and is currently negotiating an open skies agreement with
the United States.

    In Thailand, the airline industry was traditionally controlled by the Thai air force,
thus fractions between the air force and civilians were a constant problem. Civilian
executives had control of the airlines for a brief two-year period in 1992-94, before air
force officers regained control. Seven percent of Thai Airways' shares are owned by the
public, with remaining shares held by the government. Further privatization is expected,
but is likely to be slow with the military in charge. Thailand reached a new aviation
agreement with the United States in January 1996 which significantly expanded passenger,
cargo, and charter services between the two countries (Burgess, 1996).

    South Korea has two privately owned air carriers, competing in both domestic and
international routes. In this two-carrier system, international route rights were divided
between the two carriers according to the government's "guidelines for the supervision
and development of national flag carriers", established in 1990. The guidelines were
subsequently revised in 1994, due to dissatisfaction by both carriers. Most of Korea's
bilateral air services agreements are restrictive in nature, with the exception of the liberal
bilateral with the U.S. Open skies negotiations are currently ongoing with the United
States.

    Japan has only modest deregulation in place. The government is encouraging
competition, but fares are still under regulatory control. A passive attitude has generally

---

[20] US DOT News 82-97.

[21] Note that the current ASA between the U.S. and China prohibits American from operating its own aircraft
to China and from doing third country code-sharing. United Airlines and Northwest have announced partnerships
with Chinese carriers in the past, but none have amounted to anything of significance.

pted towards international air service liberalization. Japan has been tangled in a
wrangle with the US over air services agreement between the two countries, and has
rmained firm in its stance against open skies (Ballantyne 1996, and Kayal and Burgess
1996). Its concerns center on the relatively weak position of Japan Airlines and All
Nippon Airlines and on the potential growth of US carriers to markets served from Tokyo
(Kayal 1997b, 1997d) .

As the liberalization process advances, US and European carriers are demanding
more fifth freedoms in the region. Their efforts have stirred up anger among many Asian
countries. US bilateral relations with Japan, Hong Kong, and the Philippines were stalled
over this issue. The Orient Airlines Association (OAA)[22] has taken center stage in
coordinating a regional campaign against fifth freedoms to stop "uncontrolled competition
from outside", arguing that US fifth freedoms within Asia are comparable to cabotage in
the US. However, the region's position on fifth freedom is far from uniform. Attitudes
vary by geographical locations and with the nations' development strategies.

The Asia-Pacific region is comprised of countries of very different political
systems and economies of varying degrees of openness. There is no Asia-Pacific body akin
to the EC to provide a base form for uniting air transport policy in the region.
Liberalization is almost entirely confined to domestic skies, and multilateralism, where it
exists, remains within Asia-Pacific's alluring borders. There have been movements
towards liberalizing aviation among some ASEAN[23] countries, in line with the group's
move towards a trading environment akin to the European Union. For example, Malaysia,
Thailand and Indonesia signed a Memorandum of Understanding in 1995 under which their
secondary airports are opened to cross-border flights as part of the "Northern Growth
Triangle" scheme (Hooper, 1997). Each of the three countries can designate two carriers
to fly anywhere within the Indonesia-Malaysia-Thailand growth triangle with limited
government intervention. In addition, the new BIMP-EAGA (Brunei-Indonesia-Malaysia,
Philippines-East Asia Growth Area), born in 1994, is hoping to become the first Asian
group to forge a joint airline system[24]. Furthermore, 13 Asia-Pacific countries met in
January 1996 to explore regional cooperation in aviation and greater openness in the air
service market, and possibly coexistence of multilateral and bilateral approaches to
liberalization. So far, the effort to move towards a regional open-skies agreement has not
made much progress.

---

[22] OAA was recently renamed as the Association of Asia Pacific Airlines (AAPA) (Mackey, 1997).

[23] Association of South-East Asian Nations. ASEAN includes Brunei Darussalam, Indonesia, Malaysia,
Philippines, Singapore, and Thailand.

[24] "New Group on the Bloc: Brunei-Indonesia-Malaysia-Philippines East Asia Growth Area", *Airline
Business*, September, 1997, vol 12, No. 9, p.100,

3.4 Summary

This chapter reviews developments and current status of regulatory environments in the international air transport industry. In North America, particularly in the United States, domestic deregulation is firmly in place. The US government is actively seeking to create a more liberal aviation regime in the international market through its open skies initiatives. It has reached open skies agreements with 12 European countries, Canada, six central American countries, and 4 Asian countries. In Canada, the domestic market has been deregulated since 1988, however, the Canadian government has been rather cautious in its international air policy. Other than the open skies agreement with the US, Canada's bilateral agreements tend to restrict, rather than facilitate, international competition, although these bilaterals are more liberal than a decade ago.

In Europe, the single European aviation market came into existence on April 1, 1997. Any EU-registered carrier has the right to run domestic services within any of the EU's 15 member countries, as well as Norway and Iceland. National ownership rules have been replaced by EC ownership criteria. However, these changes have yet to apply to extra-EC agreements. Negotiation of access by foreign carriers to EC member states presently remains with individual members of the community.

In the Asia-Pacific region, air transport deregulation process has been much slower than that in North America and Europe. Liberalization is almost entirely confined to domestic skies, and multilateralism, when it exists, remains within Asia Pacific's alluring borders. Protectionist attitudes still prevail among governments in their policies towards aviation regulation.

Chapter 4
Operating Environment and Input Prices

This chapter gives a brief overview of selected airlines. It examines airline network characteristics and changes in input prices in order to provide a context for analysing changes in airline productivity, efficiency, and cost structures. It also examines the relationship between exchange rate fluctuations and input factor prices, as well as the growing practice of global sourcing of input factors.

4.1   Carrier Profiles

The selected airlines are all international carriers, and have significant involvement in scheduled passenger services. That is, carriers engaged mainly in cargo or charter services are excluded. The sample includes airlines from Europe, North America, and Asia-Pacific. Some of the airlines are 100 percent state owned, some are private companies, while others have mixed ownership. For example, Air France, Iberia and Thai International are government owned, while the US carriers are all private companies.

There are large variations in size, output mix, and other operating characteristics among the sample airlines. Table 4.1 provides some recent descriptive statistics for the airlines. The list is organized by continent and by revenue size. The size of the airlines, as measured by revenue tonne-kilometres (RTK) in 1995, ranges from 2.2 billion RTK for Scandinavian Airlines Systems (SAS), to 19.6 billion RTK for United Airlines. In terms of number of passengers carried in 1995, it ranges from 8.3 million (8.6 million in 1996) for Canadian Airlines International (CAI), to 87 million (97 million in 1996) for Delta.

Aside from US carriers, most of the sample airlines provide mainly international services, some do not provide domestic services at all. Qantas, Singapore Airlines (SIA), Cathay Pacific and Japan Airlines (JAL) serve mostly inter-continental traffic, as indicated by their long average stage length, while US Air and SAS have a large proportion of their business in domestic or intra-continental traffic. Figures 4.1a, 4.1b, and 4.1c plot changes in average stage length for each airline. In general, average stage length has a slight upward trend for most airlines as they expand their network into international markets. A number of exceptions, however, are noted. For example, the sharp fall in CAI's stage length between 1986[25] and 1988, was due to the integration of Canadian Pacific Air Lines, Eastern Provincial Airways, Nordair, and Pacific Western Airlines in 1987. The big drop in Qantas' average stage length in 1994 was due to its merger with Australian Airlines - a domestic carrier. Entering the domestic market also resulted in a decrease in average stage length for Thai International during the late 1980's. Similarly, an increase in intra-Europe flights has reduced average stage length for KLM since 1992. Continental's average stage length had a noticeable drop in 1994 due to expansion of short haul services.

In terms of passenger load factor, the variation among carriers is somewhat smaller, ranging from Air Canada at 63%, to KLM at 75% (76% in 1996). Figures 4.2a, 4.2b, and 4.2c show significant fluctuations in passenger load factor from 1980 to 1995. North American carriers' passenger load factors remained relatively stable during this period, indicating that carriers must have tried to adjust capacity in accordance with the

---

[25] CAI's 1986 number was for CP Air.

changing traffic. Asian carriers' load factors fell slightly from the late 1980's level, which is consistent with the dramatic capacity increases for many Asian carriers. On the other hand, European carriers' load factors showed a slight upward trend. In terms of weight load factor, KLM was able to achieve a high load factor in 1996, at 74%. On the other hand, average weight load factors for US Air, American Airlines (AA), and Air Canada (AC) were just above 50%.

Table 4.1 Descriptive Statistics of Sample Airlines, 1995

Airline	Revenue Tonne-km (millions)	Number of Passenger (thousands)	Number of Employees (units)	% Int'L RTK	Stage Length (km)	Passenger Load Factor (%)	Weight Load Factor (%)
North America							
American	17,660[1]	79,389[1]	90,980	36.9	1,799	69[1]	52
United	19,637[1]	81,945[1]	80,902	42.3	1,683	72[1]	59
Delta	15,168[1]	97,271[1]	62,832	30.7	1,224	70[1]	55
Northwest	12,821[1]	52,722[1]	44,682	47.8	1,362	73[1]	60
US Air	5,949[1]	56,893[1]	43,614	7.4	904	69[1]	52
Continental	6,009[1]	35,986[1]	32,272	20.0	1,315	68[1]	61
Air Canada	3,453	12,801	20,503	67.3	1,536	63	53
Canadian	2,948	8,578[1]	13,228[1]	70.1	1,681	71[1]	68[1]
Asia-Pacific							
Japan Airlines	10,204	28,880	20,482	85.6	2,348	68	66
All Nippon	4,583	37,870	14,649	41.2	1,112	64	51
Singapore	9,512[1]	12,022[1]	13,258	100.0	4,300	74[1]	71
Korean Air	8,261	21,422	16,478	93.9	1,714	65	56
Cathay	7,092[1]	10,985[1]	15,657[1]	100.0	3,283	74[1]	71[1]
Qantas	6,603[1]	15,551[1]	24,429[1]	79.5	2,064	72[1]	64[1]
Thai	3,795	12,821	20,718	92.0	1,559	67	69
Europe							
Lufthansa[2]	12,205	32,599	26,578	95.2	1,131	70	71
British Airways	12,215	35,000[1]	50,477	98.1	1,863	72[1]	71
Air France	9,701	14,498	36,384	91.1	1,846	71	71
SAS	2,195	19,828[1]	21,348[1]	83.1	728	64[1]	61
KLM	8,630[1]	12,285	26,385[1]	99.9	1,748	76[1]	73[1]
Swissair	3,574	8,826[1]	16,520	99.0	1,268	64	69
Iberia	2,850	14,600[1]	22,500	79.6	1,194	70	61

[1] 1996 data

[2] Lufthansa were through dramatic restructuring during 1994-1995. Its Technical Services and Cargo divisions became independent public limited companies on January 1, 1995. The parent company Lufthansa AG is now purely a scheduled passenger airline company.

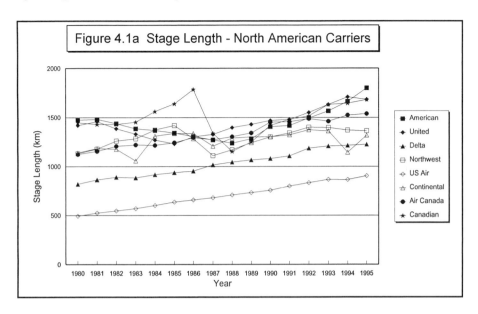

Figure 4.1a Stage Length - North American Carriers

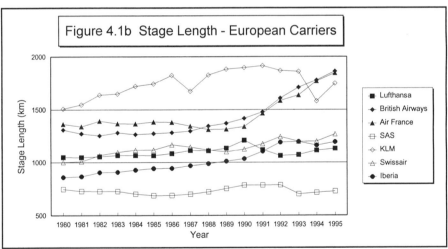

Figure 4.1b Stage Length - European Carriers

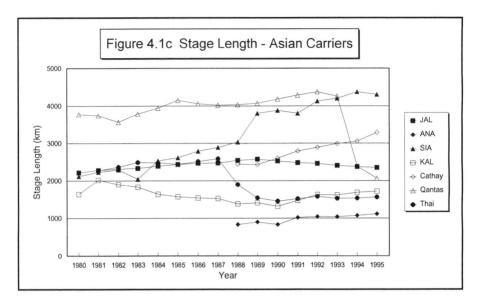

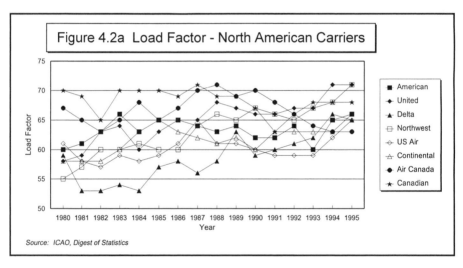

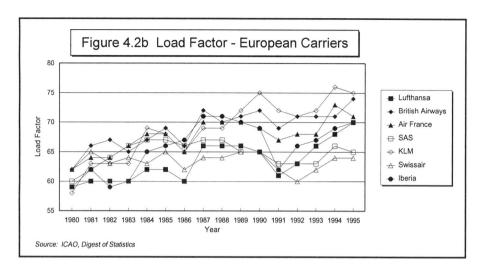

Figure 4.2b Load Factor - European Carriers

Source: ICAO, Digest of Statistics

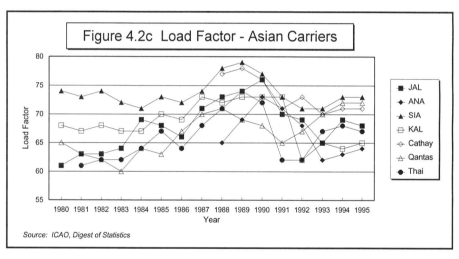

Figure 4.2c Load Factor - Asian Carriers

Source: ICAO, Digest of Statistics

The size of the airlines in terms of operating revenues ranges from US$2.3 billion for CAI, to US$15.6 billion for AA. Figure 4.3 plots the airlines' 1995 operating revenues by category. There are large variations in terms of revenue shares (output mix). Passenger revenues account for about 90 percent of operating revenues for Delta, US Air, Continental, All Nippon Airways (ANA), and British Airways (BA), but account for less than 60% for Korean Air (KAL). Korean Air, Singapore Airlines, and Cathay Pacific's cargo services contribute about 20 percent to operating revenues. Overall, compared to US carriers, many Asian carriers and some European carriers generate relatively high proportions of revenues from cargo services. Also, European carriers (except for BA), as well as KAL and Thai International, have a heavy emphasis on incidental (non-airline business) services. US carriers, on the other hand, focus primarily on scheduled passenger services.

4.2   Carrier Profitability

This section briefly examines financial performance of the airlines. Table 4.2 shows that profitability performance varies greatly among the sample airlines. In the first six months of 1996, American Airlines made an operating income of US$746 million, and a before-tax income of US$507 million. British Airways had a net income of US$649 million out of an operating income of US$852 million in the 6 months ended September 30, 1996. Among the sample airlines, British Airways, SIA and Northwest Airlines were the most profitable in 1995, with net income of US$740 million, US$622 million (US$624 million in 1996), and US$ 506 million (US$536 million in 1996), respectively. Air France suffered the biggest loss, a net loss of US$581 million, in 1995. Iberia and Canadian Airlines International (CAI) also suffered losses in 1995, at a net loss of US$361 million and US$143 million (US$137 million in 1996), respectively. CAI was the only airline in our sample incurred an operating loss. All of the Asian carriers were able to achieve a positive net income in 1995. 1995 was the best year of the decade for the airlines in terms of financial results.

Over the years, the airline industry has recorded low operating profit levels despite strong growth in traffic. This is partly due to the fact that airlines' earnings are subject to considerable fluctuation caused by external political, social and economic events, and cyclical nature of the industry. Figures 4.4a, 4.4b, and 4.4c show changes in the airlines' operating revenue/expense ratios. Strong growth in demand during the late 1980s was reflected by the higher revenue/expense ratios until economic recession and the Gulf War threw the industry into a slump in the early 1990s. A rather interesting point to note in Figures 4.4a-c is that changes in operating revenue/expense ratios for North American carriers appear to be nicely "synchronized", with the exception of US Air. However, larger discrepancies are observed among Asian carriers and European carriers. This observation partly reflects the fact that North American carriers operate in similar environments, while the operating environments for the Asian and European carriers vary greatly.

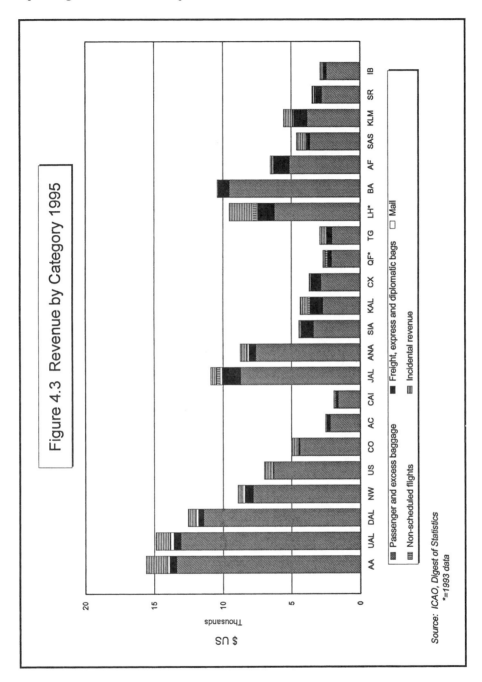

Figure 4.3 Revenue by Category 1995

Source: ICAO, Digest of Statistics
*=1993 data

Table 4.2 Profitability Indicators 1996

Airline	Total Revenue (millions)	Total Operating Expense (millions)	Operating Income (millions)	Net Income (millions)
		North America		
American[1]	15,610	14,642	968	208
United[1]	14,895	14,063	832	341
Delta	12,455	11,992	463	156
Northwest	9,881	8,827	1054	536
US Air	8,140	7,700	438	263
Continental	5,825	5,440	385	224
Air Canada	3,579	3,421	158	109
Canadian	2,271	2,344	-69	-137
		Asia-Pacific		
Japan Airlines[1]	10,883	10,724	159	5
All Nippon[1]	8,739	8,457	282	32
Singapore	4,512	4,060	452	624
Korean Air[1]	4,363	4,012	350	137
Cathay	3,819	3,370	486	490
Qantas	5,378	5,155	223	104
Thai[1]	2,926	2,550	376	130
		Europe		
Lufthansa[1][2]	9,231	9,154	77	133
British Airways[1]	10,411	9,190	1,221	740
Air France[1]	6,510	6,308	202	-581
SAS	4,993	4,482	511	260
KLM	6,144	6,091	53	252
Swissair[1]	3,482	3,442	40	4
Iberia[1]	2,902	2,699	203	-361

[1] 1995 data

[2] Lufthansa were through dramatic restructuring during 1994-1995. Its Technical Services and Cargo divisions became independent public limited companies on January 1, 1995. The parent company Lufthansa AG is now purely a scheduled passenger airline company.

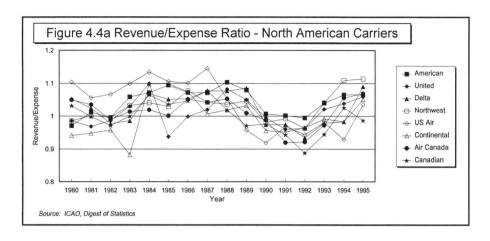

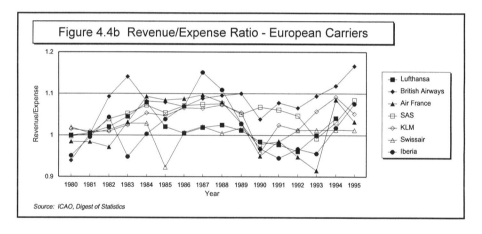

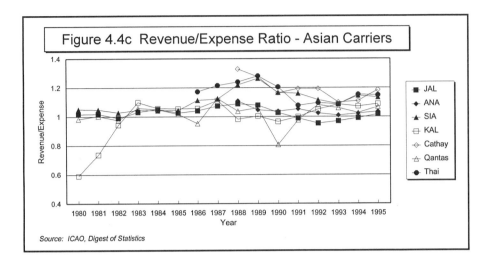

Figure 4.4c Revenue/Expense Ratio - Asian Carriers

Source: ICAO, Digest of Statistics

4.3   Input Prices

A primary determinant of the cost of providing airline services is input prices, that is, prices paid per unit of labour, fuel, aircraft and infrastructure services, as well as purchased materials and services. This section examines price changes for airline input factors.

Labor

Labour accounts for about 30 percent of an airline's total cost. Figures 4.5a, 4.5b, and 4.5c show average wage level in current US dollars. There is a clear upward trend in average labour prices for all airlines, without considering the inflation factor. However, there are substantial differences in average labour prices across airlines. Asian carriers, except for JAL and All Nippon Airways (ANA), enjoy significantly lower labour prices than European and North American carriers. JAL and ANA have the highest paid labour force among all airlines. BA, KLM, and Air France have relatively lower average labour prices than other European carriers, while Swissair has the highest average wage level in Europe. Air Canada, Canadian, and Continental enjoy relatively lower average labour prices among North American carriers. Delta, US Air, and Northwest have slightly higher labour prices than United and American. On average, European carriers pay a slightly higher price for their work force than their North American counterparts, but not as significant as often believed. This is consistent with findings by the European Commission (Comité des Sages 1994).

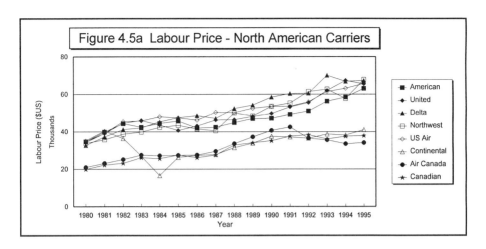

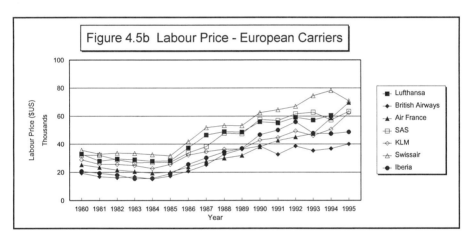

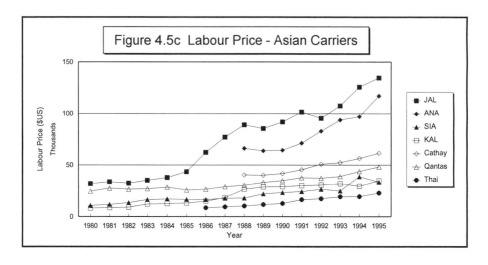

Figure 4.5c Labour Price - Asian Carriers

Fuel

Fuel accounts for about 7-20 percent of an airline's cost. Fuel prices differ substantially from one country to another due to tax and transport costs. International airlines pay fuel prices at airports they serve; therefore, average price an airline paid for fuel is a weighted average of fuel prices of destinations served.

Figures 4.6a, 4.6b, and 4.6c plot fuel price changes from 1980 to 1995. Substantial fluctuations in fuel prices occurred during this period, with a big hike during 1990-1991 due primarily to the Gulf war crisis. It appears that variations in fuel prices among the airlines are not significant. Some exceptions, however, do exist. ANA pays the highest fuel prices among the sample airlines. This is because it provides mostly Japanese domestic services where fuel prices are substantially higher than in other countries. On the other hand, a much larger proportion of JAL's traffic is in international markets, thus its average fuel price is closer to fuel prices paid by most other international airlines. Thai's average fuel price is also considerably high relative to other Asian carriers. Among European carriers, SAS has the lowest fuel price. This is a little surprising since SAS is often considered a high cost carrier. Air France, Swissair and British Airways' average fuel prices are slightly higher than those of Lufthansa and KLM. The two Canadian carriers, AC and CAI, pay noticeably higher fuel prices than US carriers. There is very little difference in average fuel prices paid by US carriers. It should be noted that fuel price differences between airlines mainly reflect the markets an airline serves, and thus has no strong implications on its cost competitiveness. All carriers face essentially the same fuel price when serving a given market.

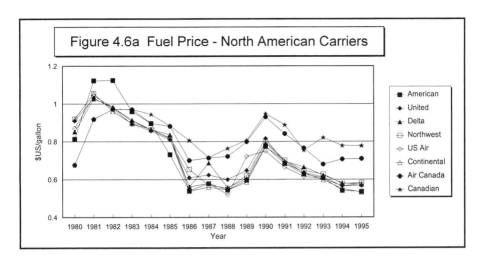

Figure 4.6a Fuel Price - North American Carriers

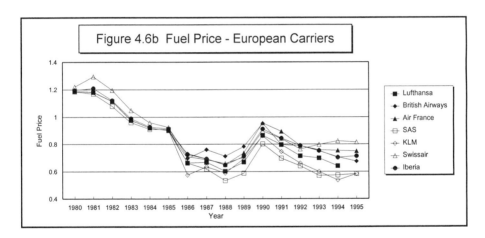

Figure 4.6b Fuel Price - European Carriers

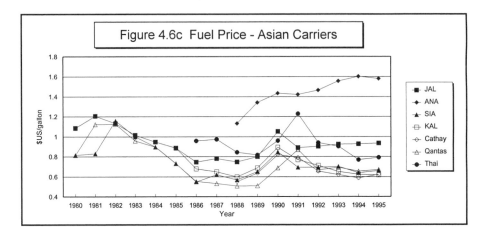

Aircraft

       Aircraft are purchased on world markets, and cost approximately the same for all airlines. Some aircraft are carrier-owned, while others are leased. However, the trends show that many airlines are leasing rather than buying their aircraft. According to AVMARK[26], about one-half of the world's fleet is operating under some kind of leasing arrangement. Leasing provides airlines with access to needed aircraft without major capital outlay. In addition, airlines operate fleets comprised of many different types of aircraft. Therefore, it is necessary to construct a meaningful measure of aircraft capital, comparable across airlines, in order to compare aircraft costs among the airlines.

       Assuming that the flow of capital services for an aircraft in a given category is independent of age, a aircraft service price index can be constructed[27] using the multi-lateral index procedure proposed by Caves, Christensen, and Diewert (1982). Since aircraft leasing is a competitive business and leasing companies generally supply aircraft to airlines all over the world, aircraft lease rates are considered to reflect the "real" capital cost of each aircraft. Thus, they can be used to approximate aircraft service prices in constructing the price index. Table 4.3 gives some examples of aircraft lease rates. These lease rates were estimated by AVMARK based on aircraft value. It assumes a five-year operating lease with aircraft returned in half-time condition. In reality, however, lease rates are highly variable, depending on lessee's credit rating, lease duration, tax consideration to the lessor, return provisions, and residual value assumptions.

---

[26] *AVMARK Newsletter*, March 1996.

[27] See Appendix for details about the construction of aircraft price index.

Table 4.3 Sample Aircraft Lease Prices

Type	Oct.1986	Sept.1988	Sept.1990	Sept.1992	Mar. 1996	Mar. 1997
			Monthly Lease Rate ($000)			
A300B4-100	295	250	300	188	95	75
A300-600R			650	580	620	680
A310-300			600	470	485	505
A340-200				888	790	735
B-727-200ADV	150	100	100	56	105	125
B-737-200ADV	125	110	95	48	85	95
B-747-200B	425	350	475	290	425	380
B-767-300			575	460	410	375
B-777-200A					850	870
DC-8-63F	145	175	200	160	80	75
DC-9-50	125	135	130	68	90	100
DC-10-30	350	425	475	300	290	295
F.28-4000	105	125	85	48	35	33
F.100			240	173	210	210
L-1011-50	240	175	225	150	70	58
L-1011-500	275	250	350	210	160	150
MD-81	225	200	175	140	250	255
MD-88			275	240	295	290

Source: AVMARK Inc. Newsletter, various issues

Figures 4.7a, 4.7b, and 4.7c plot the estimated aircraft price index. Since the same lease rates are applied to all airlines, differences in aircraft capital prices observed in Figures 4.7a-c reflect differences in fleet composition. The estimated aircraft price indices are almost the same for the North American carriers. A similar pattern is seen among Asian carriers as well. However, some noticeable differences are observed among European carriers in terms of aircraft price, particularly for SAS and Iberia. The difference is due to the fact that SAS and Iberia's fleets have a larger proportion of MD aircraft, which had relatively higher lease rates in the late 1980s, and then relatively lower lease rates in the early 1990s.

The changes in aircraft price during the study period clearly reflect the cyclical nature of the international airline industry, albeit with a lag. The first half of 1980s saw industry profitability fall considerably, which resulted in less airplane orders, and consequently falling aircraft price. The boom years of the late 1980s then brought a record number of airplane orders, naturally pushing up aircraft price during 1989-1990. However, delivery of these airplanes coincided with the economic recession of the early 1990s, resulting in excess capacity in the industry, thus lowering aircraft prices once again.

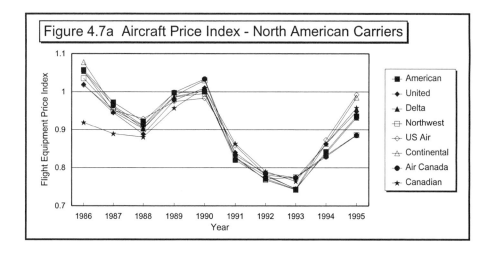

Figure 4.7a Aircraft Price Index - North American Carriers

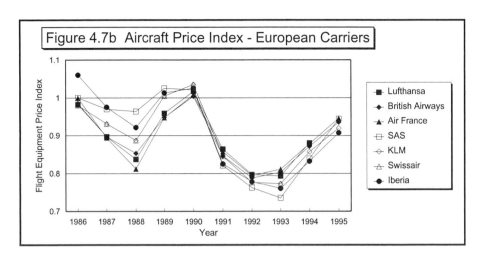

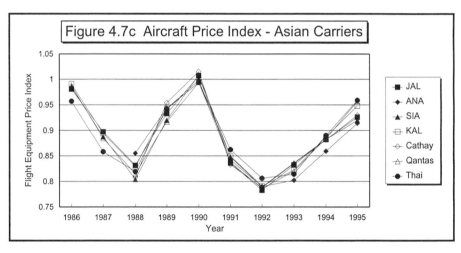

Total Capital Input

In addition to aircraft, airline capital assets also include so-called ground property and equipment (GPE), such as ramp equipment, maintenance and engineering equipment, furniture fixtures and office equipment, buildings, and other miscellaneous ground equipment. Since GPE costs are small relative to flight equipment costs, these two capital input categories are aggregated to form a total capital input series. Figures 4.8a, 4.8b, and 4.8c present price index for this total capital input. Because aircraft fleet is the dominant component of an airline's capital, total capital input price index follows an almost identical pattern as aircraft price index. Noticeable exceptions are due mostly to mergers and changes in network structure. For example, Canadian Airlines International was formed in 1987 by the merger of four airlines; and Thai Airways started to serve the domestic market in 1986.

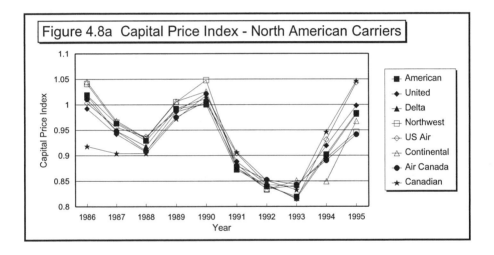

Figure 4.8a Capital Price Index - North American Carriers

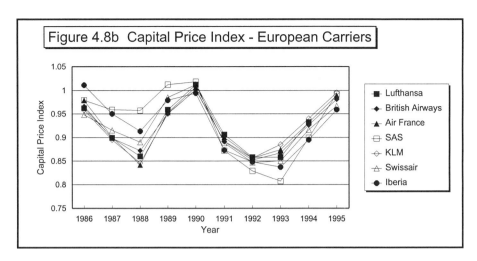

Figure 4.8b Capital Price Index - European Carriers

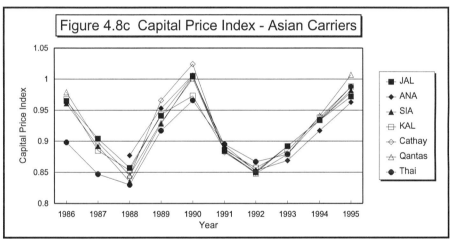

Figure 4.8c Capital Price Index - Asian Carriers

Materials

Materials input is a catch-all-expense category, it includes all other input or material costs not included in the above input categories. Materials cost is defined as the part of total operating cost not attributable to labour, fuel, or capital, and it accounts for 35-50 percent of airlines' total costs. Since materials cost includes numerous items and activities, it is very difficult, if not impossible, to construct an "exact" materials price index for each individual airline. Therefore, a GDP deflator can be used to approximate the price index for materials input. Because our sample airlines are based in different countries, the price index must also account for changes in market exchange rates and changes in real price levels of the carriers' home countries. The materials input price index in Figures 4.9a, 4.9b, and 4.9c is constructed using the Purchasing Power Parity (PPP) index for GDP[28] and the US GDP deflator. The PPP index adjusts for changes in market exchange rate and change in real price level of a country relative to the US, and the US GDP deflator ensures that the materials input quantity index is comparable over time. Note that the materials input prices are assumed to be the same for all carriers in the same country.

Materials input prices generally increased during the 1986-1995 period. Compared to prices paid by US carriers, Canadian carriers' materials input prices were lower at the beginning of the period, higher during 1989-1991, but then lower again after 1992. European carriers' materials input prices were considerably higher than those of Canadian and US carriers, especially toward the end of the period. Among them, Swissair and SAS have the highest materials input prices, while Iberia and BA have the lowest. With the exception of Japanese carriers, Asian carriers' materials input prices are substantially lower than those of North American and European carriers. Japanese carriers' materials input prices are slightly higher than those of Lufthansa, but lower than those of SAS and Swissair.

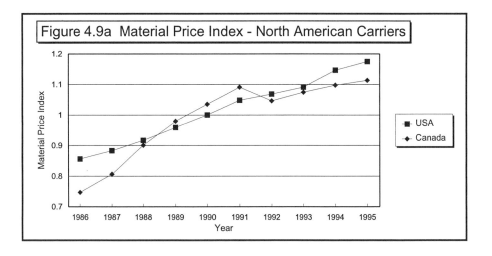

_____

[28] Obtained from the Penn World Table 5.6. Summers and Heston (1991) give a detailed description of an earlier version of the Penn World Table.

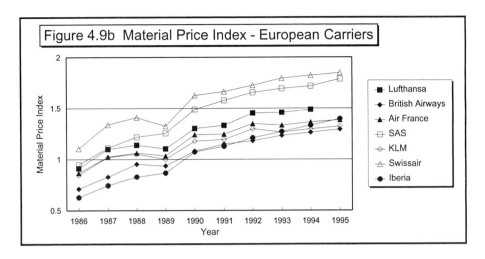

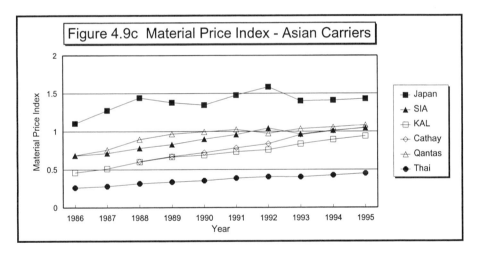

4.4 Exchange Rate Fluctuation

In previous sections, all prices were expressed using a common currency - the US dollar. Since airlines compete in international markets, it is common practice to compare their operating results in terms of a common currency. However, exchange rate fluctuations have had non-negligible impacts on inter-country cost differentials (denominated in a common currency). This section examines the effects of exchange rate fluctuations on carriers' input prices. In particular, we look at the cases of JAL, AC, SAS, AF, and Lufthansa.

Figure 4.10 shows changes in the Japanese Yen relative to the US dollar. We can see that the Yen experienced dramatic appreciation during 1985-87, and further appreciated by about 44% against US dollar between 1986 and 1995, after a brief depreciation during 1988-1990. Figure 4.11 shows changes in the Canadian dollar against the US dollar. The Canadian dollar depreciated substantially during the early 1980s. It then appreciated significantly during 1986-1991, then fell back to the 1986 level by 1994. European currencies tend to be even more volatile than both the Japanese Yen and the Canadian dollar. Figure 4.12 plots changes in the French Franc relative to the US dollar. The Franc experienced a big drop, and then a big jump during the early 1980s. Since then, there have been a number of brief ups or downs. In general, the Franc has appreciated against the US dollar since 1986. The Swedish Krona (Figure 4.13) had a similar pattern as the French Franc in the early 1980s, but a different pattern later on. It exhibited a general trend of appreciation between 1986 and 1992 despite some fluctuations, but then it depreciated dramatically between 1992-1994. The Deutsche Mark (Figure 4.14) exhibited an almost identical pattern as the French Franc: a big fall, then a big jump, followed by some fluctuations after 1986. It generally appreciated between 1986-1995.

Figures 4.15 and 4.16 plot changes in JAL's labour and non-labour input prices, respectively, in relation to Japan's exchange rate. Both JAL's labour and non-labour input prices in US dollar terms have increased substantially relative to AA because of appreciation of the Japanese Yen. The pattern of input price changes in the Japanese Yen, however, tells a different story (as shown by input prices converted using 1986 exchange rate). In fact, between 1986 and 1995, JAL's non-labour input prices decreased by about 31% in terms of the Japanese Yen, but increased by 23% in terms of US dollars. For Air Canada (Figures 4.17 and 4.18), input prices in Canadian dollars were much lower than those in US dollars during 1989-1991, when the Canadian dollar appreciated over 15 percent from its 1986 level, but moved closer to those in US dollars as the exchange rate fell back to the 1986 level. Figures 4.19 and 4.20 plot changes in Air France's input prices in relation to the French Franc. The Franc appreciated by about 28% between 1986 and 1995. Air France's labour prices doubled in terms of Francs during the period, but almost tripled in terms of US dollars. Air France's non-labour input price relative to AA actually declined in terms of Franc, but increased by 33% in US dollars. These three cases (Japan, France, and Canada) all see currency appreciation against the US dollar, thus the changes in carrier input prices in domestic currencies are lower than those measured in US dollars. The opposite occurs when a currency depreciates. Figures 4.21 and 4.22 plot labour and non-labour input prices for SAS. Since the Swedish Krona depreciated considerably against the US dollar between 1992 and 1994, SAS's input prices in Kronas are well above those measured in US dollars during the same period. The last case examined is

Lufthansa (Figures 4.23 and 4.24). As noted earlier, changes in the Deutsche Mark were very similar to those in the French Franc. The Mark appreciated by 24% between 1986 and 1993. In Deutsche Marks, Lufthansa's input prices declined considerably relative to AA (as shown by input prices measured using 1986 exchange rate). In US dollars, however, there is a clear upward trend.

The difference between input price changes measured in domestic currencies and those in US dollars is due to exchange rate changes. Exchange rate fluctuations are entirely beyond a carrier's control, but have decisive effects on some airlines', such as JAL's, competitive position.

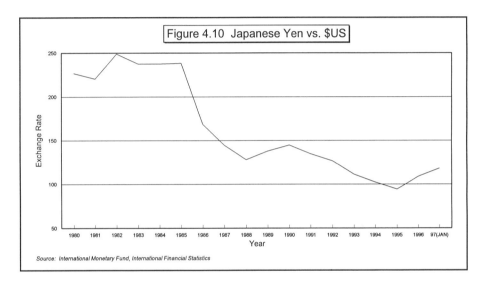

Figure 4.10 Japanese Yen vs. $US

Source: International Monetary Fund, International Financial Statistics

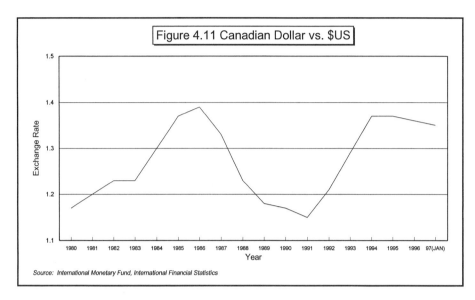

Figure 4.11 Canadian Dollar vs. $US

Source: *International Monetary Fund, International Financial Statistics*

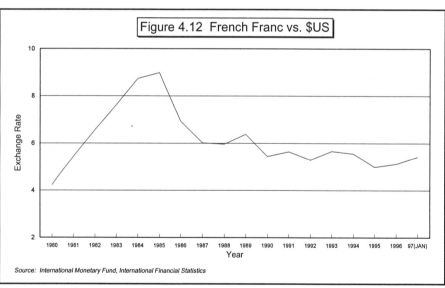

Figure 4.12 French Franc vs. $US

Source: *International Monetary Fund, International Financial Statistics*

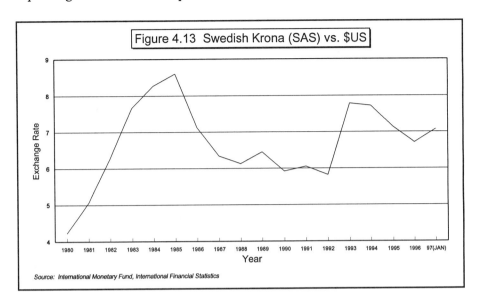

Figure 4.13 Swedish Krona (SAS) vs. $US

Source: International Monetary Fund, International Financial Statistics

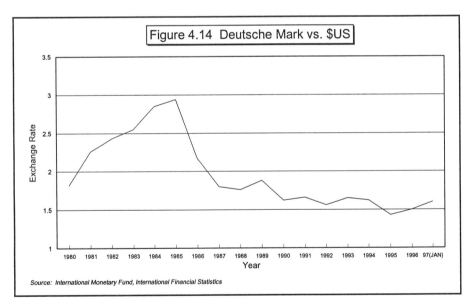

Figure 4.14 Deutsche Mark vs. $US

Source: International Monetary Fund, International Financial Statistics

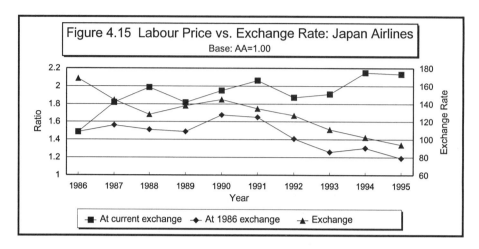

Figure 4.15 Labour Price vs. Exchange Rate: Japan Airlines
Base: AA=1.00

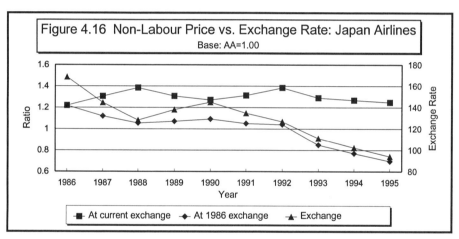

Figure 4.16 Non-Labour Price vs. Exchange Rate: Japan Airlines
Base: AA=1.00

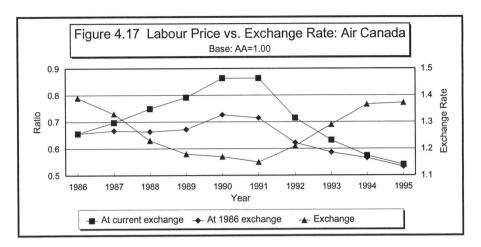

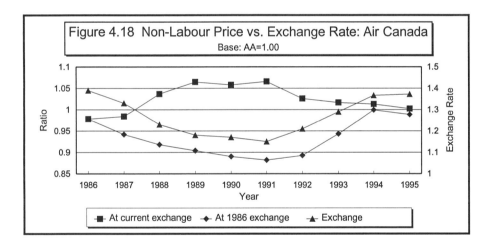

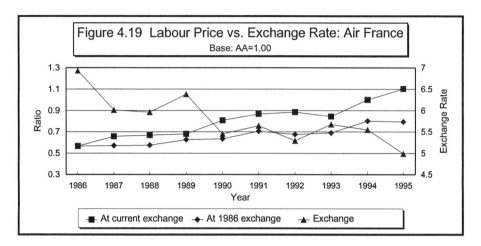

Figure 4.19 Labour Price vs. Exchange Rate: Air France
Base: AA=1.00

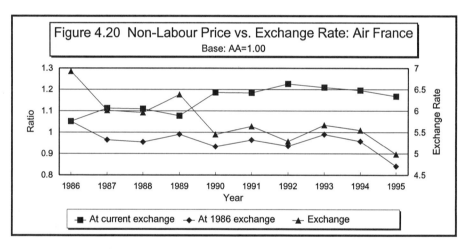

Figure 4.20 Non-Labour Price vs. Exchange Rate: Air France
Base: AA=1.00

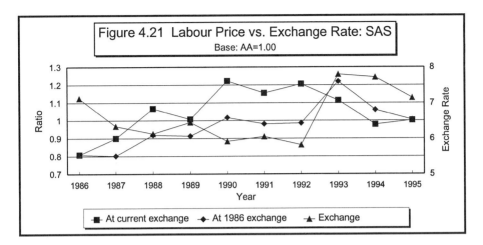

Figure 4.21 Labour Price vs. Exchange Rate: SAS
Base: AA=1.00

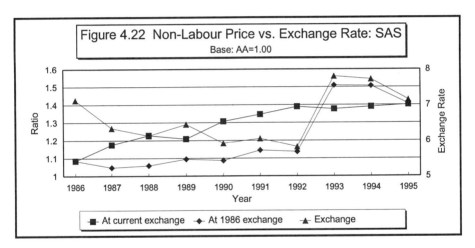

Figure 4.22 Non-Labour Price vs. Exchange Rate: SAS
Base: AA=1.00

62

Chapter 4

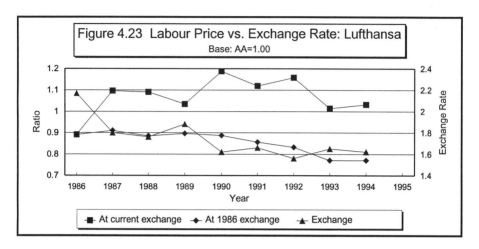

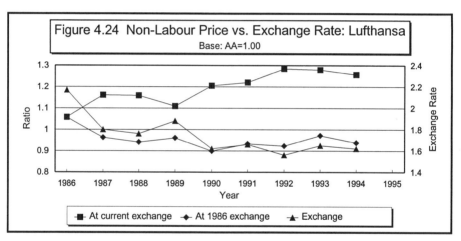

4.5 Global Sourcing

Global sourcing, also called delocating or offshoring, is the trend of moving business to where costs are lowest and potential productivity gains the highest. For airlines, this often means leasing cheaper aircraft and crews, contracting out ancillary operations to specialized companies, and sending work to lower-wage countries to the extent that labour unions allow. The main purpose of global sourcing is, therefore, to reduce cost. This section gives a brief overview of the most common global sourcing practice in the international airline industry.

Global sourcing is increasingly facilitated by growth of reliable and affordable telecommunications technology. A growing trend is for airlines in developed countries to use developing countries for electronic data processing. Many airlines are moving their key back office functions to lower cost countries due to high expense and tight labour conditions at home. Wage differentials allow airlines to add all necessary extra transportation and communication infrastructure cost and still save 30-40 percent of total operational costs. In addition, the relocated work, which is often highly repetitive in nature, is not often desired by workers in developed countries.

Table 4.4 lists some examples of global sourcing. American Airlines (AA) started to move their revenue accounting operations to the Caribbean in 1983. AA has two data management service units in Barbados and the Dominican Republic, where 1600 employees work at least two shifts a day, and sometimes 24 hours a day, to capture data. Data is then transmitted via satellite links to AA's Tulsa (Oklahoma) centre. Swissair, British Airways, Cathay Pacific, and Singapore Airlines (SIA) also moved their revenue accounting operations to places where wages are lower: Swissair and BA to Bombay, India; and Cathay and SIA to China.

Many airlines also look at crew staffing as an area of potential savings. JAL has been using foreign flight attendants since 1966. British Airways, Lufthansa, and United Airlines also use foreign cabin crew at lower cost[29]. In addition, many large Asian carriers also hire experienced, but less expensive, pilots from North America, Europe and Australia. For example, 11% of JAL's 2,600 pilots are non-Japanese. Some airlines lease pilots from codesharing partners, e.g. Northwest Airlines leases pilots to KLM, US Air to British Airways. It is estimated that savings of between 25-30% can be achieved because leased pilots fly for lower salaries than pilots from home countries.

Maintenance operations are another area for global sourcing. Swissair and Lufthansa moved part of their aircraft maintenance operations to Shannon, Ireland to capture benefits of lower wages. For the same reason, Cathay Pacific and Singapore Airlines have set up aircraft maintenance operations in China to cut costs and remain competitive.

Airlines often work together in global sourcing to achieve maximum cost savings. For example, Delta, Singapore Airlines, and Swissair announced in August 1995 that they were forming DSS World Sourcing AG, a global sourcing agency. The company sources

---

[29] Of course, there are other reasons for inducing international airlines to use foreign labour. For example, many foreign flight attendants are hired because of the airlines' need for language and special service capability to better serve ethnic passengers.

items such as flight amenities, beverages, duty free, stationary, uniforms, and office and computer equipment to the three airlines.

Table 4.4 Examples of Global Sourcing of Inputs and Services

AIRLINE	HOME COUNTRY	YEAR	LOCATION	SIZE	FUNCTION
American Airlines	USA	1983	Barbados & Dominican Republic	1,600 employees total	Revenue accounting
United Airlines	USA	1992	France	250	Flight attendants
Swissair	Switzerland	1988	Bombay, India	33 employees	Passenger Reservation Control Office
		1993	Bombay, India	370 employees	Revenue accounting services
		1995	Shannon, Ireland	35% share	Maintenance centre
Lufthansa	Germany		Bombay, India		Billing, ticketing operations
		1995	Shannon, Ireland	35% share	Maintenance centre
			various Asian countries	up to 10% of total cabin crew	Flight attendants
British Airways	UK	1992	New Delhi		System for correcting tickets
		1996	Bombay	450	Data processing
			various countries		Flight attendants
Alitalia	Italy	1995	Australia	6 Boeing 767 jets	Leased jets complete with crews
Cathay Pacific	Hong Kong	1993	Guangzhou, China	250 employees	Revenue accounting, data processing
		1995	Xiamen, China	10% share	Taikoo Aircraft Engineering (TAECO) maintenance centre
		1995	Australia	$188 million	Computer centre
JAL	Japan	1966	various countries	up to 30% of total approx. 1,000 employees	Flight attendants
		1993/94		100	Pilots, copilots, flight engineers
		1995	Xiamen, China	10% share	TAECO maintenance centre
SIA	Singapore	1994	Bombay, India	30 employees	Computer software development
		1994	Beijing, China		Revenue accounting
		1995	Xiamen, China	10% share	TAECO maintenance centre

4.6 Summary

This chapter provides a preliminary analysis of some airline operation and network characteristics, and input factor prices. It also examines the relationship between exchange rate fluctuations and input factor prices, as well as the growing practice of global sourcing of input factors.

Results from this preliminary analysis show that Asian carriers, with the exception of JAL and ANA, generally enjoy lower prices than North American and European carriers in almost all of the input categories. European carriers, on average, pay higher input prices, particularly for non-labour input categories. Labour and materials input prices illustrate a clear upward trend over the period, while fuel and flight equipment prices show considerable fluctuations. Exchange rate changes have had significant impacts on input prices for carriers where home currencies have experienced substantial changes and fluctuations.

As the international airline industry moves toward globalization, global sourcing is becoming a common practice. Global sourcing will reduce some variations in input factor prices among airlines, and increase competitive pressures on airlines.

Appendix 4
Aircraft Price Index

In our study, each airline's fleet is categorized into 14 types of aircraft. The average annual lease prices of these 14 types of aircraft are aggregated to form a single aggregate aircraft price index by using the multilateral index procedure proposed by Caves, Christensen, and Diewert (CCD, 1982). In mathematical terms, the CCD method is specified as follows:

$$\ln\frac{P_i}{P_j} = \sum \frac{W_{ki}+\bar{W}_k}{2}\ln\frac{P_{ki}}{\tilde{P}_k} - \sum \frac{W_{kj}+\bar{W}_k}{2}\ln\frac{P_{kj}}{\tilde{P}_k} \qquad\qquad A\ 4.1$$

where P_i is the price index for the i-th observation, P_{ki} is the price for type k aircraft) for i-th observation, the W_{ki} are weights, a bar over a variable indicates the arithmetic mean and a tilde over a variable indicates the geometric mean. Lease rates are used as prices for the aircraft, and cost shares based on the lease values are used as weights.

This procedure establishes transitive comparisons across all of the sample observations (time-series of a cross-section of airline companies) via a series of binary comparisons between each of the observations and the geometric mean of the data.

Chapter 5
Partial Factor Productivities
and Input Efficiency Indices

This chapter first describes airline output and input variables which are required for performance analysis. It then presents and discusses results of airline partial factor productivity and input efficiency measurement.

5.1 Airline Output and Input

Measurement of productivity and efficiency requires detailed data on outputs and inputs. Data on five categories of airline outputs are compiled for this study: scheduled passenger service (measured in revenue-passenger-kilometers or RPK), scheduled freight service (measured in revenue-tonne-kilometers or RTK), mail service (measured in RTK), non-scheduled passenger and freight services (measured in RTK), and incidental services (non-airline businesses). Incidental services include a wide variety of non-airline businesses such as catering services, ground handling, aircraft maintenance and reservation services for other airlines, technology sales, consulting services, and hotel business. These are non-core activities of an airline, but use up inputs reported in the sources of data used by most researchers. Our data show that for some years, the revenues from non-airline businesses account for up to 30 percent of total operating revenues for some airlines, with an average of 8 percent for the airlines included in our sample[30]. Therefore, omission of incidental output, without the corresponding exclusion of inputs used to produce them, would bias productivity or efficiency measures in favor of the airlines who do little non-core businesses.

In order to include incidental services in our analysis, it is necessary to construct a quantity index for incidental outputs which can be meaningfully compared across all airlines and over time. A quantity index is computed by deflating incidental revenues by an appropriate price index. As in the case of materials input price discussed in Chapter 4, incidental services include a wide variety of activities, therefore, the same general price index, used for materials input price, can be used also as the price index for incidental output. Table 5.1 presents the airlines' 1995 output levels. The last column in the table reports the percentage of incidental revenue.

Recall from Chapter 4, we distinguish five categories of input: labor, fuel, materials, flight equipment, and ground property and equipment (GPE). Labor input is measured by total number of employees. Fuel input is measured by gallons of fuel consumed. For flight equipment, a fleet quantity index is constructed by deflating total annualized aircraft cost by the aircraft capital price index discussed in Chapter 4. Annual cost for each aircraft type is estimated by the product of lease price and number of airplanes. Total annualized aircraft cost is then computed as the sum across all categories

---

[30] In 1996, incidental services accounted for seven percent of total revenue for an average airline in our sample.

	Table 5.1 Airline Revenues and Outputs, 1995								
	Revenue in US$ (million)				Output in RTK (million)				%Incid'l
	Passenger	Freight	Mail	non-sch.	Incid'l	Pax	Freight	mail	non-Sch	revenue[1]
North America										
American	13362	516	152	9	1571	14992	2446	584	10	10
United	13051	543	214	28	1059	16285	2463	834	40	7
Delta	11407	377	160	14	599	12426	1483	578	7	5
Northwest	7784	615	136	18	355	9125	2838	441	25	4
US Air	6275	79	74	27	530	5492	183	201	67	8
Continental	4364	110	54	30	361	5184	484	186	41	7
Air Canada	2179	199	21	35	98	2387	922	82	62	4
Canadian	1600	176	10	67	85	2082	715	27	124	4
Asia-Pacific										
Japan Airlines	8701	1358	142	244	439	6449	3787	179	27	4
All Nippon	7581	511	114	26	505	3625	972	87	26	6
Singapore Airlines	3376	886	26	10	142	4775	3844	91	3	3
Korean Air	2689	930	25	147	571	3229	4561	47	425	13
Cathay	2838	718	29	3	108	3366	2790	57	2	3
Qantas	3952	494	49	296	272	4697	1617	119	12	5
Thai	2038	401	18	11	458	2391	1320	38	7	16
Europe										
Lufthansa[2]	6818	1716	203	116	1051	5519	5373	173	37	11
British Air	9530	820	60	305	1	9300	3075	145	25	0.01
Air France	5139	1149	74	34	114	5331	4437	151	19	2
SAS	3629	195	37	18	718	1671	453	48	23	16
KLM	3823	991	47	1	685	4302	3690	48	0.4	12
Swissair	2762	449	26	35	211	1936	1508	53	30	6
Iberia	2424	218	28	0	232	2143	677	30	0	8

1. Revenue share of incidental services (%);   2. 1994 data;

of aircraft. The real stock of ground properties and equipment (GPE) is estimated using the perpetual inventory method. Under the assumption that the flow of capital service is proportional to the capital stock, the annual cost of using GPE is computed by multiplying the real GPE stock by a GPE service price. The GPE service price is constructed using the method proposed by Christensen and Jorgenson (1969) which accounts for interest, depreciation, corporate income and property taxes, and capital gains or losses. Since GPE costs are small relative to flight equipment costs, these two categories of capital inputs are further aggregated into a single capital stock series using the translog multilateral index procedure proposed by Caves, Christensen and Diewert (1982)[31]. The last input category, materials input, contains all other inputs not included in any of the input categories discussed above (labor, fuel, and capital). As such, materials cost is a catch-all cost category, including numerous items such as airport fees, sales commissions, passenger meals, employee travel, consultants, non-labor repair and maintenance expenses, stationery, and other purchased goods and services. Materials cost is computed by subtracting labor, fuel, flight equipment rental payment, and capital depreciation and amortization from total operating expenses, as reported in *Financial Data* published by the International Civil Aviation Organization (ICAO). As in the case of incidental output, materials cost is deflated by the materials input price index to construct a materials input quantity index. This is in order to include materials input in our analysis. Table 5.2 lists five input variables for 1995.

The five categories of outputs (inputs) are aggregated to form a single aggregate multilateral output (input) index using the translog multilateral index procedure proposed by Caves, Christensen and Diewert (1982)[32]. Figures 5.1a, 5.1b, and 5.1c plot the aggregate output index, and Figures 5.2a, 5.2b, and 5.2c plot the input index. Both series are normalized at American Airlines' 1990 data. Figures 5.1a-c show that most of the airlines had strong output growth during the 1986-1995 period, except for Air Canada and Iberia. US Air and Delta achieved high annual output growth rates of 17% and 13%, respectively, mostly because of mergers with other carriers (US Air-PSA-Piedmont; Delta-Western). Korean Air, All Nippon Airways (ANA), and Thai International are the fastest growing carriers in Asia with average annual output growth of 12%, 10% and 15%, respectively. Qantas' high output growth in 1994 was due mostly to its merger with Australian Airlines. Among the European carriers, British Airways (8%) and Lufthansa (8%) are the leaders in output growth. Air France experienced high output growth during 1991-1993 mainly due to the merger with UTA.

---

[31] This multilateral index is essentially a weighted average which uses cost shares of the capital categories as weights for aggregation . Thus, it has been widely used by economists. Please see Appendix IV for the details on constructing multilateral index from panel data.

[32] Revenue shares (cost shares) are used as weights in aggregating outputs (inputs). As a result, higher weights are given to outputs with higher yields. Similarly, more expensive input factors are given higher weights in aggregating inputs.

	Input Cost in US$ (mllion)					Input Quantity				
	Labour	Fuel	Materials	Flight	GPE	Labour (No.)	Fuel (mill.gal)	Materials (index[1])	Flight (index[1])	GPE (index[1])
North America										
American	5742	1482	5713	2098	535	90980	2772	1.163	1.456	0.892
United	5293	1583	5500	2325	348	80902	2799	1.120	1.593	0.581
Delta	4232	1368	4745	1685	301	62832	2389	0.966	1.175	0.502
Northwest	3030	1031	3340	1095	150	44682	1774	0.680	0.803	0.251
US Air	2866	605	2574	1234	139	43614	1052	0.524	0.808	0.232
Continental	1321	570	2199	840	24	32272	1073	0.448	0.554	0.040
Air Canada	699	329	1066	403	91	20503	464	0.229	0.296	0.153
Canadian	533	291	873	311	17	14088	374	0.188	0.211	0.028
Asia-Pacific										
Japan Airlines	2756	1303	5213	852	453	20482	1395	0.872	0.598	0.756
All Nippon	1715	1067	4518	737	401	14649	675	0.756	0.524	0.669
Singapore Airlines	431	577	2290	487	50	12966	874	0.524	0.344	0.084
Korean Air	571	538	2233	505	305	16478	873	0.569	0.346	0.509
Cathay	871	440	1544	352	71	14163	708	0.352	0.246	0.118
Qantas	1120	503	2389	505	69	23238	751	0.527	0.343	0.116
Thai	474	292	1300	307	294	20718	368	0.692	0.208	0.490
Europe										
Lufthansa[2]	2665	761	5105	846	202	44121	1189	0.821	0.625	0.344
British Air	2017	943	5422	1127	379	50477	1400	1.003	0.783	0.633
Air France	2531	737	2196	669	172	36384	985	0.379	0.460	0.288
SAS	1134	248	2444	350	62	17937	425	0.327	0.241	0.103
KLM	1557	485	2302	399	212	25033	831	0.417	0.271	0.353
Swissair	1170	300	1556	225	128	16520	369	0.201	0.159	0.213
Iberia	1202	272	913	349	148	24704	382	0.156	0.250	0.247

1. All indices are normalized at the American Airlines' 1990 data;   2. 1994 data;

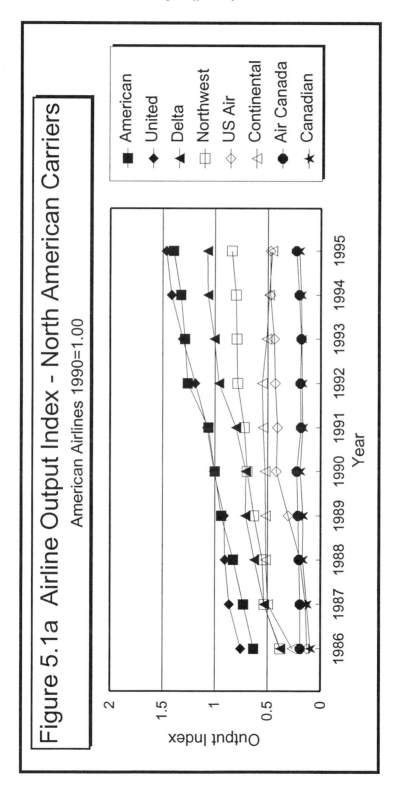

Figure 5.1a Airline Output Index - North American Carriers

American Airlines 1990=1.00

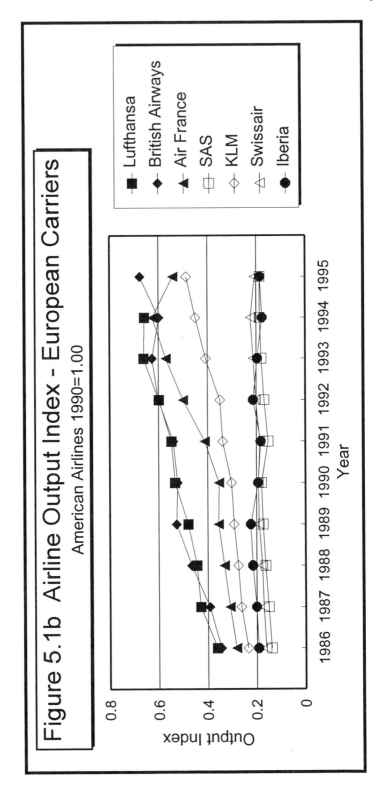

Figure 5.1b Airline Output Index - European Carriers
American Airlines 1990=1.00

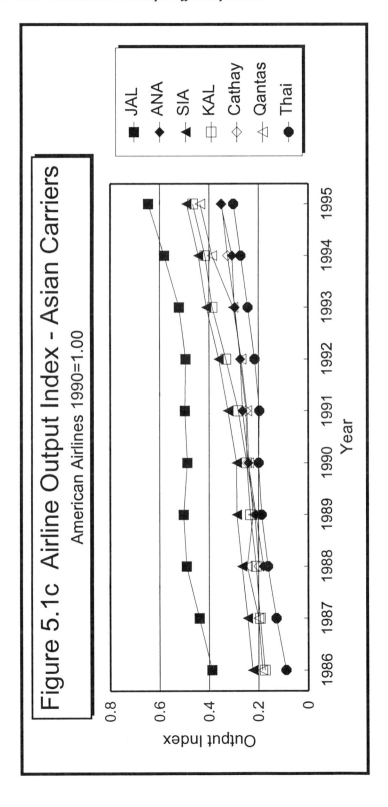

Figure 5.1c Airline Output Index - Asian Carriers

American Airlines 1990=1.00

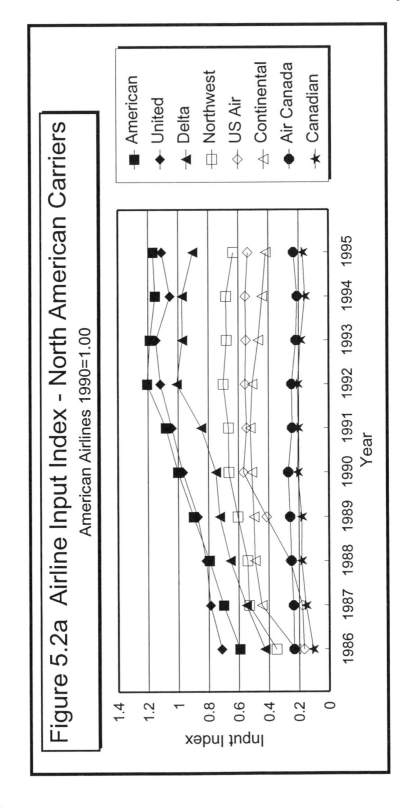

Figure 5.2a Airline Input Index - North American Carriers

American Airlines 1990=1.00

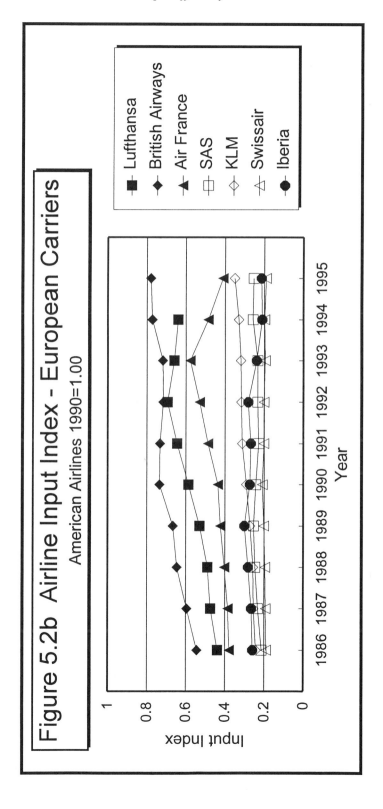

Figure 5.2b Airline Input Index - European Carriers
American Airlines 1990=1.00

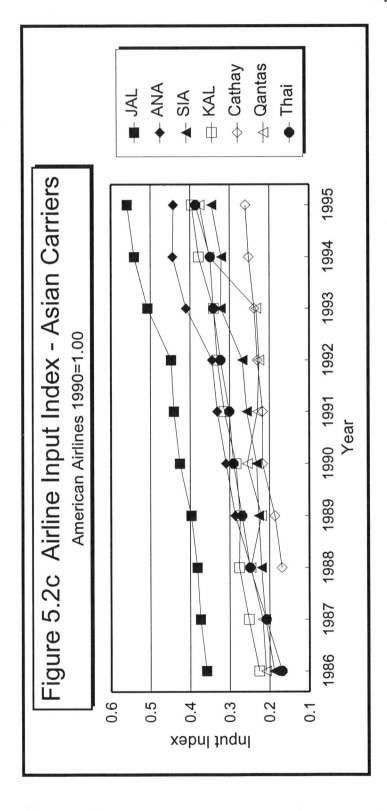

Figure 5.2c Airline Input Index - Asian Carriers

American Airlines 1990=1.00

5.2 Partial Factor Productivities and Input Efficiency Measures

Productivity of a production unit (a firm or organization) refers to the ratio of its output to input. This ratio is easy to compute if the production unit produces a single output using a single input. However, airlines use several inputs to produce several outputs, causing complications in computing productivities. Thus, partial measures of productivities are commonly used by trade and popular press, industry, and even academics to assess differences in performance. These partial measures are easier to compute and understand intuitively. However, gross or observed measures of these partial factor productivities are affected by airline network and operating variables, such as average stage length and output composition, which are largely beyond managerial control. Therefore, the effects of these uncontrollable factors must be removed in order to make a meaningful comparison of airlines' efficiency in using a particular input - airline input efficiency. It must be noted, however, that input efficiency results still need to be interpreted with caution. This is because a single input efficiency measure (for a particular input) does not tell the whole story about a firm's overall productivity or efficiency, it only reflects how that particular input is used by airlines. For example, an increase in labor input efficiency may be achieved as a result of labor being replaced by outsourcing (or automation). But this would result in a decrease in materials (capital) input efficiency.

Since productivity of an input (labor, capital, fuel, or materials) is influenced significantly by factors beyond managerial control, such as average stage length of an airline and composition of outputs, it would be meaningless to compare a gross measure of productivity across airlines and/or over time within an airline without removing the effects of variations in these uncontrollable factors between airlines and/or changes over time. Therefore, in this section, we examine airline input efficiencies[33], after removing effects of "uncontrollable" variables from gross measures of partial factor productivities. The following variables are regarded as being 'uncontrollable' in this study:

- **average stage length**: This variable depends on route and market structure of an airline's network which, in turn, depends largely on geographic location of home country, extent of regulatory control on market access, and government attitude toward bilateral air treaties. Since average cost declines with stage length, longer average stage length is expected to lead to higher productivities.
- **composition of airline outputs**: This variable is also greatly influenced by geographic location of the airline and regulatory control on the airline industry. For example, air cargo accounts for a large portion of total output for many Asian and European carriers based in export-oriented countries - such as Lufthansa, Korean Air, KLM, Air France, JAL, Singapore, and Cathay. Such carriers were economically induced to develop air cargo businesses early on. On the other hand, U.S. carriers have traditionally focused on passenger business. Cargo service is considered to require less input than passenger service, but it generates

---

[33] GPE capital is very small compared to aircraft capital, thus airline total capital is dominated by aircraft capital. Therefore, GPE capital efficiency is not examined here.

less revenue. Thus, the presence of cargo services could affect an airline's productivities in either direction. As for incidental service output, there is not yet enough empirical evidence nor theoretical ground to foresee how incidental output would affect an airline's gross productivities.

Some researchers argue that the load factor is also largely determined by type of markets an airline is allowed to enter, as well as extent of control on choice of aircraft and flight frequencies. Others argue that airline management can manage load factor by adjusting flight frequency and aircraft size to changing demand. Obviously, whether or not load factor can be managed depends largely on regulatory conditions of a specific market. Most airlines serve both regulated and unregulated markets. Thus, when a system-wide load factor is used, it can be regarded either as a controllable or uncontrollable variable. In this study, load factor is regarded as being controllable. Since higher load factor indicates better utilization of aircraft, a positive relationship is expected between load factor and productivities.

Labor Efficiency

Gross labor productivity is measured by aggregate output per employee. This gross labor productivity is regressed against a set of explanatory variables, and a labor efficiency index is then computed after removing the effects of uncontrollable variables (average stage length and output mix variables)[34]. Figures 5.3a, 5.3b, and 5.3c show changes in labor efficiency over the period. Northwest is consistently at the top in terms of labor efficiency among North American carriers, followed by Continental and United. US Air and Air Canada's labor efficiency is significantly lower than that of Northwest. During the sample period, 1986-1993, Delta made substantial improvement in its labor efficiency, average 4.2% per year, followed by United at an average of 1.7% per year. Northwest, Canadian, and Air Canada also improved labor efficiency, at annual rate of 1.2%, 1.3%, and 0.8%, respectively, while American and US Air's labor efficiency remained essentially unchanged during the period. On the other hand, Continental's labor efficiency was down by about 1.3% per year between 1986 and 1993. Continental's decline in labor efficiency may have been caused partly by their deteriorating labor relations problem.

BA had the highest labor efficiency among European carriers, followed by Lufthansa and KLM. BA also made the most significant improvement in labor efficiency, at an average rate of 4.7% per year, followed closely by Air France at 4.5% per year. It is clear that BA's restructuring process made a significant difference. Iberia and SAS had relatively low labor efficiency among European carriers throughout the period. Except for Iberia, labor efficiency has generally improved for European carriers during the 1986-1993 period. Iberia's labor efficiency remained essentially unchanged during the period.

---

[34] See Table 5A.1, in Appendix V, for the regression results.

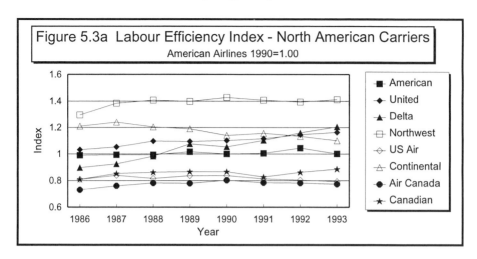

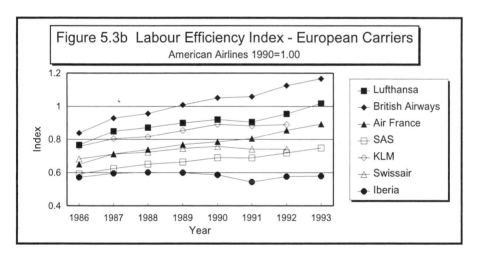

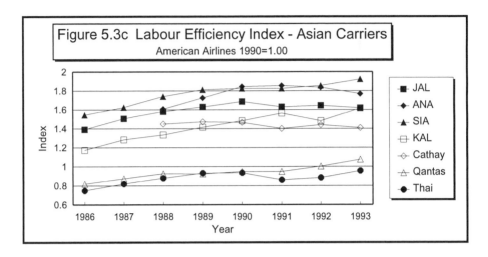

Asian carriers' labor efficiencies are patchy and marked by substantial variations between carriers. Singapore Airlines achieved the highest labor efficiency among Asian carriers, followed by ANA and JAL. Thai and Qantas' labor efficiency is substantially lower than that of SIA and other Asian carriers. For the most part though, Asian carriers improved their labor efficiency considerably during the sample period, with KAL as the leader. KAL improved its labor efficiency at an average rate of 4.6% per year, followed by Qantas at 3.9% per year.

The average labor efficiency indices in 1993 are shown in Table 5.3. Asian carriers, on average, have higher labor efficiency than North American carriers, which in turn have higher labor efficiency than European carriers. This result appears to be contrary to the perception that Asian carriers are likely to use more labor because of lower wage levels at home. One of the explanations for this result is that number of employees is used to measure labor input rather than number of employee-hours, and employees of Asian carriers tend to work more hours. Furthermore, the standard deviation for Asian carriers is much higher than that of North American carriers, indicating that variations in labor efficiency among Asian carriers is much larger than among North American carriers. In terms of labor efficiency improvement, European carriers had a higher average growth rate than Asian carriers, while North American carriers' labor efficiency growth rate was substantially lower than European or Asian carriers.

Table 5.3 Average Labour Efficiency, 1993			
	North America	**Europe**	**Asia**
Mean	1.041	0.925	1.480
STD	0.206	0.212	0.330
N	8	6	7

* American Airlines 1990=1.00

Fuel Efficiency

Gross fuel productivity is measured by aggregate output per gallon of fuel consumed. Similar to labor efficiency, a fuel efficiency index is estimated after removing effects of uncontrollable variables (stage length and output mix) from gross fuel productivity[35]. Figures 5.4a, 5.4b, and 5.4c plots the fuel efficiency index. Fuel productivity is mostly determined by type of aircraft used and aircraft operating procedures, and is affected by network structure. Fuel price differentials among airlines and short term fuel price fluctuations are not considered as influential factors of fuel productivity. Among North American carriers, Canadian (CAI) and United achieved relatively high fuel efficiency, while US Air and Continental had relatively low fuel efficiency. Fuel efficiency showed a general upward trend among North American carriers, with Canadian achieving the most significant fuel efficiency improvement at an average rate of 3.9% per year.

BA had the highest fuel efficiency among European carriers. Moreover, there was a noticeable gap between BA and other European carriers. Air France had the lowest fuel efficiency before its merger with UTA, but made continuous improvement over the period. Lufthansa also made substantial fuel efficiency improvement. Iberia's fuel efficiency dropped considerably in 1990, and had not been able to return to its previous level by 1993. SAS's fuel efficiency also declined over the period, at an average diminution of 0.5% per year, and became the lowest between 1992 and 1993.

Thai Airways appeared to have the highest fuel efficiency among Asian carriers. This may be partly due to the fact that its fleet is made up mostly of Airbus aircraft, which

---

[35] The regression results are listed in Table 5A.1 in Appendix V.

are generally more fuel efficient than Boeing and Douglas aircraft[36]. ANA, Thai and KAL's fuel efficiency increased during the period, while SIA and Cathay's fuel efficiency declined considerably. This decline in fuel efficiency is consistent with the falling load factor (see Figures 4.2a-c). ANA's improvement in fuel efficiency can be partly explained by its improving load factor and the introduction of Airbus aircraft into its fleet. JAL had the lowest fuel efficiency among the Asian carriers. This is partly because JAL's fleet consists mostly of Boeing 747s and Douglas DC-10s, both among the least fuel efficient aircraft.

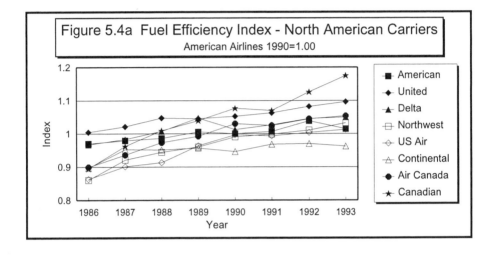

Figure 5.4a Fuel Efficiency Index - North American Carriers
American Airlines 1990=1.00

---

[36] Note that the fuel consumption data for Thai was estimated through regression. Estimated fuel quantities from regression are surprisingly accurate for most airlines. However, Thai is the only airline in our sample which has a fleet made up mostly of Airbus aircraft. Airbus planes, in general, are more fuel efficient than other aircraft. The fuel quantity variable for Thai appears to be underestimated, thus Thai's fuel productivity is likely to be somewhat overestimated. This may also partly explain the noticeably higher fuel price for Thai (Figure 4.6c).

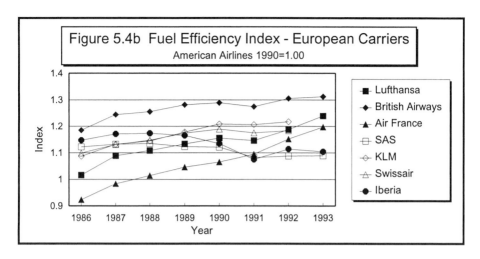

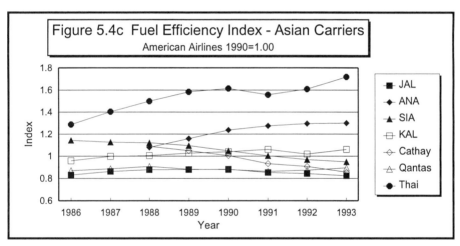

Table 5.4 shows average regional fuel efficiencies in 1993[37]. European carriers, on average, had higher fuel efficiency than Asian carriers, who in turn had higher fuel efficiency than North American carriers. Perhaps, North American carriers pay less attention to fuel efficiency because their fuel prices are cheaper relative to those in Asia or Europe. However, North American carriers, on average, had higher fuel efficiency growth. It is further noted that large variations in fuel efficiency exist among Asian carriers.

Table 5.4 Average Fuel Efficiency, 1993			
	North America	Europe	Asia
Mean	1.049	1.191	1.086
STD	0.060	0.067	0.299
N	8	6	7

* American Airlines 1990=1.00

Aircraft Efficiency

Gross aircraft productivity is measured by the ratio of aggregate output to the aggregate fleet quantity index. And, an aircraft efficiency index is constructed after removing the effects of stage length and output mix from gross aircraft productivity[38], and is plotted in Figures 5.5a, 5.5b, and 5.5c. United Airlines had relatively high aircraft efficiency than most other North American carriers prior to 1991, when its aircraft efficiency came to par with American Airlines, Northwest, and Delta. Continental's aircraft efficiency remained relatively high among North American carriers, even though it declined substantially during the period. US Air had the lowest aircraft productivity among North American carriers, even after removing the effect of its shorter stage length. In general, aircraft efficiency exhibited a downward trend for North American carriers, especially US Air and Air Canada, over the sample period, except for Northwest, which registered a slight improvement.

Level of aircraft efficiency is widespread among European carriers. Prior to 1989, Iberia appeared to have the highest aircraft efficiency. However, its aircraft efficiency fell dramatically between 1987 and 1993. During the same period, SAS, Lufthansa, Air France and BA similarly experienced falling aircraft efficiency of varying degrees. On the other hand, KLM and Swissair did not record any significant drops in

---

[37] The effects of stage length on fuel productivity appear to be overestimated by the regression analysis (Table 5A.1), thus efficiency estimates for airlines with long stage length, such as SIA and Cathay which had relatively high gross fuel productivity, may be underestimated.

[38] The regression results are presented in Table 5A.1 in Appendix V.

aircraft efficiency, but rather slight improvements.

There was also a widespread drop in aircraft efficiency among Asian carriers with SIA, Cathay, and Thai having relatively higher aircraft efficiency than other carriers. ANA's aircraft productivity was substantially lower than other Asian carriers, even after accounting for its short haul network. KAL experienced some fluctuation in its aircraft efficiency, but did not record any significant drop during the period. Other airlines' aircraft efficiency, however, fell in the early 1990s, though to varying extent.

Aircraft efficiency index is closely related to daily average aircraft utilization rate as measured by average hours an aircraft flies per day. Figure 5.6 examines the relationship between the two. It is obvious that high daily aircraft utilization rate generally leads to high aircraft efficiency. For example, KLM had the highest daily aircraft utilization rate among all the carriers, and it also had the highest aircraft efficiency as well. On the other hand, US Air and ANA had rather low daily aircraft utilization rates, thus very low aircraft efficiency (even after removing effects of their shorter haul networks).

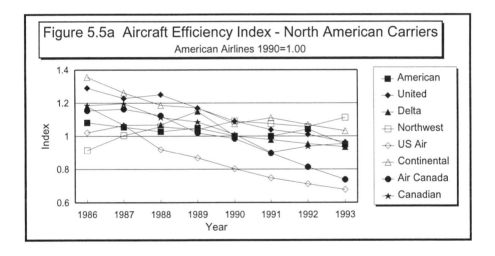

Figure 5.5a Aircraft Efficiency Index - North American Carriers
American Airlines 1990=1.00

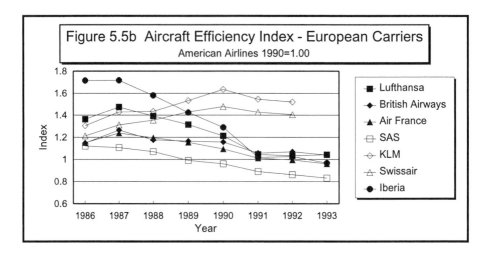

Figure 5.5b Aircraft Efficiency Index - European Carriers
American Airlines 1990=1.00

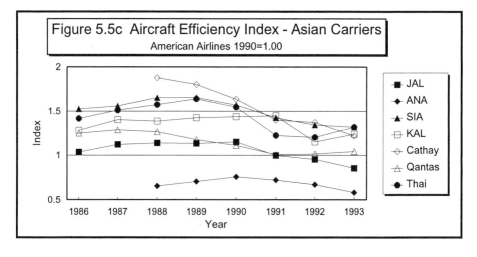

Figure 5.5c Aircraft Efficiency Index - Asian Carriers
American Airlines 1990=1.00

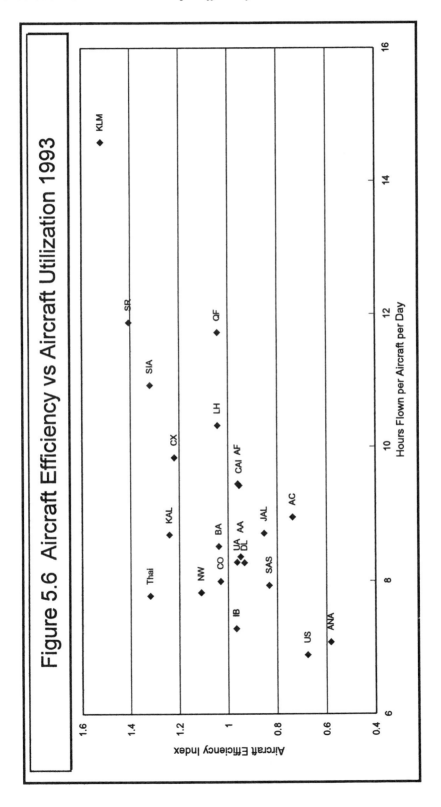

Figure 5.6 Aircraft Efficiency vs Aircraft Utilization 1993

Table 5.5 shows average regional aircraft efficiencies in 1993. Comparing aircraft efficiency between the three geographical regions produces similar results as fuel efficiency. Again, European carriers, on average, had higher aircraft efficiency than North American or Asian carriers. Asian carriers generally had higher aircraft efficiency than North American carriers. And, the results on fuel and aircraft efficiency for North American carriers are consistent with the fact that they tend to provide more frequent services, generally resulting in lower aircraft utilization, and higher fuel consumption. However, this may be optimal for North American carriers whose major markets are on short to medium distance routes requiring frequent services.

Table 5.5 Average Aircraft Efficiency, 1993			
	North America	Europe	Asia
Mean	0.920	1.139	1.082
STD	0.135	0.232	0.256
N	8	6	7

* American Airlines 1990=1.00

Materials Efficiency

The last input category is the materials input. Gross materials input productivity is the ratio of aggregate output to the materials input quantity index. Again, a materials efficiency index is constructed through a regression analysis[39]. Figures 5.7a, 5.7b, and 5.7c plot materials efficiency index. American had the highest materials efficiency among North American carriers during the 1989-1993 period. Prior to 1989, Delta had the highest materials efficiency, but it then declined substantially to be on par with Northwest, United and Continental. Air Canada and Canadian had relatively lower materials efficiency than US carriers. Except for Canadian, all North American carriers' materials input efficiency declined during the sample period.

KLM and Swissair were the most efficient European carriers in terms of materials input, however, Iberia was catching up rather quickly. Air France and Lufthansa were virtually the same in materials efficiency. And, BA and SAS' materials efficiency were considerably lower than other European carriers. Iberia achieved the most significant materials efficiency improvements, followed by BA and SAS.

In Asia, JAL appeared to have the most efficient use of materials input prior to 1991, while Qantas and Cathay later became more efficient. Thai was the least efficient carrier in terms of materials input. Qantas and Korean Air (KAL) made the most significant improvement in materials efficiency, followed by Thai and Cathay. SIA's materials efficiency remained essentially unchanged over the period, while JAL and ANA experienced decline in their materials efficiency.

---

[39] The regression results are listed in Table 5A.1 in Appendix V.

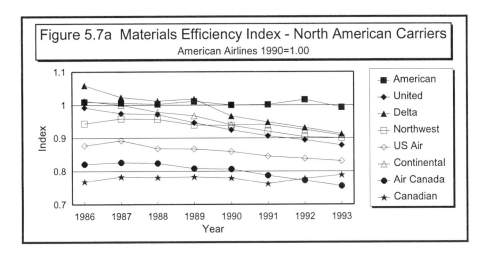

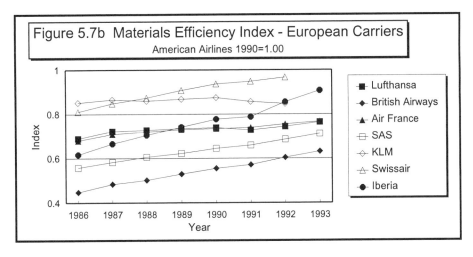

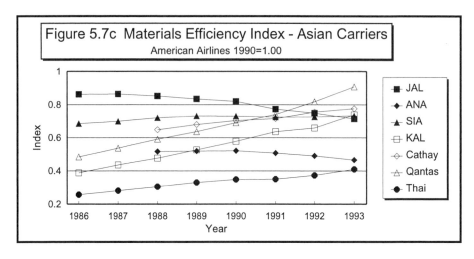

Comparison of 1993 average regional materials efficiencies is presented in Table 5.6. Unlike the previous input efficiency measures, Asian carriers were generally the least efficient in materials input, far behind average North American or European carriers. North American carriers appeared to be the most efficient in materials input.

Table 5.6 Average Materials Efficiency, 1993			
	North America	Europe	Asia
Mean	0.871	0.802	0.677
STD	0.071	0.101	0.163
N	8	6	7

* American Airlines 1990=1.00

5.3 Summary

This chapter examines airline input efficiencies after removing effects of the variables which are beyond airlines' managerial control. In general, Asian carriers had higher labor efficiency than North American and European carriers. European carriers, however, had higher fuel and aircraft efficiencies than North American and Asian carriers. North American carriers, on the other hand, had higher materials efficiency. From the discussions in this chapter, it can be seen that each input efficiency measure tells a somewhat different story regarding an airline's relative performance. High labor efficiency may be a result of labor being replaced by outsourcing or by automation. As an airline uses more outsourcing, which is reflected by the materials input, one may expect to see increase in labor efficiency, but decrease in materials efficiency at the same time. For a complete picture of an airline's productive performance, the efficiency of using all inputs should be considered in an integrated manner. The following chapter, therefore, examines airlines' total factor productivity and overall efficiency measures.

Appendix 5
Partial Factor Productivity Regression Results

	Table 5A.1 Partial Factor Productivity Regression Results*			
	Level: Dep = LPFP=log(PFP)			
Parameter	Labour	Fuel	Aircraft	Materials
Constant	-4.239 (4.36)	-3.155 (4.90)	-6.721 (5.82)	-2.938 (2.66)
Output	0.091 (1.96)	0.106 (3.44)	-0.020 (0.36)	0.019 (0.36)
Stage Length	0.218 (2.42)	0.247 (4.13)	0.114 (1.06)	0.181 (1.77)
%Freight	-0.009 (0.12)	0.036 (0.68)	-0.002 (0.02)	0.003 (0.03)
%Non-Sch.	0.007 (0.63)	0.011 (1.47)	-0.007 (0.56)	-0.012 (0.99)
%Incidental	0.068 (7.20)	0.063 (10.1)	0.519 (4.60)	-0.008 (0.72)
load factor	0.672 (4.75)	0.389 (4.14)	1.449 (8.61)	0.372 (2.31)
	+firm dummy + firm dummy*time	+firm dummy + firm dummy*time	+firm dummy + firm dummy*time	+firm dummy + firm dummy*time
No. of Obs.	178	178	178	178
R- Square	0.982	0.970	0.951	0.962
Log-Likelihood	290.31	363.42	259.47	267.57

* T-values in parenthese
- all variables except dummies are in natural log ;
- the parameter estimates for the firm dummies, and firm dummy* time trend are not reported here due to space limitation.

Chapter 6
Airline Productivity and Efficiency

This chapter examines airline overall productive efficiency using such methods as Total Factor Productivity (TFP), residual TFP, and Stochastic frontier method. These concepts and methodologies are also described briefly.

6.1 Total Factor Productivity

Total factor productivity (TFP) is a widely used measure of productivity of all input factors. TFP recognizes that multiple outputs are produced using various inputs.

TFP is defined as the amount of aggregate output produced by a unit of aggregate input. Caves, Christensen and Diewert (CCD, 1982) proposed the following well-known multilateral index procedure for computing TFP and making comparisons across firms, and over time:

$$
\begin{aligned}
\ln TFP_k - \ln TFP_j &= (\ln Y_k - \ln Y_j) - (\ln X_k - \ln X_j) \\
&= \sum_i \frac{R_{ik} + \bar{R}_i}{2} \ln \frac{Y_{ik}}{\tilde{Y}_i} - \sum_i \frac{R_{ij} - \bar{R}_i}{2} \ln \frac{Y}{\tilde{Y}} \\
&\quad - \sum_i \frac{W_{ik} + \bar{W}_i}{2} \ln \frac{X_{ik}}{\tilde{X}_i} + \sum_i \frac{W_{ij} + \bar{W}_i}{2} \ln
\end{aligned}
\tag{6-1}
$$

where Y_{ik} is the output I for observation k, R_{ik} is the revenue share of output I for observation k, $\bar{R}_i$ is the arithmetic mean of revenue share of output I over all observations in the sample, and $\tilde{Y}_i$ is the geometric mean of output I over all observations, X_{ik} are input quantities, and W_{ik} are input cost shares.

The TFP formula (equation 6-1) essentially shows that TFP index, for comparing between observations k and j, is computed by dividing the aggregate output index (see Figures 5.1a-c) by aggregate input index (see Figures 5.2a-c). Since multiple outputs are aggregated using their respective revenue shares as weights, high-valued outputs are given higher weights than low-priced outputs when forming the aggregate output index.

Figures 6.1a, 6.1b and 6.1c show the TFP index (normalized at American Airlines 1990). This TFP index reflects observed airline productivity. It is referred to as 'gross' TFP index, as it may not indicate airlines' "true" productive efficiency. 'Gross' TFP can be influenced by numerous factors including stage length, composition of outputs, and state of economy, which are largely beyond managerial control. Therefore, one should refrain from making inferences on productive efficiency from "gross" TFP results. With this note of caution, the gross TFP results reported in Figures 6.1a, 6.1b and 6.1c are summarized below.

- Most airlines' gross TFP levels improved during the 1986-1995 period. On average, European carriers, whose 1986 TFP levels were significantly lower than most US carriers, achieved higher TFP growth rate (3.4%

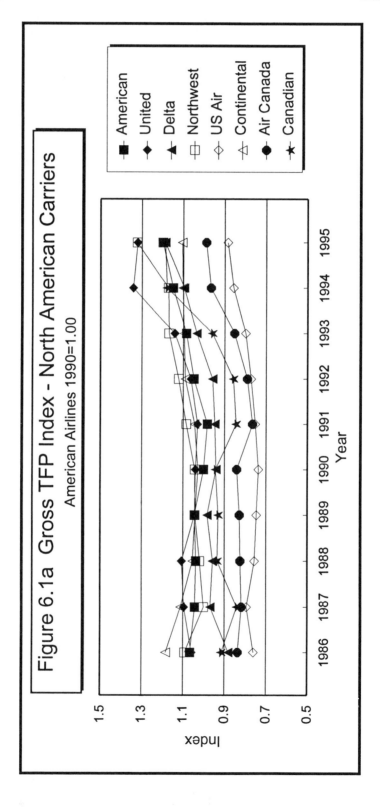

Figure 6.1a Gross TFP Index - North American Carriers

American Airlines 1990=1.00

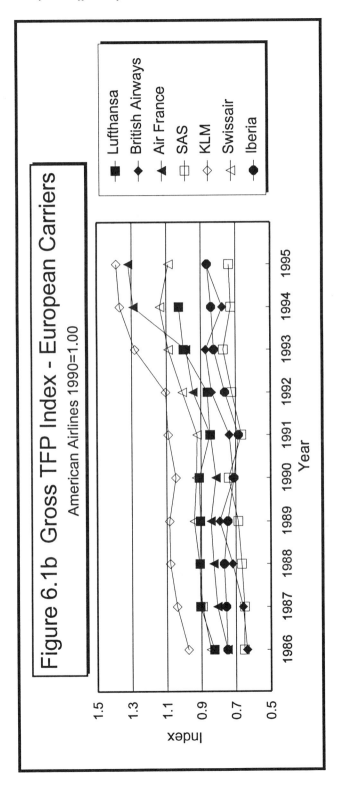

Figure 6.1b Gross TFP Index - European Carriers
American Airlines 1990=1.00

96

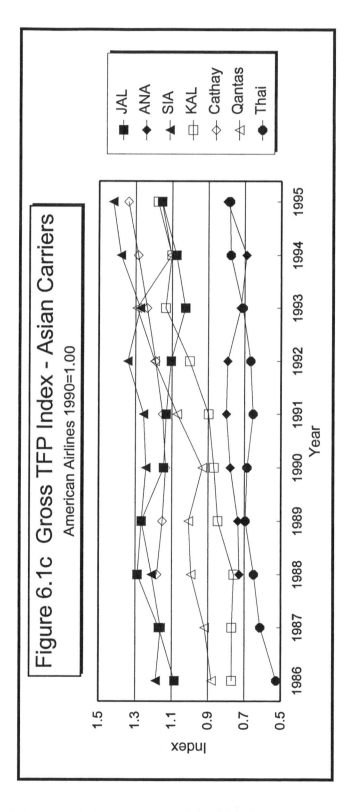

Figure 6.1c Gross TFP Index - Asian Carriers
American Airlines 1990=1.00

Chapter 6

per year) than US carriers (2.1%). Major regulatory and institutional changes in the European aviation market since 1986[40] may have contributed to European carrier improvements. Among Asian carriers, Korean Air (KAL) had consistent gross TFP improvements throughout the sample period (5.0% per year). Qantas and Thai had substantial productivity improvements, with average annual growth rates of 3.5% and 4.7%, respectively. Delta achieved the highest productivity growth rate (3.5% per year) among North American carriers, similar to the average growth rate for European carriers.

- Observed TFP growth is closely associated with output growth. Comparing Figure 5.1 with Figure 6.1, it is noted that carriers with high output growth also experienced strong TFP growth. For example, Korean Air's continuous TFP growth was fueled by its continuous strong output growth. Air France saw a substantial improvement in its TFP after its merger with UTA and as a result of both output growth and changes in output mix.

- Many airlines experienced a reduction in TFP between 1990 and 1992, probably due to the reduced demand caused by the economic recession and Gulf war. Continental experienced a slight decline in its gross TFP over the period, with an average TFP diminution of 0.7% per year.

- In 1995, the following airlines had higher gross TFP levels than other airlines in the region:
  North America: Northwest (1.32), United (1.32), American (1.20), Delta (1.19)
  Asia: Singapore (1.42), Cathay (1.34), Korean Air (1.18), Qantas (1.16);
  Europe: KLM (1.39), Air France (1.31), Swissair (1.09)

- US Air, All Nippon Airways, Thai, and SAS had considerably lower gross TFP than other airlines throughout our sample period.

6.2 Productivity and Efficiency

Productivity varies due to differences in production technology, productive efficiency, and network and production environments (Lovell 1993). Efficiency of a production unit, such as a firm, refers to the efficiency with which the production unit uses its inputs to produce outputs. TFP is the most widely used technique to assess firms' productive efficiency, and has also been used in many airline studies including Caves, Christensen and Tretheway (1981), Caves, Christensen, Tretheway and Windle (1987), Gillen, Oum and Tretheway (1985, 1990), Windle (1991), and Encaoua (1991). The traditional TFP method, however, does not account for or changes in the network and production environment. As discussed previously, the gross TFP measures are affected by many factors beyond managerial control, such as /changes in network, operating and market conditions. Therefore, separating effects of productive efficiency from those of network and production environment is a pre-requisite for making a proper inter-firm efficiency comparison. Many researchers use second-stage regression analysis on the TFP index to decompose TFP differentials into various sources, including efficiency. Examples

---

[40] Studies using pre-1986 data, such as Good et al (1995), found that US airlines had higher productivity growth than European airlines before liberalization measures were introduced by the European Union. EU introduced packages 1, 2, and 3 liberalization measures in 1987, 1989 and 1993, respectively.

of using this two-step procedure can be found in Caves, Christensen, and Tretheway (1981), Gillen, Oum and Tretheway (1989), and Ehrlich, Gallais-Hamonno, Liu and Lutter (1994).

In recent years, the use of frontier methods to estimate efficiency has become widespread (Bauer, 1990, and Greene, 1993)[41]. For example, Barla and Perelman (1989) were among the first to apply the stochastic frontier method to measure airline productive performance. Good, Nadiri, Röller, and Sickles (1993) and Good, Röller, and Sickles (1995) used the stochastic frontier method to compare performance of the largest European carriers and their American counterparts. Other studies that used stochastic frontier methods to examine airline efficiency include Bruning (1991), Jha and Sahni (1992), Loeb, Bruning and Hu (1994), and Coelli, Perelman and Romano (1996). One advantage of frontier methods over the TFP method is that the former makes use of the fact that some firms may not be on efficiency frontier, and thus, attempts to measure the distance between efficient 'frontier' and the observed performance of a firm.

Below, the two-step TFP method and stochastic frontier method are used to measure productive efficiency of our sample airlines.

6.3 Two-Step TFP Method for Computing Residual TFP

With the two-step TFP method, the gross TFP index is regressed against a set of explanatory variables. A residual TFP index is then computed by removing the effects of variations in the variables beyond managerial control (henceforth, referred to as 'uncontrollable' variables) from the gross TFP measure. This residual TFP index is used to compare productive efficiency across firms and over time within a firm.

In this study, a log-linear regression is run on a number of output and network variables. As described in Chapter 5, average stage length and composition of airline outputs are regarded as being 'uncontrollable' in this study. *Ceteris paribus,* an airline with a longer average stage length is expected to have higher 'gross' TFP than an airline with shorter stage length because average cost per unit of output decreases with stage length. Also, an airline with high load factor is expected to have a high gross TFP if other things are equal.

Table 6.1 reports four alternative TFP regression models. %Freight, %Non-Sch., and %Incidental variables are revenue shares for freight, non-scheduled and incidental services, respectively, reflecting mix of outputs. All four models include six basic variables. The difference between the models lies in the way in which year and firm dummy and/or time trend variables are incorporated. *TFP1* has the simplest model specification, including year dummies only. *TFP2* includes both year dummies and firm dummies. *TFP3* specifies unique time trend variable for each airline. *TFP4* includes both firm dummies and firm-specific time trend. Statistical tests show that TFP4 model is the best model to

---

[41] Some studies have used the Data Envelopment Analysis (DEA) method, a non-parametric method, for measuring airline efficiency (see, for example, Oum and Yu (1994)). The DEA method is not used here because the results of Monte Carlo studies such as Gong and Sickles (1992) and Yu (1997) indicate that DEA is dominated by the stochastic frontier method in most cases.

use.[42] Accordingly, only the TFP4 results are to be reported.

Table 6.1 TFP Regression Results*				
	Level: Dep = LTFP=log(TFP)			
Parameter	TFP1	TFP2	TFP3	TFP4
Constant	-1.991 (2.45)	-2.972 (4.44)	-2.436 (3.46)	-3.422 (4.59)
Output	0.156 (8.76)	0.071 (2.03)	0.154 (6.60)	0.049 (1.38)
Stage Length	0.273 (9.38)	0.065 (1.14)	0.184 (4.80)	0.173 (2.51)
%Freight	-0.024 (1.85)	-0.224 (4.58)	-0.060 (2.30)	0.002 (0.03)
%Non-Sch.	0.018 (2.12)	0.002 (0.24)	0.014 (1.43)	-0.008 (0.99)
%Incidental	0.047 (5.34)	0.035 (4.55)	0.033 (3.75)	0.032 (4.38)
load factor	0.012 (0.06)	0.446 (3.60)	0.242 (1.54)	0.523 (4.83)
1987	-0.002 (0.06)	-0.028 (1.49)		
1988	0.019 (0.48)	-0.015 (0.72)		
1989	0.014 (0.35)	-0.021 (0.89)		
1990	-0.029 (0.72)	-0.048 (1.90)		
1991	-0.053 (1.39)	-0.046 (1.89)		
1992	-0.026 (0.66)	-0.009 (0.31)		
1993	0.001 (0.02)	0.030 (1.01)		
		+ firm dummies	+ firm dummy *time	+ firm dummy + firm dummy*time
No. of Obs.	178	178	178	178
R- Square	0.620	0.943	0.827	0.964
Log-Likelihood	128.87	297.45	198.65	337.94

* T-values in parenthese
- all variables except dummies are in natural log ;
- the parameter estimates for the firm dummies, and firm dummy* time trend are not reported here due to space limitation.

---

[42]TFP1 is nested in TFP2, and is obviously statistically dominated by TFP2. Similarly, TFP3 is nested in TFP4, and is statistically dominated by TFP4. The log likelihood ratio test between TFP2 and TFP4 yields a test statistic of 80.98 (=2* (337.94-297.45)), which is significantly larger than 33.92 - the critical value of χ^2 distribution with 22 degrees of freedom at 5% level of significance. Therefore, TFP4 is statistically preferred over the other three models. It is worth noting that the residual TFP index from TFP1 (the model with lowest goodness of fit) is similar to those from TFP4. In fact, the correlation coefficient between the two sets is over 91%. This shows robustness of our empirical results.

The regression results show that:

- The fact that TFP4 model is chosen implies that different airlines have different residual TFP level and growth rates over time.
- Average stage length has a positive effects on the observed (gross) TFP level while output level does not have a statistically significant effect. The load factor has a statistically significant positive effect on the gross TFP.
- %Incidental is significant and has a positive coefficient, indicating that there is a strong positive relationship between %Incidental and the gross TFP level. This implies that, *ceteris paribus,* an airline with a large share of incidental revenue is expected to have high gross TFP. Other output mix variables (%Freight and %Non-scheduled) do not have statistically significant effects on the gross TFP level.

Residual TFP index is computed by removing effects of uncontrollable variables (average stage length and output mix variables) from "gross" TFP values. Figures 6.2a, 6.2b and 6.2c plot the residual TFP index from TFP4. Comparing these with the gross TFP index reported in Figures 6.1a, 6.1b and 6.1c, it is noted that residual TFPs have a much smaller spread between airlines than gross TFP. This happens because much of the spread in the gross TFP index was explained by the uncontrollable variables. Furthermore, growth rate of residual TFPs is much smaller than that of gross TFP because changes in airline networks and output mix accounted for a large portion of TFP growth. The residual TFP results are summarized below.

Overall, European carriers have improved productive efficiency and achieved much higher growth rates than North American carriers. In particular, British Airways (4% per year) achieved the most significant productivity growth. The Asian carriers, however, are divided into two groups. One group, including Korean Air (5.6%), Qantas (5.2%), and Thai (4.6%), achieved high growth in productive efficiency, while the rest experienced slow growth in residual TFP. SIA also made some improvement in its productive efficiency during the period, an average of 0.8% per year.

Among the North American carriers, Northwest (0.3~1.3%), Delta (0.8~1.3%) and Canadian (1%) achieved modest productive efficiency growth, while Continental and US Air experienced a slight decline in productive efficiency. There was no significant improvement or decline in the productive efficiencies of other North American carriers. Furthermore, efficiency levels of the three US mega carriers (American, United, and Delta) were very close. Similarly, the major Asian carriers (Singapore, Korean Air, and Cathay as well as Qantas) essentially converged to the same efficiency level in 1993, from substantial performance at the beginning of our sample period.

Although the residual TFP index has a smaller spread than the gross TFP index, there appear to be considerable efficiency among the sample carriers. In order to see whether there are any significant difference in productive efficiency between carriers in different geographic regions, we computed regional average residual TFP index for North America, Europe, and Asia. These average TFP indices are reported in Figure 6.3a. Figure 6.3a shows that European carriers, on average, were about 12% less efficient than US carriers in 1993. However, they have made significant improvement since European aviation liberalization began in 1987, and the efficiency gap between European carriers and North

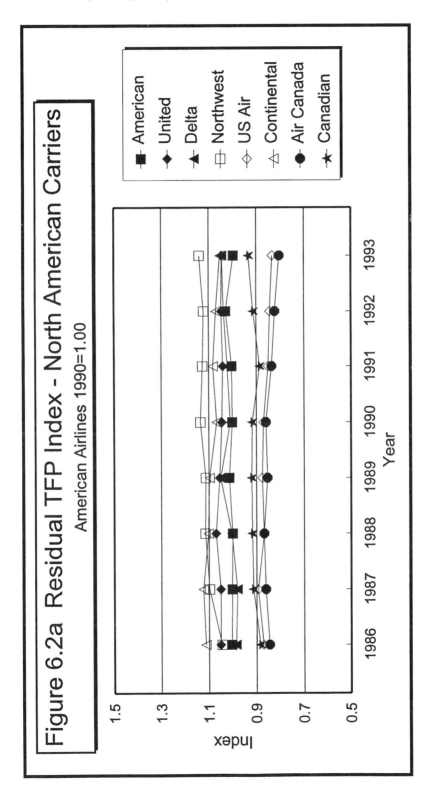

Figure 6.2a Residual TFP Index - North American Carriers

American Airlines 1990=1.00

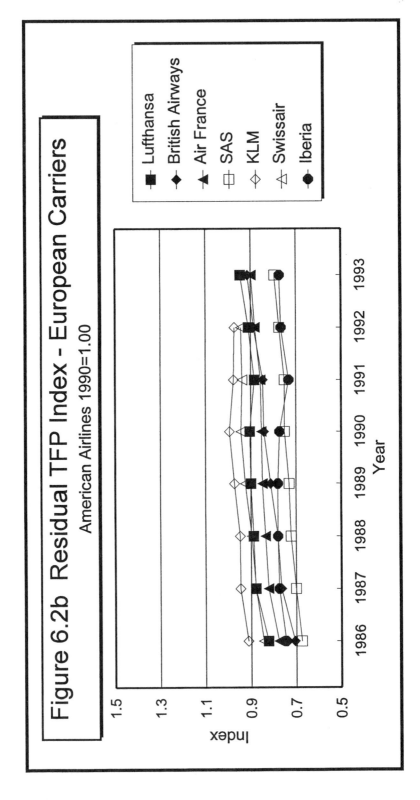

Figure 6.2b Residual TFP Index - European Carriers
American Airlines 1990=1.00

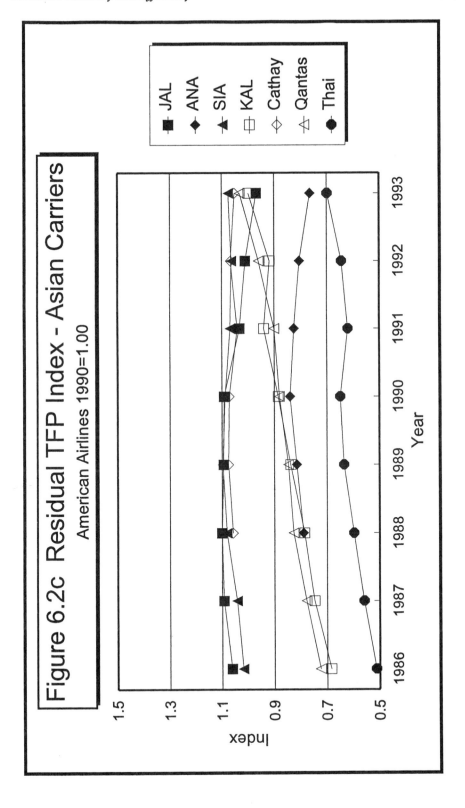

Figure 6.2c Residual TFP Index - Asian Carriers
American Airlines 1990=1.00

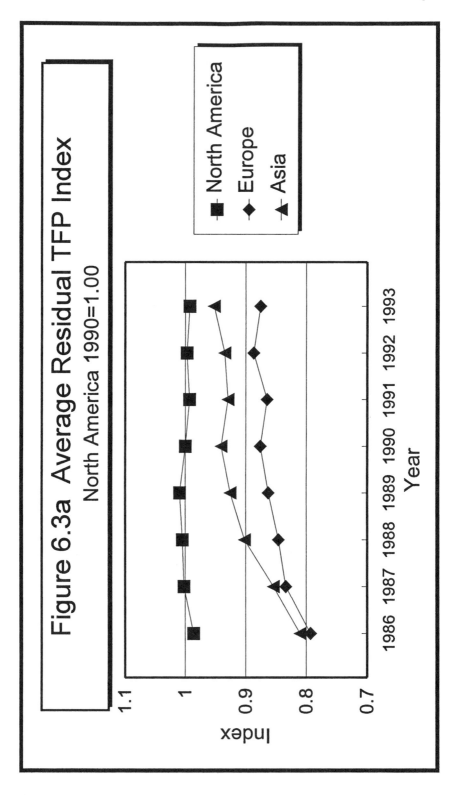

Figure 6.3a Average Residual TFP Index

North America 1990=1.00

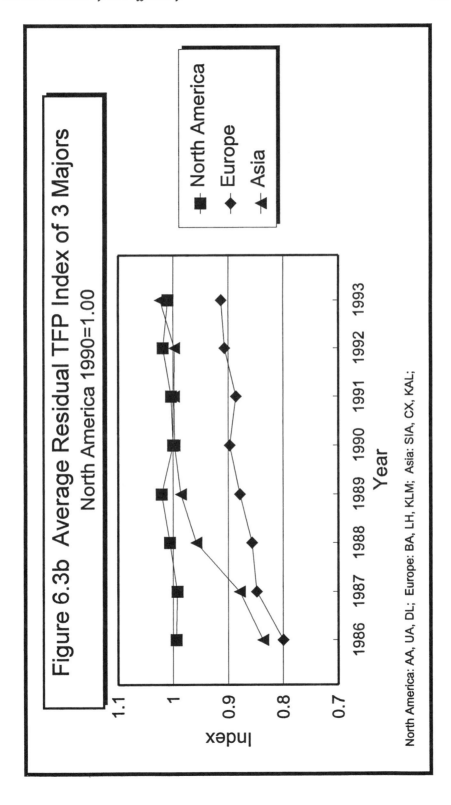

Figure 6.3b Average Residual TFP Index of 3 Majors
North America 1990=1.00

North America: AA, UA, DL; Europe: BA, LH, KLM; Asia: SIA, CX, KAL;

American carriers is becoming smaller. Figure 6.3a also shows that US carriers, on average, outperformed Asian carriers during the period, but Asian carriers made considerable improvement to close the efficiency gap between them and North American carriers, from an 18% difference in 1986 to a 5% difference in 1993. North American carriers, on the other hand, did not make any significant improvement in their productive efficiency.

Although it is useful to compare average residual TFP index of all airlines, it is more interesting to examine how the winning carriers of each region perform relative to their counterparts in other regions. This is so because these carriers are likely to play an important role in shaping the future of the global airline industry. Therefore, we computed an average residual TFP index of three major carriers in each of the three regions. They are: American Airlines, United Airlines, and Delta in North America (the three mega carriers); British Airways, Lufthansa, and KLM in Europe; Singapore Airlines, Cathay Pacific, and Korean Air in Asia[43]. The average residual TFP index of the three majors is plotted in Figure 6.3b. It shows that the 3 European majors were about 9% less efficient than the US mega carriers in 1993, a significant improvement from the 20% efficiency gap in 1986. The 3 Asian majors were 16% less efficient than the US mega carriers at the beginning of our sample period, but was able to reach the same, if not higher, efficiency level as the US mega carriers by 1993. The US mega carriers, in line with other North American carriers, achieved little efficiency improvement.

6.4   Stochastic Frontier Method

The stochastic frontier method postulates that some firms fail to achieve the production (cost) frontier. That is, inefficiencies exist, and these inefficiencies cannot be fully explained by measurable variables. Thus, a one-sided error term, in addition to the traditional symmetric noise term, is incorporated in the model to capture inefficiencies which can not be explicitly explained. This method was first proposed by Aigner, Lovell and Schmidt (1977) and Meeusen and van den Broeck (1977), and has been extended by Jondrow, Lovell, Materov, and Schmidt (1982), and Battese and Coelli (1991), among others. Specific distributional assumptions about disturbance terms must be made in order to obtain estimates of individual firm efficiencies[44]. A number of distributions have been assumed for the one-sided (inefficiency) term. Aigner, Lovell and Schmidt (1977) proposed half-normal and exponential distributions. These specifications have been used widely by subsequent researchers. Stevenson (1980) proposed a truncated normal distribution, while Greene (1990) proposed a two-parameter Gamma distribution[45].

The basic stochastic frontier model is given by:

---

[43] The choice of the three major carriers in each region is based on our subjective evaluation of their importance in shaping future pattern of the world's airline industry.

[44] When panel data are available, estimates of the inefficiency can be obtained without assuming a particular distribution for the efficiency terms (Schmidt and Sickles, 1984). However, one must specify how efficiency changes over time instead.

[45] There are a number of survey papers which cover alternative frontier procedures, such as Greene (1993), Bauer (1990), Lovell and Schmidt (1988), Schmidt (1986), and Forsund, Lovell and Schmidt (1980).

$$y = f(x,\beta)e^{v}e^{-u}, \qquad\qquad u \geq 0 \qquad\qquad 6\text{-}2$$

where y represents output, $f(x,\beta)$ is the deterministic core of the frontier production function, β are the parameters to be estimated, v is a random variable that takes values over the range $(-\infty,+\infty)$ and represents the effects of measurement errors, non-observable explanatory variables and random shocks, and u is a random variable that takes nonnegative values which captures inefficiency. In other words, $f(x,\beta)e^{v}$ is the stochastic frontier while e^{-u} is the measure of deviation of each observation (firm) from the frontier, i.e. the inefficiency. The condition $u \geq 0$ ensures that all observations lie on or below the production frontier.

In this study, we consider four alternative model specifications: the original cross-sectional, half-normal formulation of Aigner, Lovell and Schmidt (1977), the (unbalanced) panel data , half-normal and truncated normal formulations of Battese and Coelli (1992), and the so-called technical efficiency effect model of Battese and Coelli (1995). The Aigner, Lovell, and Schmidt (ALS) model estimates a stochastic production frontier with assumptions that efficiency term u in equation (6-2) follows a half normal distribution, and each observation is an independent decision making unit or an independent firm. The efficiency measure e^{-u} is then estimated using conditional expectations of e^{-u} given residuals from equation (6-2) (Battese and Coelli, 1988). The Battese and Coelli (1992) formulations estimate stochastic frontier production functions for (unbalanced) panel data in which firm effects are assumed to follow a truncated (or half) normal distribution, and vary systematically with time. The model can be specified as:

$$
\begin{aligned}
y_{it} &= f(x_{it},b)e^{v_{it}}e^{-u_{it}} \qquad i = 1,\ldots,N,\, t = 1,\ldots,T \\
u_{it} &= (u_i \exp(-\eta(t-T)))
\end{aligned}
\qquad 6\text{-}3
$$

where y_{it} (x_{it}) is the output (input) of the I-th firm in the t-th time period; u are non-negative random variables which are assumed to account for technical inefficiencies, and are assumed to be independently identifically distributed (*iid*) with truncations at zero of the $N(\mu,\, \sigma_u^2)$ distribution; η is a parameter to be estimated. If μ is assumed to be zero, then u_i follows a half-normal distribution.

The technical efficiency effect model of Battese and Coelli (1995) extends models proposed by Reifschneider and Stevenson (1991) and Kumbhakar, Ghosh and McGukin (1991), it assumes that efficiency term u is an explicit function of a vector of firm-specific variables. The model can be expressed as:

$$
\begin{aligned}
y &= f(x,\beta)e^{v}e^{-u}, \\
u &= h\delta + w
\end{aligned}
\qquad 6\text{-}4
$$

where u is a non-negative truncation of the $N(h\delta,\, \sigma^2)$ distribution, h is a vector of explanatory variables which may influence firm efficiency, δ is a vector of parameters to be estimated, and w is a random variable which is defined by the truncation of the normal distribution with zero mean and variance, σ^2, such that the point of truncation is $- h\delta$.

The Cobb-Douglas production with four inputs producing a single output - the aggregate output index is estimated in this study[46]. In particular, the deterministic core of the production frontiers is specified as:

$$\ln y_j = \alpha_0 + \sum_i \alpha_i \ln x_{ij} + \sum_k \beta_k \ln z_{kj} \qquad\qquad 6\text{-}5$$

where y_j is the output index for observation j, x are the input variables, z are characteristic variables including stage length and output mix variables, and α and β are coefficients to be estimated. For the technical efficiency effect model, a government majority ownership dummy is included as one of the h variables in equation (6-4) along with load factor and a time trend variable.

Table 6.2 reports four alternative models of the stochastic frontier production functions. Statistical tests indicate that model SF2 (with a half-normal inefficiency term) is the most appropriate model to use.[47] Therefore, the empirical results will be discussed primarily from the model SF2. The four input variables all have statistically significant positive coefficients. As expected, stage length has statistically significant positive coefficients in all four models. Load factor also has statistically significant positive coefficients in the first three models. %Incidental has a statistically significant positive coefficient in all four models, indicating that an airline with high %Incidental output is expected to have a high productive efficiency as compared to airlines with low involvement in incidental businesses. Other output mix variables (%Freight and %Non-scheduled) are not statistically significant.

Efficiency estimates from stochastic frontier model SF2 are plotted in Figures 6.4a, 6.4b and 6.4c. United and Northwest were the most efficient North American carriers, followed by Delta, American, and Continental. US Air was the least efficient, but it improved considerably over the period. Air Canada also made considerable performance improvements. KLM was again shown to be the most efficient European carrier, followed by BA, while SAS was the least efficient[48]. Again, similar to the residual TFP results, European carriers are shown to have improved productive efficiency the most during our sample period (1986-93 period) as compared to North American or Asian carriers. Singapore Airlines was the most efficient among Asian carriers, followed by Cathay Pacific. However, these two carriers' productive efficiency did not improve significantly during the 1985-93 period while other Asian carriers (JAL, Qantas, KAL, ANA and Thai)

---

[46] Madala (1979) noted that measurement of technological change and efficiency are quite insensitive to the choice of functional form of production since these measures are related to the shifts of the isoquants rather than their shapes.

[47] SF2 is nested in SF3, since SF3 becomes SF2 when μ is restricted to zero. The log likelihood ratio test between these two models yields a test statistic of 2.518 (=2*(286.287-285.028)). Since the test statistic is smaller than 3.841, the critical value of the χ^2 distribution with 1 degree of freedom at 5% significance level, SF2 is preferred over SF3. SF1, SF2 and SF4 are not nested. Oum (1980) shows that by using Bayesian criterion, for cases involving different numbers of parameters, one can choose *a posteriori*, which model is most likely to generate observed data through a likelihood ratio test. And, for cases involving the same number of parameters, one compare values of likelihood functions. A significance level of 0.05 is used in the tests. Testing SF1 and SF2 yields a test statistic of -87.104 which is smaller than $\chi^2_6 = 12.59$, thus SF2 is favoured over SF1; similarly testing SF1 and SF4 yields a test statistic of 7.968 which is larger than $\chi^2_3 = 6.251$, thus SF1 is favored over SF4. Therefore, SF2 is statistically the best among the four models.

[48] This result is supported by Norman and Strandenes (1994)

have improved their efficiency significantly.

Parameter	ALS model	Battese and Coelli (1992) Models		Battese and Coelli (1995)
	(Half-Normal) SF1	Half-normal SF2	Truncated Normal SF3	(Tech. Effi. Effects) SF4
Constant	-9.300 (20.57)	-9.177 (16.74)	-9.132 (17.49)	-8.306 (8.32)
Labour	0.128 (6.95)	0.098 (2.69)	0.111 (3.22)	0.129 (1.34)
Fuel	0.622 (30.20)	0.552 (15.79)	0.567 (13.36)	0.587 (11.03)
Material	0.242 (10.94)	0.251 (6.07)	0.226 (4.96)	0.279 (1.54)
Capital	0.024 (0.79)	0.108 (2.28)	0.104 (2.48)	0.017 (0.18)
Stage length	0.198 (10.99)	0.146 (4.80)	0.135 (4.70)	0.191 (3.67)
%Freight	0.036 (2.81)	0.019 (0.77)	0.020 (0.75)	0.053 (1.49)
%Non-sch.	-0.011 (2.55)	0.004 (0.78)	0.006 (1.12)	-0.013 (1.28)
%Incidental	0.049 (12.35)	0.058 (9.18)	0.061 (10.06)	0.040 (4.91)
Load Factor	0.230 (2.34)	0.484 (4.94)	0.495 (5.59)	
1987	0.023 (1.26)			
1988	0.035 (1.86)			
1989	0.045 (2.39)			
1990	0.033 (1.68)			
1991	0.031 (1.56)			
1992	0.074 (3.79)			
1993	0.103 (5.04)			
σ^2	0.010	0.008	0.004	0.008
μ	0	0	0.093 (2.06)	
η	0	0.100 (3.73)	0.080 (2.56)	
δ_0				0.058 (0.11)
Load factor				-0.051 (0.061)
GMAJ				0.094 (0.67)
time				-0.024 (1.29)
Log-likelihood	241.476	285.028	286.287	237.492

Table 6.2
Stochastic Frontier Production Functions

* t-values in parentheses

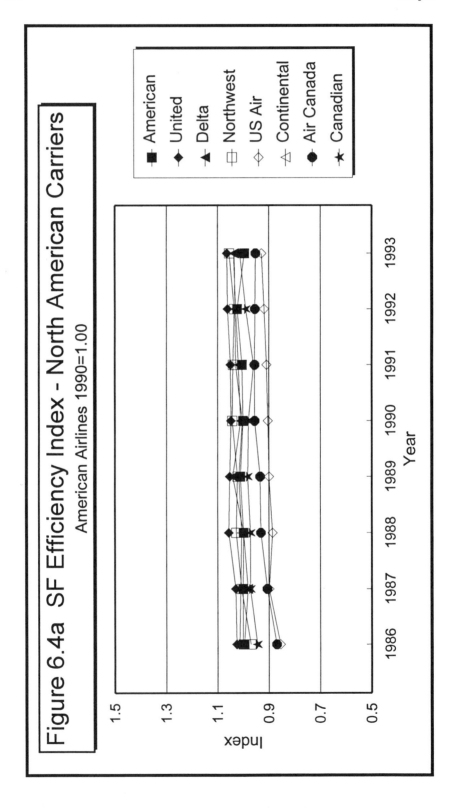

Figure 6.4a SF Efficiency Index - North American Carriers

American Airlines 1990=1.00

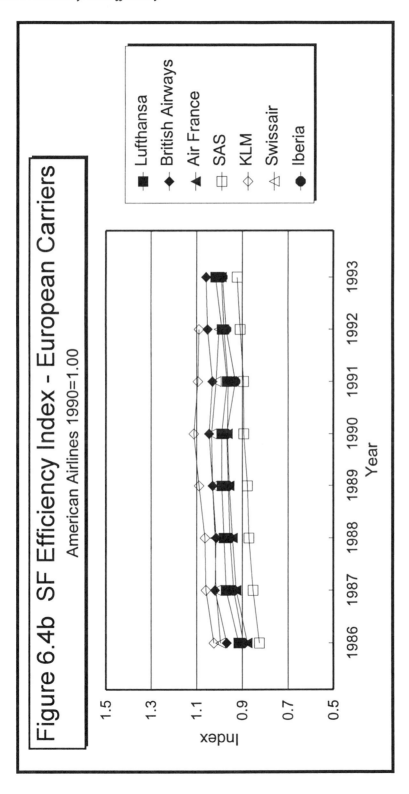

Figure 6.4b SF Efficiency Index - European Carriers

American Airlines 1990=1.00

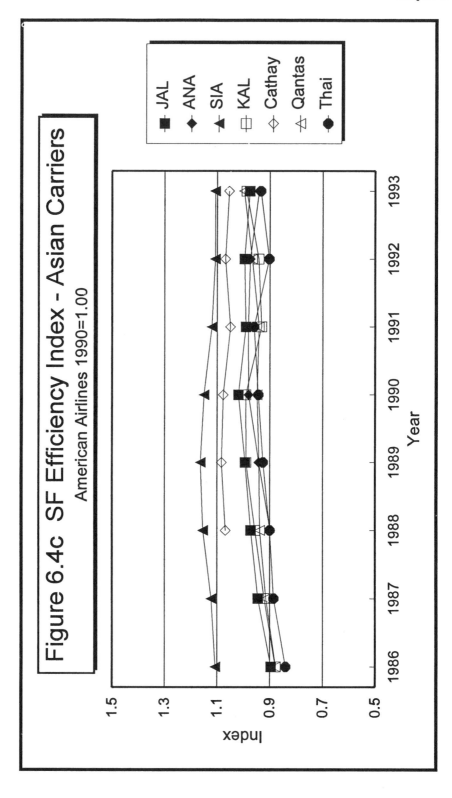

Figure 6.4c SF Efficiency Index - Asian Carriers
American Airlines 1990=1.00

6.5 Effects of Government Ownership on Efficiency

The question of relative efficiency of alternate forms of ownership is becoming largely an empirical one, since economic theory fails to provide unequivocal propositions on the issue. The principal-agent theory argues that government ownership does not provide the same level of managerial incentives and adequate monitoring arrangements as private ownership does. Thus, government-owned enterprises are inherently less efficient than private enterprises. Commonly cited consequences of government ownership include over-capitalization, low productivity, high wages, inefficient capital-labor mix, in output characteristics of public firms, and a tendency to favor business over consumer groups and organized groups over unorganized groups. However, a number of economists, for example Estrin and Pérontin (1991), have questioned the strength of this argument. They suggest that principal-agent problems may also arise in the private sector as a result of capital market imperfections. Empirical studies have tested hypotheses regarding effects of government ownership on efficiency, but their results have been mixed. For example, Gillen, Oum and Tretheway (1989) found that government ownership of Air Canada resulted in reduced productive efficiency, on average, 23 percent of the carrier's total cost during the period 1964-1981. On the other hand, in the case of British Ports, Liu (1995) failed to identify ownership as a significant factor of production. He found that efficiency between alternate forms of port ownership are negligible and insignificant.

In order to identify effects of government ownership on efficiency, a one-way analysis of variance (ANOVA) was conducted on the residual TFP scores (TFP4 model) and the inefficiency index estimated from the stochastic frontier production function (SF2 model). The results (Table 6.3) show that majority government ownership does have a statistically significant negative effect on airline efficiency. For example, airlines with majority government ownership achieved an average residual TFP of 0.836 compared to 0.962 for other airlines. Similarly, average efficiency estimates from SF2 are 0.971 for airlines with majority government ownership versus 0.997 for other airlines. Average efficiency difference is between 3 to 13 percent.

Table 6.3 The Effects of Government Ownership on Efficiency Results from One-Way ANOVA		
	Residual TFP Index	SF Efficiency Index
Means		
Gmaj=1	0.836	0.971
Gmaj=0	0.962	0.997
F-Value $(1,176)$	47.42	6.96
p-value	0.0001	0.0091

Note that GMAJ = 1, if government ownership is over 50%;
= 0, otherwise

6.6 Summary

This chapter measures and compares the airlines' productive efficiency using residual TFP index and efficiency estimates from stochastic frontier production functions. Results can be summarized as follows:

- Average stage length and output mix have substantial effects on airlines' observed productivity. Changes in these variables account for a large portion of the observed productivity growth.
- After removing effects of stage length and output mix, U.S. carriers are generally more efficient than Asian carriers, while Asian carriers, in turn, are more efficient than European carriers. In 1993, US carriers, on average, were 12% more efficient than European carriers, and 4% more efficient than Asian carriers.
- During our study period, major European and Asian carriers have achieved considerably higher productivity growth than their North American counterparts. As a result, the productivity gap between North American carriers and other carriers has diminished significantly. Also, European aviation liberalization, which began in 1987, appears to have produced substantial productivity gains for the European carriers.
- The 3 European majors (BA, Lufthansa, and KLM) were about 9% less efficient than the US mega carriers in 1993, a significant improvement from the 20% efficiency gap in 1986. The 3 Asian majors (SIA, Cathay, and KAL) were 16% less efficient than the US mega carriers at the beginning of our sample period, but was able to reach the same, if not higher, efficiency level as the US mega carriers by 1993.
- Over time, productive efficiency of carriers competing in the same or similar markets tend to converge. For example, in 1993 there was little difference between residual TFP levels of American, United, and Delta in North America - the three US mega carriers. This was also the case for Singapore, Korean Air, and Cathay in Asia. Similar trends were seen in Europe, although there are still substantial in productive efficiency among European airlines.
- Majority government ownership is shown to have a significant negative impact on productive efficiency of an airline.

Before leaving this chapter, a word of caution is in order. It is noted that the productive efficiency reported in this chapter does not take into account of any difference in quality of output between airlines (or changes over time), the intensity of airport congestion an airline is subjected to, and other uncontrollable variables except average stage length and mix of outputs. Therefore, our productive efficiency measures are likely to under-estimate true efficiencies of the airlines that produce high quality (input-intensive) services and/or airlines, with a majority of flights moving through very congested hub airports (and thus requiring more inputs).

Appendix 6
Alternative Efficiency Estimates

Figures 6.5-6.26 compare residual TFP indices obtained from TFP4 model and the efficiency indices estimated from the stochastic frontier production function SF2 for each of the airlines. Results are generally consistent between the two models. However, there are two noticeable exceptions, BA and Thai. While the residual TFP indices suggest both airlines as relatively inefficient, efficiency estimates from stochastic frontier models show otherwise. Because of data limitations, we were able to remove only the effects of stage length and output mix variables when computing the residual TFP indices. Other factors, which are not incorporated in the TFP regression model, may have significant effects on an airline's gross TFP. For example, the effect of difference in service quality between carriers is not considered because of lack of consistent data on service quality indicator. Effects of airport congestion on carrier performance are also neglected because of lack of data. Omission of these two factors, among other things, could be partly responsible for BA's low residual TFP scores, since BA is generally considered a high quality carrier, and a majority of BA flights originate from highly congested Heathrow Airport[49]. Stochastic frontier models take into account effects of unspecifiable random factors when measuring productive efficiency, while the two-step TFP procedure cannot. The between the two sets of efficiency estimates indicate that factors not explicitly reflected in our model appear to have resulted in a relatively low efficiency rating for BA when the residual TFP indices were used.

---

[49] According to Dr. DeAnne Julius, then chief economist of BA, over 70% of BA's traffic go through Heathrow Airport.

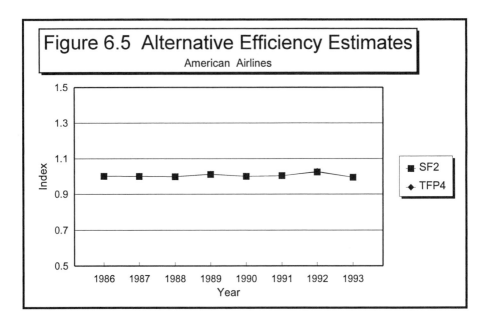

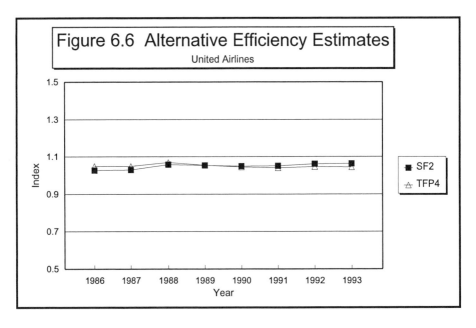

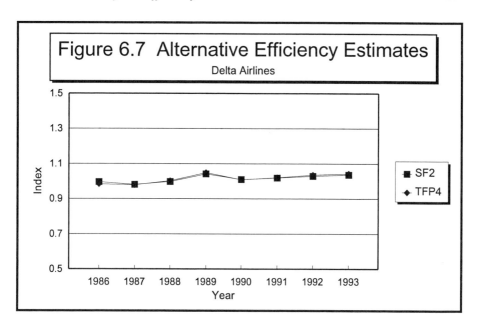

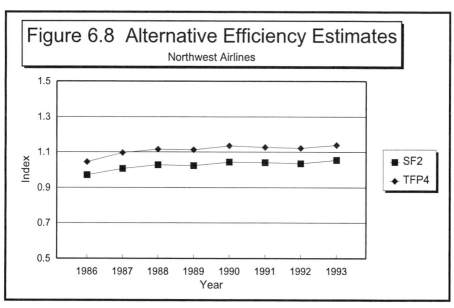

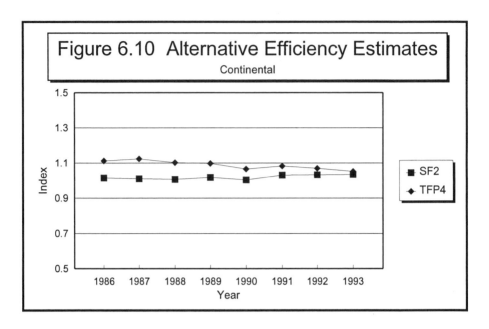

Figure 6.10 Alternative Efficiency Estimates
Continental

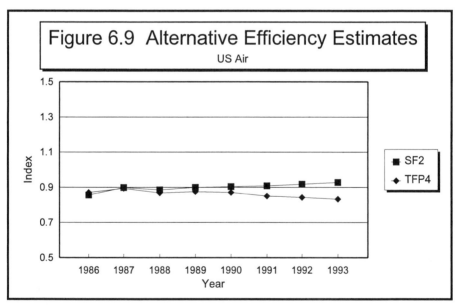

Figure 6.9 Alternative Efficiency Estimates
US Air

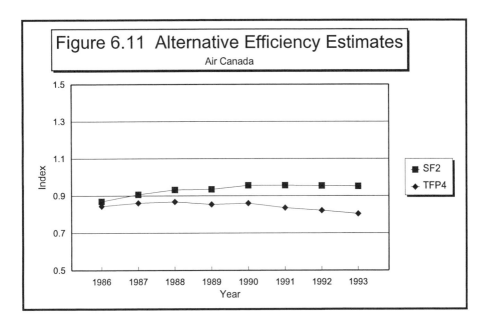

Figure 6.11 Alternative Efficiency Estimates
Air Canada

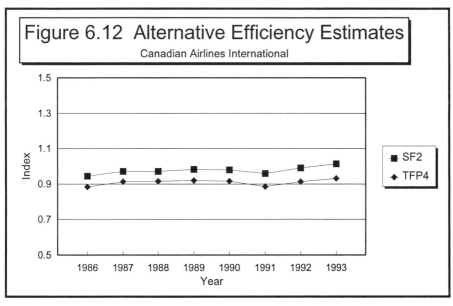

Figure 6.12 Alternative Efficiency Estimates
Canadian Airlines International

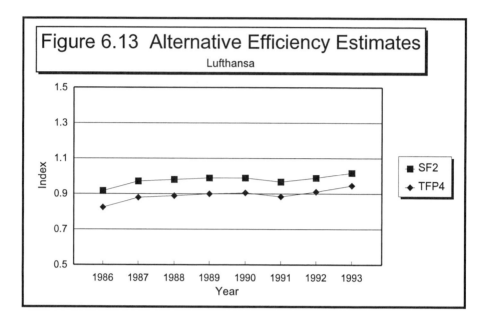

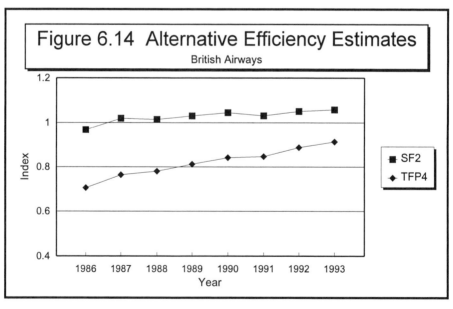

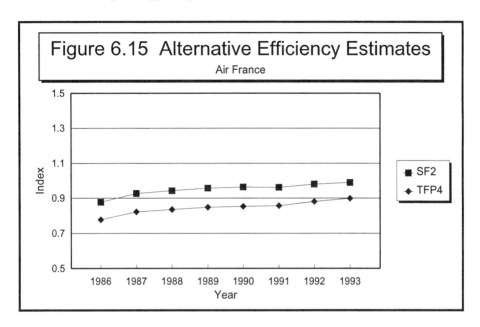

Figure 6.15 Alternative Efficiency Estimates
Air France

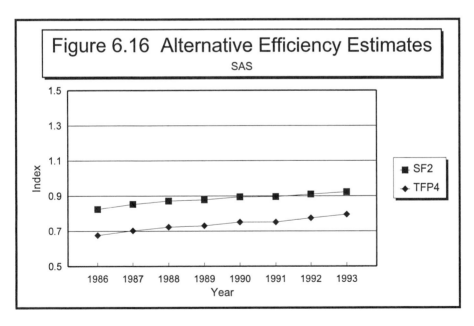

Figure 6.16 Alternative Efficiency Estimates
SAS

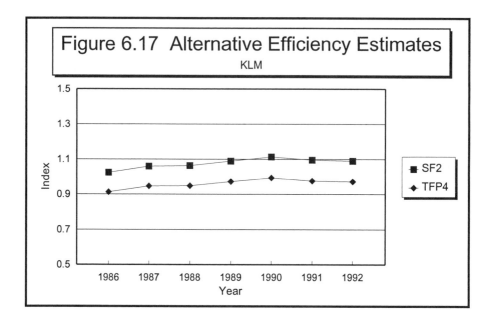

Figure 6.17 Alternative Efficiency Estimates

KLM

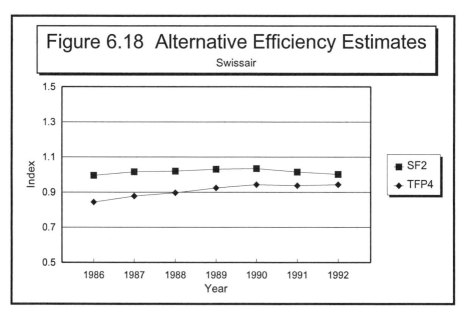

Figure 6.18 Alternative Efficiency Estimates

Swissair

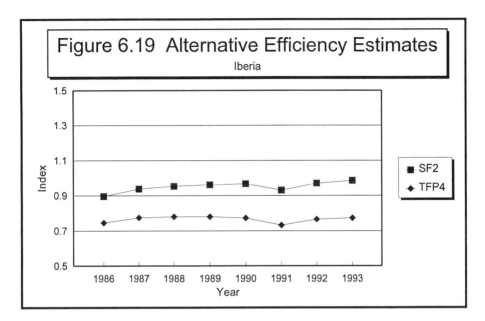

Figure 6.19 Alternative Efficiency Estimates
Iberia

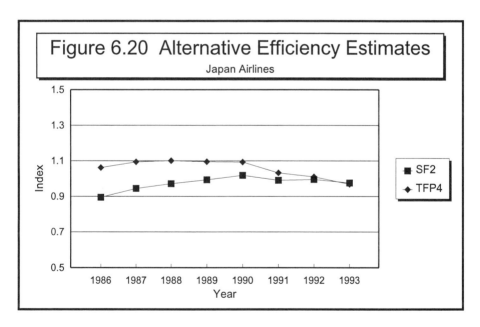

Figure 6.20 Alternative Efficiency Estimates
Japan Airlines

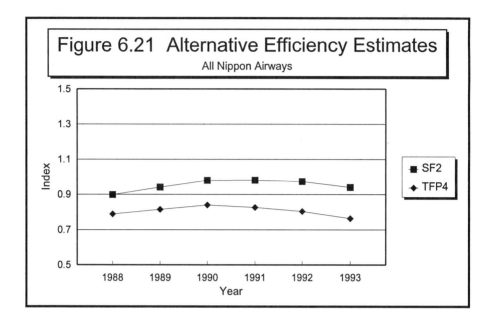

Figure 6.21 Alternative Efficiency Estimates
All Nippon Airways

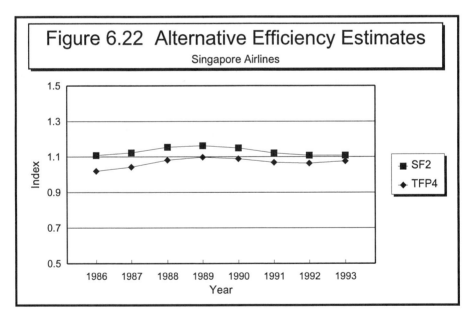

Figure 6.22 Alternative Efficiency Estimates
Singapore Airlines

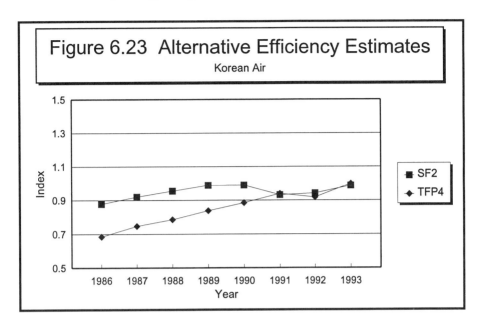

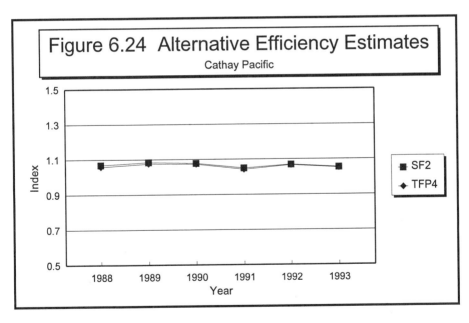

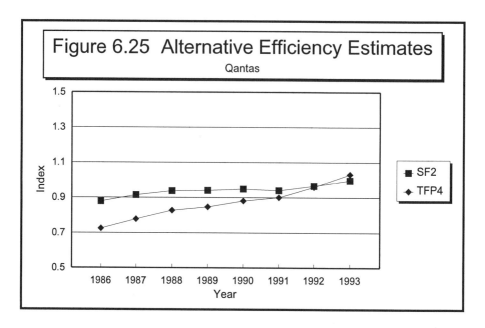

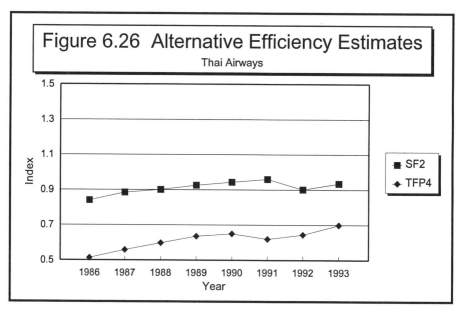

Chapter 7
Preliminary Cost Analysis

This chapter examines airline cost structures and its changes over time. It provides a preliminary analysis of the effects of network and operating characteristics, and exchange rate fluctuations on airline costs. Thus, it prepares ground for further analysis of airline cost competitiveness.

7.1 Airline Cost Structure

How an airline's costs are broken down and categorized depends on the purpose for which they are being used. No single cost categorization is capable of simultaneously satisfying all management or policy analysis requirements. As a result, most airlines break down their costs in various ways in order to use them for different aspects of management. For example, a common practice is to divide airline accounts into operating and non-operating cost categories. The former can be further subdivided into direct operating and indirect operating costs. In practice, however, distinctions between direct and indirect operating costs are not clear cut. Certain cost items are categorized as direct costs by some airlines, but as indirect costs by others. According to Doganis (1991), direct costs account for approximately half of total operating costs for world scheduled airlines as a whole. This highlights the importance of indirect costs which may not be assignable to specific traffic.

This chapter examines airline system-wide aggregate annual costs, and classifies costs by factors of production. Recall from earlier chapters, we distinguished five categories of airline costs: labour, fuel, materials, flight equipment, and ground property and equipment. Figure 7.1 gives an indication of each airline's 1995 total cost and contribution of different cost elements to total cost. Note that total cost here refers to an airline's total input costs which include costs of flight equipment and GPE capital[50]. The cost of materials inputs (purchased goods and services) accounts for between 35 percent (Iberia) to 57 percent (SIA) of total cost, thus being the most important component. Many factors contribute to the large variations in the share of materials cost, including differences in airport charges and *en route* charges (Comité des Sages,1994), and varying degrees of operations and services outsourcing.

Labor costs represent between 11 percent (SIA) to 42 percent (Iberia) of total airline costs. Variations in labor cost are partly attributable to differences in prevailing wage levels and labor market conditions in carriers' home countries. Some countries, particularly the developing and newly industrialized countries in Asia, have significantly lower national wage levels. Airlines employing relatively cheaper labour can obtain significant cost advantages for labor intensive elements of operations. However, the ultimate cost of labor depends not only on wage levels but also on labor productivity. When measured by output per employee, labor productivity is affected by institutional factors such as number of work days per week, number of holidays, maximum duty periods

---

[50] Note that this total input cost does not consider "extra"-financing costs incurred by some financially troubled airlines, such as Canadian Airlines International, because of difficulty in compiling consistent data. As a result, total cost for such airlines is very likely underestimated.

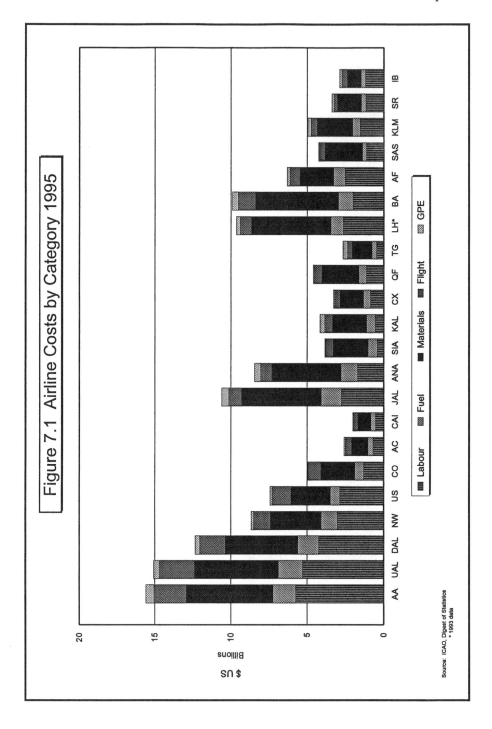

Figure 7.1 Airline Costs by Category 1995

Source: ICAO, Digest of Statistics
* 1993 data

for flight staff and others, and also by operational factors such as aircraft size, stage length, and frequencies operated. Within these constraints, management has a role to play in trying to achieve the highest productivity possible among its workforce. Airlines with relatively low wages and high labor productivity are in a very strong competitive position. SIA is such an example, having the smallest labor cost share. Another contributing factor to differences in labor costs is the extent of out-sourcing operations and services, which are accounted for in materials input cost.

Fuel costs account for a much smaller portion of total airline costs, ranging from 6 percent for SAS to 15 percent for SIA in 1995. Airlines have very limited power over fuel prices they pay, therefore they must depend on reducing fuel consumption to lower fuel costs. Note that airlines with longer stage lengths, such as SIA and Cathay, have relatively higher fuel costs as a proportion of total costs than airlines with shorter stage lengths, such as SAS. Fuel consumption, however, is not uniform during all stages of aircraft operations: more fuel is burned during landing and take-off than while an aircraft is cruising. Thus, airlines with above average fuel costs as a proportion of total costs, may have longer average stage lengths, greater landing and take-off movements, or both, over other airlines.

Airlines consider flight equipment depreciation as aircraft costs in their accounting systems. Annual depreciation charge or cost of a particular aircraft depends on aircraft value (historic purchase price or current replacement cost), depreciation period adopted , assumptions on aircraft residual values, and so on. Because of different accounting systems, airlines may obtain different cost measures for the same aircraft. A more complicating factor is that many airlines lease aircraft, with lease payments usually categorized as another cost item. In order to consistently account for economic costs of an airline's entire fleet (both owned and leased aircraft), therefore, this study estimates aircraft costs using market lease prices and number of airplanes in each aircraft category. Aircraft costs reflect economic costs of the fleet, not accounting costs, and account for about the same proportion of total costs as fuel. Aircraft costs also vary with fleet size and composition. Ground property and equipment account for a very small proportion of total costs. Therefore, for the purpose of our analysis, these two capital input categories are aggregated into a single item - total capital cost.

Labor Cost

Relative importance of various cost components have been fluctuating over time, but have also shown certain trends. Figures 7.2a, 7.2b, and 7.2c show changes in labour cost shares over the sample period. Delta and US Air had the highest labour cost shares among the North American carriers, consistent with their relatively high labour prices (see Figures 4.5a). Delta showed a clear trend in reducing labour costs, while US Air's labour cost shares rose slightly. Northwest also paid relatively high labour prices (see Figures 4.5a). Its labour cost share, however, was below average among the North American carriers because of its high labour productivity. American and United had almost identical labor cost shares until 1991. Since then, United's labour cost share dropped slightly, while American's labor cost share went up. Continental had the lowest labor cost shares in North America, but it shows a clear rising trend. Air Canada's labor cost share fell substantially in 1992 when it started to reduce its workforce.

Iberia had the highest labor cost share among European carriers, closely followed by Swissair. Swissair's high labor cost share is consistent with its high labor prices (see

Figures 4.5b), while Iberia's high labor cost share is due mostly to its low labor productivity (Figure 5.3b). British Airways had the lowest labor cost share due mostly to its low labor prices. Most European carriers showed a slight upward trend in their labor cost shares, though SAS and Swissair's labor cost shares appeared to fall from 1992.

JAL had the highest labor cost share among Asian carriers. This is largely attributable to two factors: high labor price and less use of operations/services out-sourcing. However, JAL's labor cost share appears to be falling slightly. SIA had the lowest labor cost share because of its low labor prices, high labor productivity, and increasing use of out-sourcing services. SIA's labor cost share remained relatively stable at about 11 percent during the sample period. Besides JAL and SIA, labor cost shares for other Asian carriers showed a slight upward trend, with Thai having the most significant increase.

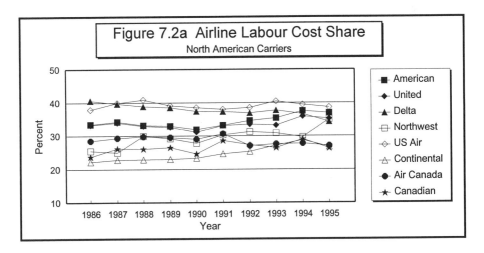

Figure 7.2a Airline Labour Cost Share
North American Carriers

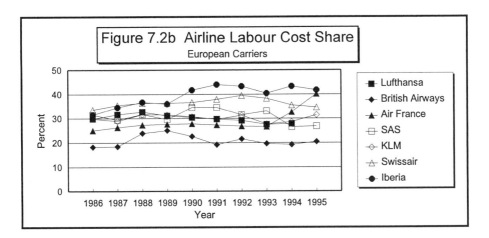

Figure 7.2b Airline Labour Cost Share
European Carriers

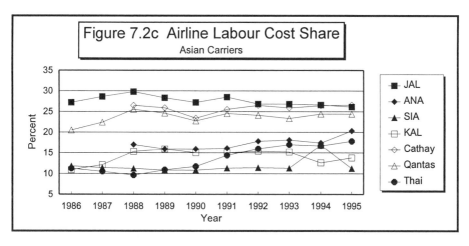

Figure 7.2c Airline Labour Cost Share
Asian Carriers

Table 7.1 shows 1995 average labor cost shares by geographical region. Labor costs contributed about 20 percent to Asian carriers' total costs, and 32.5 percent to both North American and European carriers' total costs.

Table 7.1 Average Labour Cost Shares, 1995			
	North America	**Europe**	**Asia**
Mean	32.5	32.5	20.1
STD	0.05	0.07	0.06
N	8	6	7

Fuel Cost

Figures 7.3a, 7.3b, and 7.3c show changes in fuel cost shares. Comparison of Figures 4.6a-c (fuel price) and Figures 7.3a-c indicates that changes in fuel cost shares are largely dictated by changes in fuel prices. The two "synchronized" fairly well. Continental had a relatively higher fuel cost share over other North American carriers, partly because of its relatively lower labor costs. United and American's fuel cost shares were almost the same, except in 1995. US Air had the lowest fuel cost share in North America even though it had the lowest fuel productivity. This is mainly because it incurred relatively higher labor costs, and had shorter average stage length. Consistent with improving fuel productivity, fuel cost shares for North American carriers showed a general downward trend.

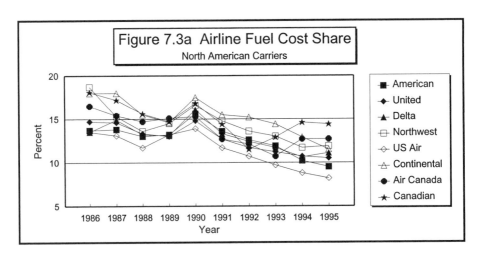

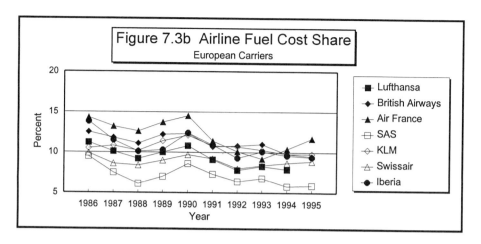

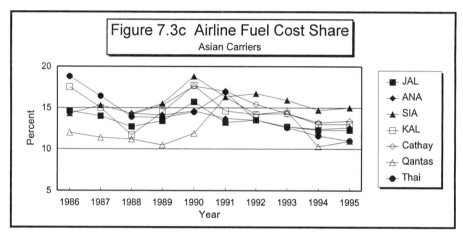

Air France had the highest fuel cost share among the European carriers, except in 1992 and 1993, due to low fuel productivity. Its fuel cost share dropped by more than 25 percent following the merger with UTA, corresponding to a 24 percent increase in fuel productivity. But it has since gone up again. SAS had the lowest fuel cost share in Europe. Overall, a slight downward trend in fuel cost shares was observed for European carriers during the sample period.

Thai and SIA had relatively high fuel cost shares, partly because of low labour costs. Qantas' fuel cost share was the lowest prior to 1990, but later went up. In general, Asian carriers' fuel cost shares have declined since 1990.

Table 7.2 compares 1995 average fuel cost shares between the three geographical regions. European carriers generally have smaller fuel cost shares than their North American and Asian counterparts. Average fuel cost shares for North American and Asian carriers are fairly similar.

Table 7.2 Average Fuel Cost Shares, 1995			
	North America	Europe	Asia
Mean	11.2	9.2	12.6
STD	0.02	0.02	0.01
N	8	6	7

Capital Cost

Total capital cost share is similar to fuel cost share. Figures 7.4a, 7.4b, and 7.4c plot changes in total capital cost share. Air Canada had the highest capital cost share among North American carriers, consistent with its low capital productivity. Northwest started the sample period with the largest capital cost share at 22 percent, but it has since reduced to about 14 percent, the lowest in North America. US Air's capital cost share remained rather stable at about 15 percent until 1994, then increased to 18% in 1995. United had the lowest capital cost share prior to 1993, consistent with its high capital productivity (see Figure 5.6a). Overall, capital cost shares have taken a slight upward trend since 1993.

Prior to 1993, British Airways had the largest capital cost share among European carriers, while SAS and Swissair had the smallest. Capital cost shares generally experienced a significant drop between 1986 and 1988, but remained relatively stable since the late 1980s. Iberia appears to be the only European carrier showing an upward trend in capital cost share since 1988.

Thai Airways had the largest capital cost share in Asia (also in the entire sample as a matter of fact) at 25 percent. JAL and ANA's capital costs accounted for a relatively small portion of their total costs, since their variable input costs were rather high. Again, between 1986 and 1988, a small drop in Asian carriers' capital cost shares was observed, but no significant changes since then.

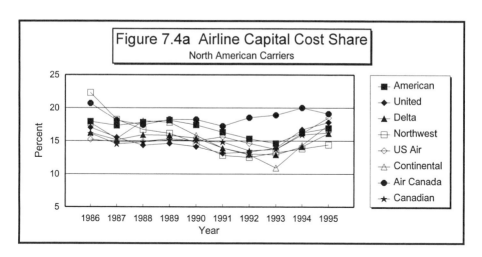

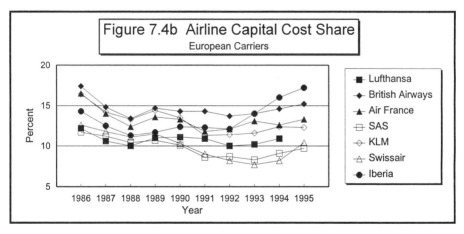

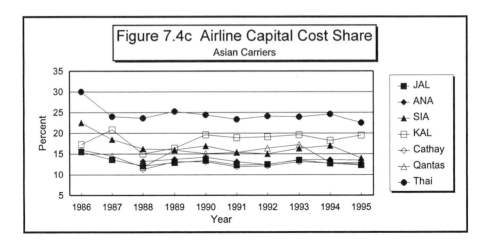

Table 7.3 compares 1995 average capital cost shares between the regions. North American carriers generally had higher capital cost shares over Asian carriers. European carriers, on average, had noticeably smaller capital cost shares than both North American and Asian carriers.

Table 7.3 Average Capital Cost Shares, 1995			
	North America	**Europe**	**Asia**
Mean	17.1	13.1	15.3
STD	0.01	0.03	0.04
N	8	6	7

Materials Cost

The last cost category is materials input cost. Recall that this item is a catch-all (residual) cost category, including numerous unaccountable items. For some carriers, it accounts for more than half of total airline costs (Figures 7.5a, 7.5b, and 7.5c). Canadian Airlines and Continental had the largest materials cost shares among North American carriers, while Delta and US Air had the smallest. There was an upward trend in materials cost shares during the period, supported by growing popularity of outsourcing/global sourcing activities (Figure 7.5a).

Change patterns in materials cost share among European carriers were a little different (Figure 7.5b). A downward trend was observed between 1987 and 1989/1990, later followed by an upward trend. The only noticeable exceptions were Iberia and Air France. Iberia experienced a dramatic drop in materials cost share in 1990, while Air France's materials cost shares fell substantially from 1993. British Airways had the largest materials cost share in Europe, with Swissair and Iberia at the opposite end of the scale. This is probably because BA outsources its operations and services more than most other carriers.

For Asian carriers, materials cost shares peaked around 1988 (Figure 7.5c). SIA and ANA had the highest materials cost shares, while JAL, Cathay, and Thai's materials cost shares were relatively low. Qantas experienced sizable declines in materials cost share between 1986 and 1993, but by 1995, its materials cost share had returned to the 1986 level.

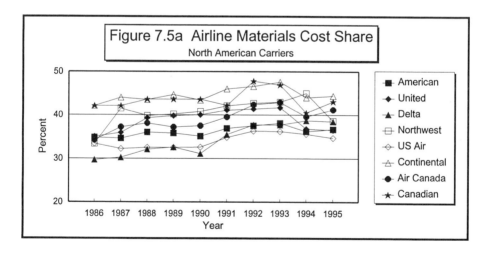

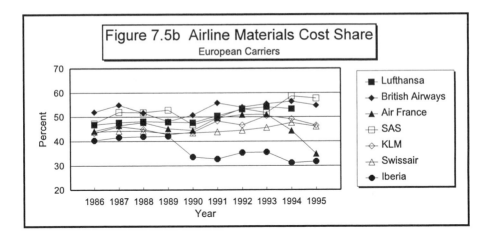

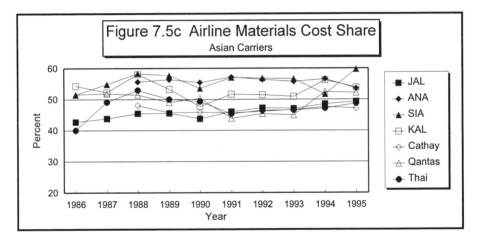

Table 7.4 lists the 1995 average materials cost shares for the three regions. Asian carriers, on average, had substantially larger materials cost shares than European and North American carriers. Furthermore, North American carriers' materials cost shares were significantly lower than those of European carriers.

Table 7.4 Average Materials Cost Shares, 1995			
	North America	Europe	Asia
Mean	39.2	45.2	52.1
STD	0.03	0.09	0.04
N	8	6	7

7.2 Unit Cost Measurement

A unit cost index is constructed by dividing total input cost by aggregate output index (see Figures 5.1a-c), and is plotted in Figures 7.6a, 7.6b, and 7.6c. The index is normalized at American Airlines' 1990 data for comparison across airlines and over time. Total cost includes annual costs of labor, fuel, capital (aircraft and ground property and equipment), and materials input. It is important to exercise caution when comparing this unit cost index as it is affected by factors beyond airline control.

North American carriers' unit cost indices ranged from 0.66 to 1.40. Prior to 1993, Continental had the lowest unit costs among North American carriers. It is interesting to note that, with exception of US Air, unit costs of most North American carriers approached similar levels in 1995. US Air had considerably high unit costs throughout the period. European carriers' unit cost indices ranged from 1.0 to 1.9, except for KLM and Air France. KLM's unit cost index was below 1.0 during the entire period, while Air France's unit costs fell below 1.0 after 1994. KLM had the lowest unit costs among European carriers, while SAS had the highest unit costs. On average, European carriers had noticeably higher unit costs than North American carriers (see Table 7.5). With the exception of Japan Airlines (JAL) and All Nippon Airways (ANA), Asian carriers generally had considerably lower unit costs than European and North American carriers. Their unit cost indices were well below 1.0. In 1995, ANA had the highest unit costs among all sample airlines, with its unit cost more than double American Airlines'. JAL's unit cost level was similar to that of European carriers, and was about 50% higher than that of American Airlines.

JAL and ANA have experienced increasing unit costs since the early 1990s, which is at least partially attributable to appreciation of the Japanese Yen against the US dollar. For other airlines, an upward trend in unit costs was observed prior to 1990-1991, followed by a downward trend thereafter. This downward trend, in part, reflects tremendous efforts by many airlines to reduce costs and improve efficiency during the economic recession.

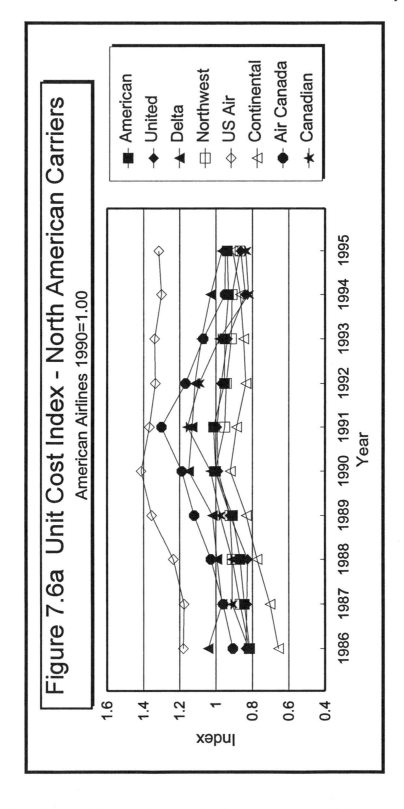

Figure 7.6a Unit Cost Index - North American Carriers

American Airlines 1990=1.00

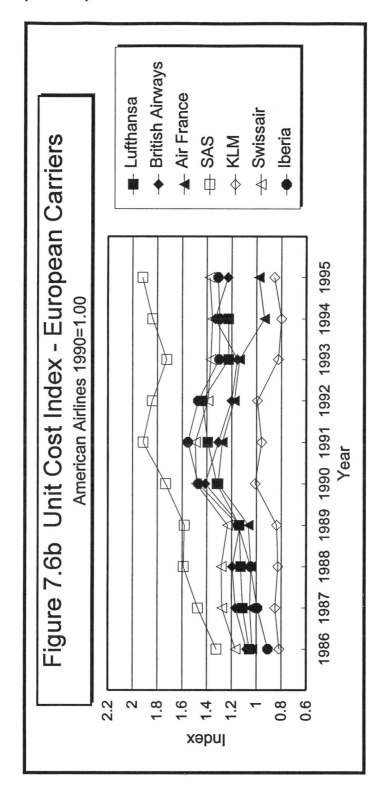

Figure 7.6b Unit Cost Index - European Carriers

American Airlines 1990=1.00

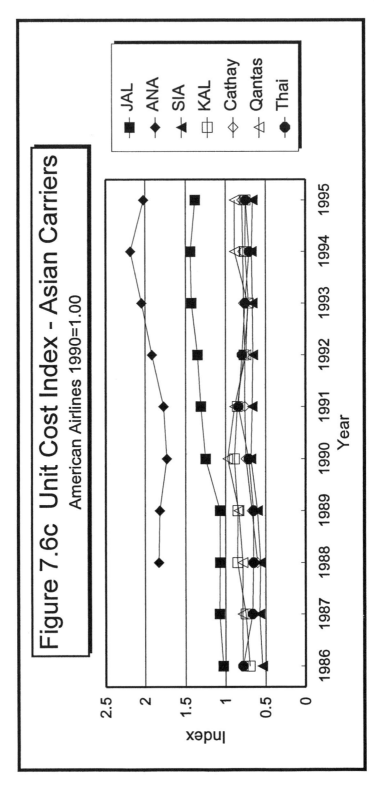

Figure 7.6c Unit Cost Index - Asian Carriers
American Airlines 1990=1.00

Table 7.5 Average Unit Cost, 1995			
	North America	**Europe**	**Asia**
Mean	0.95	1.28	1.03
STD	0.14	0.34	0.46
N	8	6	7

7.3 Factors Affecting Unit Costs

Airline unit costs are influenced by variations in network, operating and market conditions, and regulatory and institutional environment, of which airlines have none or limited control. Therefore, it is necessary to examine the effects of these variables on observed unit costs in order to make proper inferences about cost competitiveness. This section provides a preliminary analysis of effects on airline unit costs by the following influential factors:

Stage Length
Stage length is one of the most important operating characteristics that may influence airline costs. For the same aircraft type, longer stage length corresponds with lower direct operating cost per unit. Rapid decline of unit costs with increasing stage length is a fundamental characteristic of airline economics. This is because airport charges and station costs, and costs associated with ground maneuvering, and take-off and landing activities become relatively smaller per passenger kilometer or cargo tonne kilometer as stage length increases. Also, longer stage length leads to higher aircraft and crew utilization.

Figure 7.7 shows that unit costs initially fall rapidly as stage length increases, but then gradually flattens out. Therefore, airlines at the low end of the average stage length axis, such as ANA and SAS, have substantially higher unit costs than similar airlines. However, unit costs for airlines at the other end of the average stage length axis, such as SIA and Cathay, are not dramatically lower than those of similar airlines. This seems to indicate that most cost savings are exhausted once average stage length surpasses 1200 kilometers. It should be noted that optimal aircraft type depends on stage length, and airlines try to operate each aircraft at or near the stage length where costs are minimized.

Load Factor
High load factor indicates better utilization of aircraft and crew. Aircraft have very high initial costs, and a large proportion of crew costs are fixed. Therefore, unit costs should decline as load factor increases, as shown in Figure 7.8.

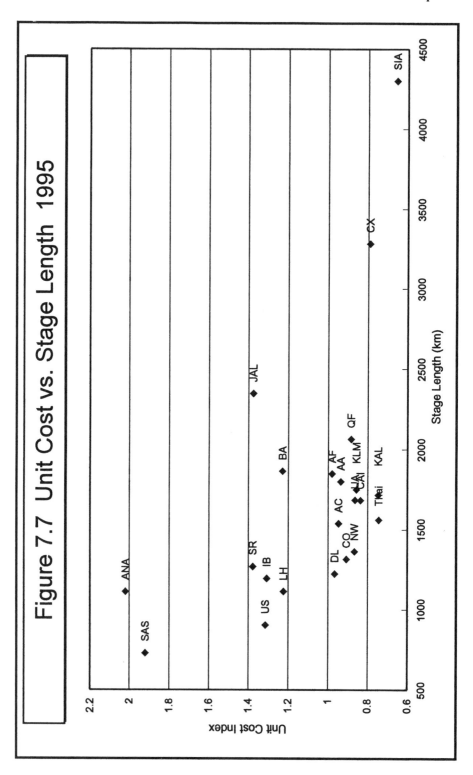

Figure 7.7 Unit Cost vs. Stage Length 1995

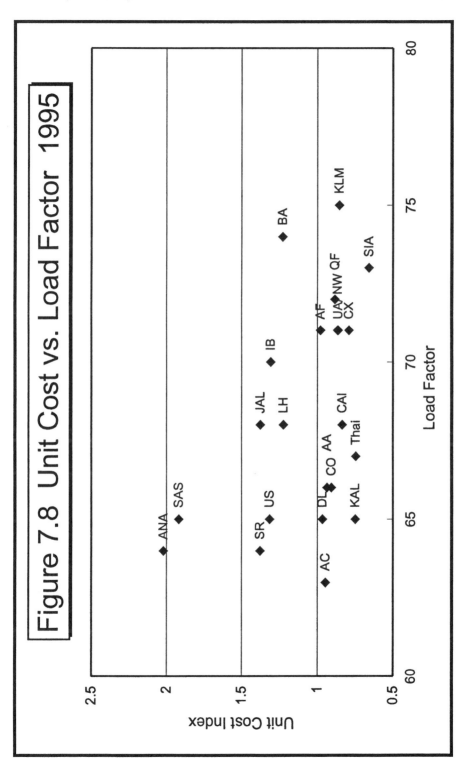

Figure 7.8 Unit Cost vs. Load Factor 1995

Input Price

Observed differences in unit costs may be partly due to differences in input prices. Figure 7.9 plots unit costs in relation to the input price index. There are substantial input price differences among European and Asian carriers, but it is easily observed that unit costs rise as input prices rise. However, variations in unit costs for North American carriers cannot be fully explained by differences in input prices. For example, US Air had considerably higher unit costs than other major U.S. carriers, but its input prices were at a similar level as United, Northwest, and Delta. Similarly, Air Canada's unit costs were noticeably higher than those of Continental and Canadian, while its input prices were comparatively lower.

Efficiency

Unit cost depends not only on stage length and input prices, but also on other factors, including productive efficiency. Theoretically, efficiency should explain cost differences between airlines which cannot be attributed to variations in input prices, operating characteristics, or any other cost variable. Figure 7.10a plots unit costs in relation to the residual TFP index presented in Chapter 6 (Figures 6.2a-c), and Figure 7.10b plots unit costs in relation to the SF efficiency index (Figures 6.3a-c). These figures show a clear pattern that unit costs decline as efficiency increases. Thai appears to be an outlier in the residual TFP index. Thai's input price is dramatically lower than those of other airlines, even by Asian carriers' standards. Its cost advantages from low input prices may more than off-set extra costs caused by low productive efficiency.

7.4 Effects of Exchange Rate Fluctuations on Unit Cost

Chapter 4 examined effects of exchange rate fluctuations on input prices. Following a similar approach, this section examines effects of exchange rate fluctuations on unit cost. Again, we look at the cases of JAL, Air Canada, SAS, Air France, and Lufthansa.

Figure 7.11 shows JAL's unit costs in relation to the Japanese Yen. Note that unit cost here is expressed in terms of the ratio of JAL's unit cost index over American Airlines' unit cost for the same year. For example, the 1986 figure 1.27 means that in 1986, JAL's unit cost was 1.27 times that of American Airlines. In US dollar terms (at current exchange rate), JAL's unit cost increased by 34 percent between 1986 and 1995. In 1995, its unit cost was 1.5 times that of American Airlines[51]. However, in Japanese Yen (at 1986 exchange rate), its unit cost decreased by 25 percent during the same period, and was 17 percent lower than that of American Airlines in 1995.

Figure 7.12 shows Air Canada's unit costs in relation to changes in the Canadian dollar. AC's unit cost was about 11 percent higher than that of American Airlines in 1986. Between 1986 and 1991, the Canadian dollar appreciated by more than 17 percent. In 1991, this resulted in a 17 percent disadvantage in AC's unit costs. Specifically, in 1991, AC's unit cost was 29 percent higher than that of AA's in US dollar terms, although it would have been only 6 percent higher had there not been changes in exchange rates (between Canadian dollar and US dollar) since 1986. As the Canadian dollar fell back to

---

[51] This also reflects changes in American Airlines' unit cost.

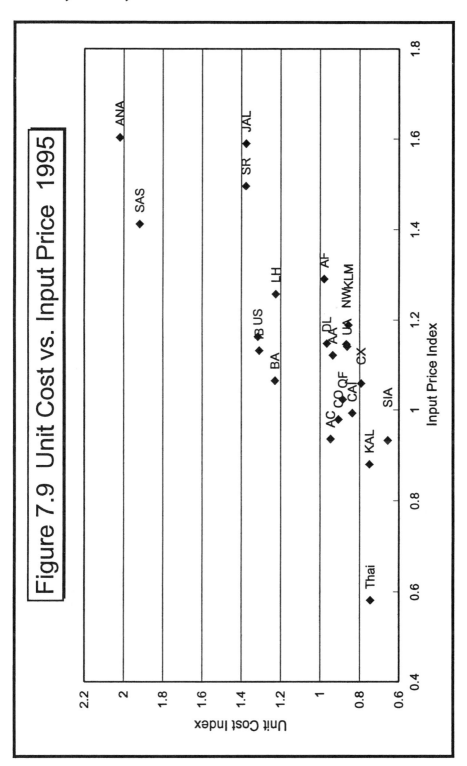

Figure 7.9 Unit Cost vs. Input Price 1995

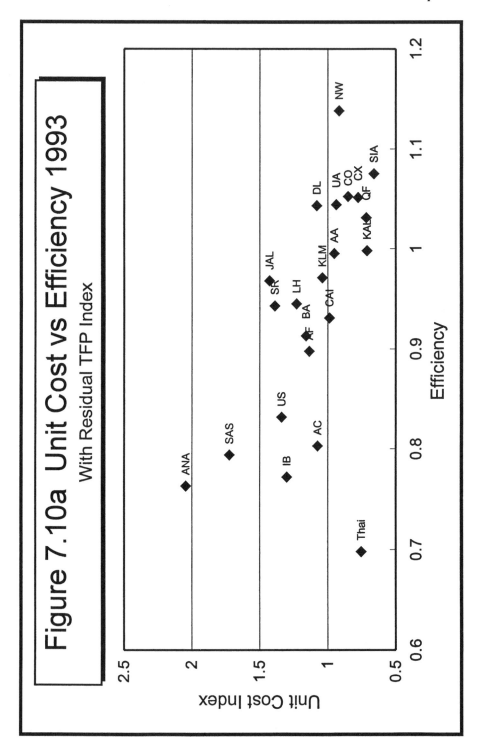

Figure 7.10a Unit Cost vs Efficiency 1993
With Residual TFP Index

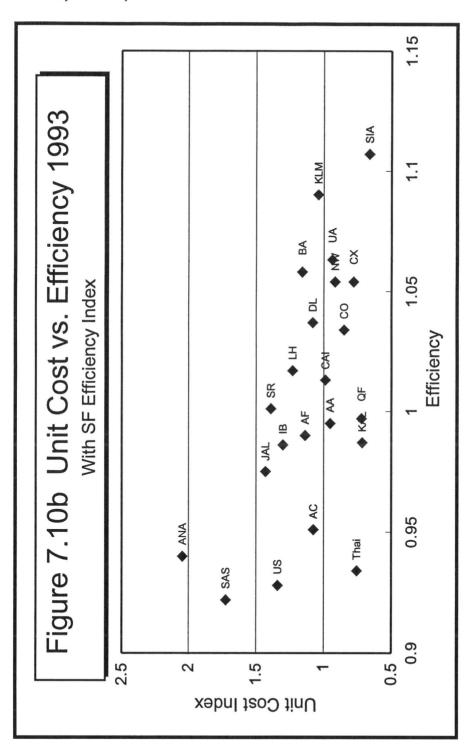

Figure 7.10b Unit Cost vs. Efficiency 1993

With SF Efficiency Index

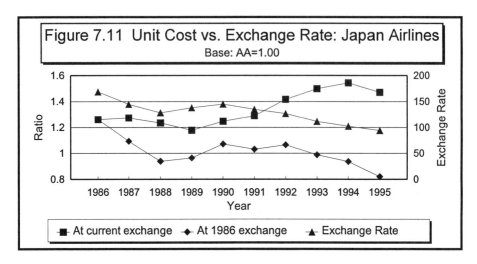

Figure 7.11 Unit Cost vs. Exchange Rate: Japan Airlines
Base: AA=1.00

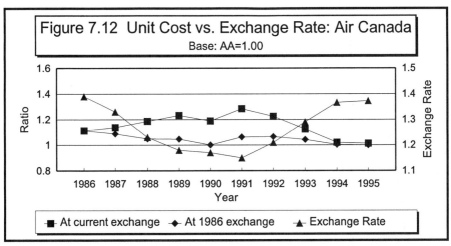

Figure 7.12 Unit Cost vs. Exchange Rate: Air Canada
Base: AA=1.00

its 1986 level, the difference became smaller - only a 1 percent difference in 1995.

Figure 7.13 plots changes in Air France's unit costs in relation to the French Franc. In 1986, AF's unit cost was 27 percent higher than that of AA. In 1995, Air France's unit cost was only about 5 percent higher than AA's in terms of the US dollar, even though the Franc appreciated by about 28 percent between 1986 and 1995. Had there been no change in the exchange rate, AF's 1995 unit cost would have been 24 percent lower than AA's. That is, Air France improved its unit cost performance more than AA[52].

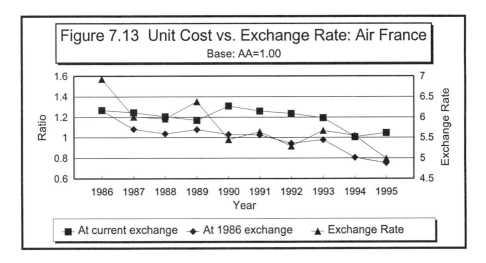

The next set of figures (Figure 7.14) examines the case of SAS. As is commonly known, SAS is a high-cost carrier. Its 1986 unit cost was 62 percent higher than that of AA. The Swedish Krona appreciated between 1986 and 1992, but then dramatically depreciated in 1993. SAS' unit cost increased by 39 percent between 1986 and 1992, and in 1992, was 93 percent higher than that of AA in US dollar terms. In Swedish Krona terms (at the 1986 constant exchange rate), however, SAS' unit costs increased by 14 percent, and would have been 58 percent higher than AA's. Because of depreciation of the Krona in 1993, SAS' unit cost was 81 percent higher than that of AA in US dollar terms, while it would have been 100 percent higher had there not been any exchange rate change since 1986.

---

[52] Please see Treppo (1997) for Air France's recent efforts on restructuring.

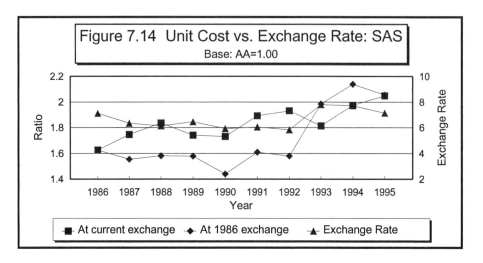

Figure 7.14 Unit Cost vs. Exchange Rate: SAS
Base: AA=1.00

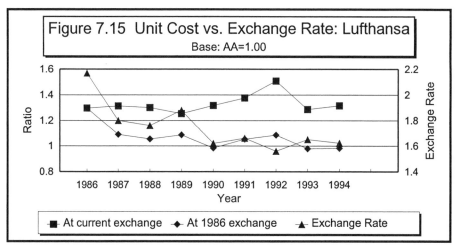

Figure 7.15 Unit Cost vs. Exchange Rate: Lufthansa
Base: AA=1.00

Figure 7.15 shows Lufthansa's unit costs in relation to the Deutsche Mark. As noted in Chapter 4, changes in the Deutsche Mark were very similar to those in the French Franc. Lufthansa's 1986 unit costs were 30 percent higher AA's. The Deutsche Mark then appreciated by about 24 percent from 1986 to 1994, increasing Lufthansa' unit cost by 16 percent. In 1994, its unit costs were 32 percent higher than AA's in US dollar terms. In Deutsche Marks (at constant 1986 exchange rate), however, Lufthansa's unit costs decreased by almost 13 percent between 1986 and 1994, which would put its unit cost at 2 percent lower than AA's in 1994, had there not been any change in exchange rates since 1986.

From the above discussion, it is obvious that exchange rate fluctuations have had non-negligible impacts on airline cost differentials between carriers from different countries. The effects could be both positive and negative. Home currency appreciation increases carrier unit costs in the short term, but may force carriers to improve productivity and efficiency. On the other hand, home currency depreciation generally reduces carrier unit costs, at least in the short term, but the subsequent reduction in competitive pressures may lead to decreased productivity of home carriers.

7.5 Summary

This chapter provides a preliminary analysis of airline cost structures and effects of some exogenous factors on airline costs. The results can be summarized as follows:

- Labor costs account for 20 percent of total cost for Asian carriers, and 32 percent for European and North American carriers. Changes in labor costs' shares over time indicate mixed patterns. For example, SIA and United's labor cost shares remained relatively stable during the period, Lufthansa's labor cost share slightly declined, while Thai's labor cost became a larger portion of its total costs.
- Fuel costs account for 9 percent of total cost for European carriers, and 11-13 percent for North American and Asian carriers. With a few exceptional cases, fuel cost shares generally declined during the sample period.
- Capital cost accounts for 13 percent of total cost for European carriers, and 15-17 percent for Asian and North American carriers. Capital costs shares have shown a general downward trend for North American and European carriers, but have remained mostly unchanged for Asian carriers.
- Materials cost shares range from 39 percent for North American carriers to 52 percent for Asian carriers. Materials cost shares have generally increased over time, probably due to the growing practice of out-sourcing in the airline industry.
- Asian carriers, excluding JAL and ANA, generally have considerably lower unit costs than European and North American carriers. And European carriers, on average, have noticeably higher unit costs than their North American counterparts. For most airlines, unit costs peaked around 1990-1991, and declined thereafter.
- Unit costs fall with increasing stage length and load factor, but rise with input prices. In addition, a clear pattern is observed between declining unit costs and improving efficiencies.
- Exchange rate fluctuations have had significant impacts on some carriers' costs. For example, JAL's rising unit cost was largely due to appreciation of the Japanese Yen.

Chapter 8
Cost Competitiveness

Widely-based airline deregulation and liberalization have intensified competition in the international airline industry. This in turn has forced airlines to undertake major restructuring in order to improve efficiency of operations, and thereby, reduce costs. Judging from industry trends, airlines' real yields will not likely increase under competitive pressures for market share. Therefore, airlines must remain cost competitive in order to survive and prosper in the globalizing airline industry. This chapter investigates issues related to cost competitiveness, focusing on identifying sources of airline cost competitiveness.

8.1 Introduction

What constitutes cost competitiveness of an airline? In simplest terms, an airline is cost competitive if its unit costs (average costs) are lower than that of its competitors on a sustainable basis. An airline may enjoy lower unit costs than its competitors because it is more efficient, pays less for its inputs, or both. That is, airline cost differentials are determined by differences in factor prices (including exchange rates) and productive efficiency. Knowledge about existing levels and sources of cost differentials are essential for analyzing public policy options and carrier strategies designed to enhance competitive positions. It is important to measure these differentials and to ascertain their sources. The policies and strategies government and firms should pursue depend on the relative importance of factors determining cost competitiveness.

To the best of our knowledge, no well-established measure for cost competitiveness exists. Few studies have systematically examined the issue of cost competitiveness, even fewer on airlines. Windle (1991) attempted to attribute unit cost differences between carriers to various sources, namely output scale, input prices, operating characteristics, non-optimal capital investment, technical efficiency, government ownership, and firm-specific effects. His study was based mainly on 1983 annual data for 14 US and 27 non-US airlines. Good and Rhodes (1991) examined three aspects of competitiveness and profitability of airlines in the Pacific region: input prices, output prices and productive efficiency, using a panel of 37 airlines over the 1976-86 period. A recent study by Baltagi, Griffin and Rich (1995) applied a translog variable cost function to a panel of 24 US airlines over the 1971-86 period to analyse cost changes in the pre- and post-deregulation US airline industry , and to identify cost changes due to technical change, economies of scale and density, and input prices.

This chapter focuses on identifying *sources* of airline cost competitiveness. We adopt the analytical framework proposed by Denny and Fuss (1983) and Caves and Christensen (1988). They proposed to estimate an econometric cost function, and use it to decompose total or unit costs into various sources. Specifically, a *translog* variable cost function is estimated, and its results are used to decompose sample airlines' observed unit cost differentials into potential sources: firm attributes (network characteristics and output mix), input prices, and efficiency. The results of the unit cost decomposition are used to assess and compare cost competitiveness across the sample airlines.

8.2 Specification of Cost Function

This section describes methodologies for estimating a neoclassical cost function and for decomposing airline unit cost differentials into potential sources.

Since the capital input in the airline industry is not always in equilibrium, we follow Caves, Christensen and Tretheway (1984) and Gillen, Oum and Tretheway (1990), by employing the following translog variable cost function (with the usual restrictions on symmetry and homogeneity imposed[53]) to reflect the short run cost minimization process:

$$
\begin{aligned}
\ln VC = a_0 &+ \sum_T a_T + b_y \ln Y + \sum_i \delta_i \ln R_i + \sum_i b_i \ln W_i \\
&+ b_e \ln E + c \ln Z + \frac{1}{2} d_{yy} (\ln Y)^2 + \frac{1}{2} \sum d_{ij} \ln W_i \ln W_j \\
&+ \frac{1}{2} d_{ee} (\ln E)^2 + \frac{1}{2} d_{zz} (\ln Z)^2 + \sum e_{yi} \ln Y \ln W_i + e_{yk} \ln \\
&+ e_{yz} \ln Y \ln Z + \sum f_{ki} \ln(uK) \ln W_i + f_{ke} \ln(uK) \ln E + \\
&+ \sum g_{ei} \ln E \ln W_i + \sum g_{zi} \ln Z \ln W_i
\end{aligned}
\qquad \text{8-1}
$$

where VC is cost of variable inputs, Y is aggregate output index, W is a vector of input prices, K is capital stock, u is utilization of capital stock (in this case, weight load factor), R_i are revenue shares of freight and mail, non-scheduled services, and incidental services, respectively, Z is stage length, E is an efficiency index, and a_T are dummy variables capturing the effects of technical shifts over time. Revenue share variables (reflecting output mix), R_i, are incorporated only in the first-order terms to keep the cost function simple.

Note that the variable cost function (8-1) includes variable E for efficiency. E is the efficiency measure estimated in Chapter 6, reflecting the overall efficiency level of airlines. By including E in the cost function estimation, we recognize the fact that some airlines fail to be on the production frontier, that is, some firms are more efficient than others. Once we recognize this, failure to include an efficiency indicator may lead to mis-specification of the model, and thus bias parameter estimates of the cost function. Therefore, we essentially use a two-step procedure to estimate the cost function. In the first stage, an efficiency index is estimated, and in the second stage, the estimated efficiency index is used as an explanatory variable in the cost function estimation. In this way, we can explicitly examine efficiency effects on airline cost.

It should also be noted that a capacity utilization rate is applied to capital stock in the cost function. This is done to reflect, in the cost function, the amount of capital service flow from the capital stock, as proposed by Oum and Zhang (1991, 1995) and Oum, Tretheway and Zhang (1991).

The following cost minimizing variable input cost share equations can be derived by applying Shephard's lemma to the variable cost function (8-1):

---

[53] See Gillen, Oum and Tretheway (1990) for an example of restrictions on symmetry and linear homogeneity of the cost function in input prices as well as application of Shephard's lemma.

$$S_i = \frac{\partial \ln VC}{\partial \ln W_i} = b_i + \sum_j d_{ij} \ln W_j + e_{yi} \ln Y + f_{ki} \ln(uK) + g_{ei} \qquad 8\text{-}2$$

To improve estimation efficiency, it is customary to estimate the translog variable cost function (8-1) jointly with variable input cost share equations (8-2). In order to further improve estimation efficiency, Oum and Zhang (1991, 1995) proposed to add the following expression to reflect the shadow value of capital stock:

$$\frac{C_k}{VC} = -\frac{\partial \ln VC}{\partial \ln(uK)} = -(b_k + d_{kk} \ln(uK) + e_{yk} \ln Y + \sum_j f_{kj} \ln W_j + \qquad 8\text{-}3$$

where C_k is depreciated capital cost approximated by total capital cost multiplied by the utilization rate. Equation (8-3) is basically the first order condition for short-run total cost minimization which endogenizes capacity utilization. Following Oum and Zhang (1991), we jointly estimate the translog variable cost function (8-1), cost share equations[54] (8-2), and the shadow price of capital input equation (8-3) as a system of multivariate equations using a Maximum Likelihood method.

Drawing on properties of a translog variable cost function, Caves and Christensen (1988) and Fuss and Waverman (1992) showed that the (total) unit cost differentials (including capital costs) between any two observations, 1 and 0, can be decomposed into various sources using the following formula:

$$
\begin{aligned}
c^1 - c^0 = {} & S[1/2(d_y^1 C_v + d_y^0 C_v) - 1] \cdot (Y^1 - Y^0) \\
& \left. \begin{array}{l} + S[1/2(d_k^1 C_v + d_k^0 C_v) \cdot (K^1 - K^0)] \\ + (1-S)[(K^1 - K^0) - (Y^1 - Y^0)] \end{array} \right\} \; size \\
& + S[1/2(d_r^1 C_v + d_r^0 C_v) \cdot (R^1 - R^0)] \quad output\ mix \qquad 8\text{-}4 \\
& \left. \begin{array}{l} + S[1/2(d_w^1 C_v + d_w^0 C_v) \cdot (W^1 - W^0)] \\ + (1-S)(W_k^1 - W_k^0) \end{array} \right\} \; input\ prices \\
& + S[1/2(d_z^1 C_v + d_z^0 C_v) \cdot (Z^1 - Z^0)] \quad operating\ characteristics \\
& + S[1/2(d_t^1 C_v + d_t^0 C_v) \cdot (t^1 - t^0) \quad\ time\ effects \\
& + S[1/2(d_e^1 C_v + d_e^0 C_v) \cdot (E^1 - E^0) \quad efficiency
\end{aligned}
$$

where S denotes average share of variable cost (in total cost) for observations 1 and 0, and $d_x^i C_v$ denotes the partial derivative of variable cost for observation i with respect to variable x. For ease of presentation, American Airlines (AA) is used as the benchmark firm against which to compare other airlines.

---

[54] To avoid singularity of variance-covariance matrix, the materials cost share equation was dropped from estimation. It is well known that maximum likelihood estimates are invariant to choice of share equation dropped.

8.3 Empirical Results

Using the residual TFP index and the SF efficiency index from Chapter 6, alternative variable cost functions are estimated using the Maximum Likelihood method. Since they have exactly the same number of explanatory variables, the model with the largest log-likelihood function value, when residual TFP index is used, was chosen for analysis and discussion in this Chapter.

In the following, we present the estimated variable cost function, and use it to decompose sources of unit cost differentials. The results are used to identify effects on unit cost of input prices, output mix, average stage length, and efficiency, and to evaluate and compare cost competitiveness in the following section.

Cost Function Estimation

The Maximum Likelihood parameter estimates, t-statistics, and other summary statistics on the variable cost function estimation (equation 8-1) are reported in Table 8.1. First-order coefficients for input prices indicate that at mean data, labour and fuel inputs account for 32 percent and 15 percent, respectively, of total variable cost. This leaves material inputs to account for 53 percent of total variable cost. The first-order coefficient for the capital input variable is negative, implying a positive capital input shadow value.[55] Stage length has a statistically significant negative coefficient, implying that variable cost decreases with stage length. The coefficient for the efficiency variable is negative and statistically significant, indicating that efficient firms are likely to have considerably lower costs. The coefficient for the 1993 time shift dummy indicates that the efficiency of using variable input improved by 3.3% between 1986 and 1993, due to industry-wide technical progress. The negative coefficients for %Incidental and %Non-Scheduled indicate that, other things being equal, carriers with high concentration on non-airline (incidental) businesses and non-scheduled services are expected to have low variable costs. On the other hand, carriers with higher concentration on freight services may suffer cost disadvantages[56].

Unit Cost Decomposition

1993 unit cost (cost per unit of aggregate output) differentials between each airline and American Airlines (AA) are decomposed into different sources using equation (4). The results are summarized in Table 8.2, where Column (1) lists observed unit cost differences, expressed in percentage difference of airline unit costs relative to American Airlines (AA).

---

[55] Many empirical studies on airline variable cost function report a positive first-coefficient for the capital stock variable, which implies a negative value of the shadow price of capital. See, for example, Gillen, Oum and Tretheway (1985 & 1990), and Caves, Christensen, Tretheway and Windle (1987) which was used extensively by Windle (1991).

[56] At first glance, this appears to be contrary to our intuition that freight services require less input than passenger services. However, this result is plausible for the following reasons. Since cargo yields per RTK are far lower than passenger yield per RTK (average yield for our sample is US$1.03 per RTK for passenger vs US$0.33 per RTK for freight), cargo output receives very low weight in aggregating outputs. Therefore, the amount of increase in output index caused by cargo output is relatively small as compared to the amount of increase in input cost caused by cargo output. If this is the case, %Freight variable would have a positive coefficient, as in our case.

Table 8.1
Variable Cost Function Estimates

Parameter	Coefficient	T-value	Parameter	Coefficient	T-value
Constant	8.109	1316.2	Output*Output	-0.013	0.70
Output	1.123	235.96	Labour*Fuel	-0.038	5.14
Labour	0.318	70.08	Labour*Capital	0.036	4.85
Fuel	0.153	89.38	Labour*Stage	-0.088	8.07
Capital[1]	-0.106	67.48	Labour*Labour	0.188	7.65
Stage Length	-0.305	37.61	Fuel*Capital	-0.059	12.12
%Freight.	0.055	11.80	Fuel*Stage	0.008	2.00
%Non-Sch.	-0.007	6.95	Fuel*Fuel	0.088	15.19
%Incidentl	-0.040	25.83	Capital*Stage	-0.028	7.34
Efficiency[2]	-1.138	64.63	Capital*Capital	-0.012	1.21
Eff. * Output	0.050	1.02	Stage*Stage	0.036	2.09
Eff. * Labour	0.090	2.47	1987	-0.003	0.42
Effi. * Fuel	0.100	5.92	1988	-0.014	2.16
Eff. *Capital	-0.063	3.72	1989	-0.009	1.42
Eff. * Efficiency	0.723	3.50	1990	-0.010	1.34
Labour*Output	-0.054	4.59	1991	-0.021	3.25
Fuel*Output	0.059	9.93	1992	-0.029	4.34
Capital *Output	0.017	1.54	1993	-0.033	4.87
Stage*Output	0.028	2.30			

Number of Observations: 178

Log-Likelihood Function: 1572.28

Note that all variables except time dummies are in natural log with mean removed.

In addition to the cost shares equations, the equation for the ratio of depreciated capital cost to variable cost, which is equal to negative partial derivative $d_k C_v$, is included in the regression.

1. Capital is Capital stock multiplied by weight load factor.

2. Residual TFP index from Chapter 6 is used as E (efficiency).

For example, Delta's 1993 unit costs were 14% higher than AA's, while Singapore Airlines' unit costs were 31% lower than AA's. Asian carriers, excluding Japan Airlines (JAL) and All Nippon Airways (ANA), had substantially lower unit costs than major U.S. carriers, while most U.S. carriers, in turn, had substantially lower unit costs than European carriers. KLM is an exception in that its unit costs were about 10% lower than Delta's.

Columns (2) - (7) in Table 8.2 report decomposition of unit cost differences, that is, contribution of each source to observed unit cost differences. Each entry listed under "Sources of Difference" is the percentage difference in total unit cost between AA and a particular airline caused by a single source. For example, for United, in column (4) under "labour price", 3.3 indicates that if price of labor was the only difference between United and AA in 1993, then United's unit cost would have been 3.3% higher than AA's.

Columns (2) and (3) show effects of stage length and output mix (scheduled passenger, freight, non-scheduled, and incidental businesses). Variations in stage length alone account for a substantial portion of observed system-wide unit cost differences, especially for carriers at extreme ends of the scale. For example, if other things being equal, Singapore Airlines' and Qantas' system-wide unit costs would be 23% and 25% lower than AA's, respectively, because of their long stage lengths. SAS and US Air, on the other hand, would have 25% and 18% higher system-wide unit costs than AA, respectively, again if other things being equal. Output mix generally has only limited effects on observed unit cost. The only noticeable exception is British Airways (BA). BA has very little incidental and non-scheduled services, thus its system-wide unit costs would be 11% higher than AA's, other things being equal.

Columns (4), (5) and (6) in Table 8.2 are percentage differences in unit costs between each airline and AA, attributable to differences in labor price, other input prices, and all input prices together, respectively. Asian carriers, with the exception of JAL and ANA, enjoyed significant cost advantages relative to AA, due to lower labor and non-labor input prices. For example, over 90% of Korean Air's unit cost advantage over AA came from lower input prices. On the other hand, JAL's high labour prices caused a 23% unit cost disadvantage while their higher non-labour input prices (fuel, capital and materials) were responsible for a further 16% unit cost disadvantage. Major US carriers, excluding Continental, incurred 3% - 8% higher costs relative to AA, due to high labour prices. Continental's lower labour prices gave it an 11% cost advantage over AA. The two Canadian carriers, Air Canada and CAI, also enjoyed a cost advantage of about 12% over AA, due to their lower labour prices. Effects of other input prices were very small for North American carriers, except CAI, which had a 3.7% cost disadvantage relative to AA due to slightly higher non-labour prices. All European carriers suffered substantial cost disadvantages relative to AA because of significantly high non-labour input prices, ranging from 10% for both BA and Iberia, to 26% for Swissair. Labor price effects, on the other hand, varied across airlines. For example, British Airways enjoyed a 13% cost advantage over AA due to lower labour prices, while Swissair suffered a 10% cost disadvantage due to higher labour prices.

Column (7) lists the contribution of efficiency to unit cost differences. The results show that, if all other things equal, in 1993, most of the major U.S. carriers (except US Air) would have enjoyed some unit cost advantage relative to AA due to their higher productive efficiencies. This advantage ranges from 1% for Continental to 10% for Northwest. KLM would have enjoyed about 5% unit cost advantage over AA, due to its

Table 8.2 Unit Cost Decomposition and Cost Competitiveness, 1993 (% Above and Below AA's Unit Cost)

| | Observed Unit Cost Difference (1) | Sources of Difference | | | | | | Cost Competitiveness (8)=(6)+(7) |
| | | Firm Characteristics | | Input Prices | | | Efficiency (7) | |
		Stage (2)	Output Mix (3)	Labour (4)	Other inputs (5)	All inputs (6)		
North America								
American	0.0	0.0	0.0	0.0	0.0	0.0	0.0	0.0
United	-1.7	-1.2	0.2	3.3	0.4	3.7	-3.8	-0.1
Delta	13.5	7.7	3.1	7.7	-0.3	7.4	-5.6	1.8
Northwest	-3.7	3.3	2.1	3.9	0.7	4.6	-9.9	-5.3
Continental	-10.7	3.8	-2.6	-10.7	-0.7	-11.4	-0.7	-12.1
US Air	40.9	17.6	-4.2	3.0	-0.4	2.6	17.4	19.9
Air Canada	12.7	1.9	3.1	-12.4	0.9	-11.5	19.9	8.5
Canadian	3.6	-1.1	1.5	-12.3	3.7	-8.6	13.7	5.0
Asia-Pacific								
Japan Airlines	50.1	-13.0	3.0	22.6	15.9	38.4	14.3	52.7
All Nippon	114.8	13.0	3.9	18.8	21.5	40.4	23.1	63.5
Singapore Airlines	-30.6	-23.0	6.8	-16.9	-3.3	-20.3	3.9	-16.3
Korean Air	-25.2	-0.8	0.1	-14.7	-9.0	-23.8	0.8	-22.9
Cathay	-18.3	-17.4	4.4	-2.1	-4.2	-6.4	2.6	-3.8
Qantas	-24.6	-24.9	0.5	-8.9	-0.1	-8.9	11.6	2.7
Thai	-20.8	0.6	-0.1	-22.4	-29.8	-52.1	42.9	-9.3
Europe								
Air France	19.3	-1.2	-0.8	-5.2	14.0	8.8	12.4	21.2
Lufthansa	29.2	11.2	-2.0	0.6	16.3	16.8	3.8	20.6
British Airways	21.9	-2.4	11.0	-12.8	9.9	-2.9	10.2	7.3
SAS	81.5	25.0	-4.7	4.4	21.0	25.4	17.0	42.4
KLM[a]	3.3	-6.2	1.7	0.6	15.5	16.0	-5.3	10.7
Swissair[a]	46.4	5.4	-2.2	9.4	26.1	35.5	2.8	38.3
Iberia	36.9	7.6	2.8	-4.9	10.0	5.1	16.4	21.5

a. 1992

higher productive efficiency. However, all other carriers in our sample would have had unit cost disadvantages of varying degrees relative to AA because of their lower productive efficiencies. For example, inefficiency alone accounted for a 20% higher unit cost for Air Canada, overpowering the 12% cost advantage it had over AA from lower input prices. Similarly, Thai's inefficiency would have led to a 43% higher unit cost, were it not for the favourable impact of its significantly lower input prices. ANA's lower efficiency level led to a further 23% cost disadvantage, in addition to the 40% cost disadvantage caused by higher input prices.

8.4 Unit Cost Competitiveness

As discussed earlier, observed unit cost differences do not reflect true comparative cost competitiveness between airlines, as airlines have different operating and network characteristics. What one needs to ask is how carriers would be able to compete in a given market such as the trans-Pacific and trans-Atlantic markets. A low system-wide unit cost for an airline, with heavy concentration on incidental services and with long average stage length, may not constitute cost competitiveness in a given market. When an airline competes in a given market, particularly in an inter-continental market, what is relevant is the marginal cost of providing a given level of service in that market. What determines cost competitiveness is input prices paid by the airline and how efficiently the airline produces and markets their services. Therefore, a cost competitiveness (CC) indicator is constructed by summing input price effects and efficiency effects reported in columns (6) and (7) of Table 8.2. Since unit cost decomposition disentangles effects of output mix and stage length from effects of input prices and efficiency, this indicator approximates the "true" comparative cost competitiveness of airlines.

Column (8) of Table 8.2 presents the 1993 cost competitiveness indicator. This indicator is measured in terms of percentage above (-) or below (+) that of AA. A negative number indicates that the airline is cost competitive relative to AA, while a positive number indicates the opposite.

Continental (CO) enjoyed an over 12% cost competitive advantage over AA in 1993. Most of its cost competitiveness came from lower labour prices. Northwest enjoyed a 5% advantage over AA. Although high efficiency gave it a 10% cost advantage, higher input prices reduced its cost competitiveness. United and Delta were similar to AA in terms of cost competitiveness (with CC at -0.1% and 1.8%, respectively). Although high efficiency gave them a 3.8% and 5.6 % cost advantage, respectively, high input prices created a 3.7% cost disadvantage for United and 7.4% for Delta. US Air was 20% less cost competitive relative to AA. This consists of 17% and 3% due to low efficiency and high input prices, respectively.

Air Canada (AC) was about 8.5% less cost competitive than AA because of its substantially lower efficiency. And Canadian Airlines International (CAI) was about 5% less cost competitive, also due to its low efficiency level. Both AC and CAI's cost advantages from lower labour prices were canceled by effects of low efficiency.

Among Asian carriers, Singapore, Korean, Cathay, and Thai enjoyed high cost competitiveness relative to AA, by factors of 16%, 23%, 4% and 9%, respectively. Their cost competitiveness came entirely from significantly lower input prices, but their relatively low efficiency levels diminished any cost advantages. Qantas was slightly less cost competitive (2.7%) than AA because its cost advantage from lower input prices was more than off-set by its lower efficiency level. JAL and ANA were significantly less cost competitive because of the combined effects of higher input prices and lower efficiency.

BA was about 7% less cost competitive relative to AA due to higher non-labour prices and lower efficiency. And KLM was 10% less cost competitive, due entirely to the cost disadvantage caused by higher input prices. However, its higher efficiency helped alleviate some of this cost disadvantage. Swissair was 38% less cost competitive relative to AA, due mainly to high input prices.

Lufthansa was 21% less cost competitive relative to AA. Their cost disadvantage was caused mostly by high input prices. Air France was also about 21% less cost competitive relative to AA, due to the combined effects of high non-labor input prices and low efficiency. SAS and Iberia were, respectively, 42% and 32% less cost competitive than AA. Their cost disadvantages resulted from high input prices and low efficiency levels[57].

Overall, European carriers were less cost competitive than US airlines, caused by both higher input prices and lower efficiency. Asian carriers, with the exception of JAL and ANA, were more cost competitive than US airlines. However, their cost competitiveness was entirely the result of low input prices rather than high efficiency.

8.5 Changes in Cost Competitiveness

Airline cost competitiveness positions may change due to changes in input factor prices, changes in productive efficiency, or both. Figures 8.1a-8.3c show changes in sample airlines' cost competitiveness and its components over time. Comparisons are made between each airline and AA in the same year, so changes reflect changes in airline cost competitiveness positions relative to AA. Note that changes in AA's unit cost may exaggerate or understate real (absolute) changes in the airlines' unit costs.

Figures 8.1a, 8.1b, and 8.1c indicate past fluctuations in airline cost competitiveness. However, relative airline rankings remained fairly stable. Continental retained its position as the most cost competitive North American carrier throughout the sample period, while US Air and Air Canada were consistently least cost competitive. American, United, and Delta were very close in their cost competitive positions, with Northwest enjoying a small advantage over them.

During the sample period, KLM was the most cost competitive European carrier, while SAS and Swissair were least cost competitive. BA made considerable improvements in its relative cost competitive position, particularly after 1990. However, Iberia and Air France's cost competitive positions deteriorated somewhat.

SIA remained the most cost competitive Asian carrier until 1992, when it was overtaken by KAL. JAL and ANA were least cost competitive in Asia, and their situations have notably worsened since 1990. Qantas and KAL, on the other hand, have made substantial improvements in their relative cost competitive positions.

---

[57] It is noteworthy that our results on unit cost differentials are, by and large, consistent with the findings of Bureau of Industry Economics (1994) and Commité de Sages (1994).

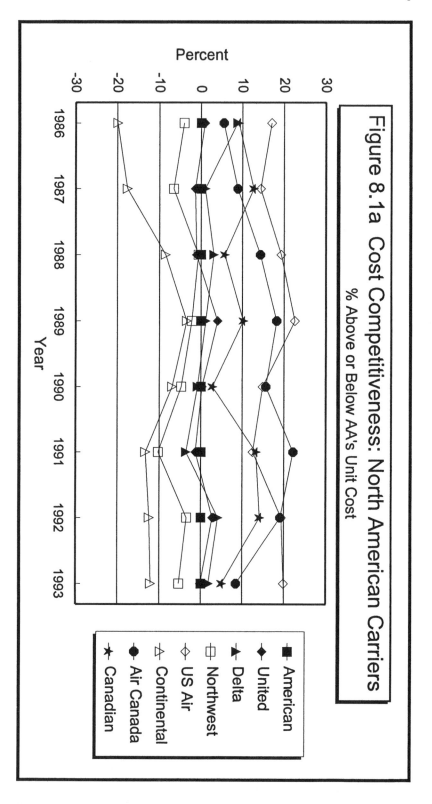

Figure 8.1a Cost Competitiveness: North American Carriers
% Above or Below AA's Unit Cost

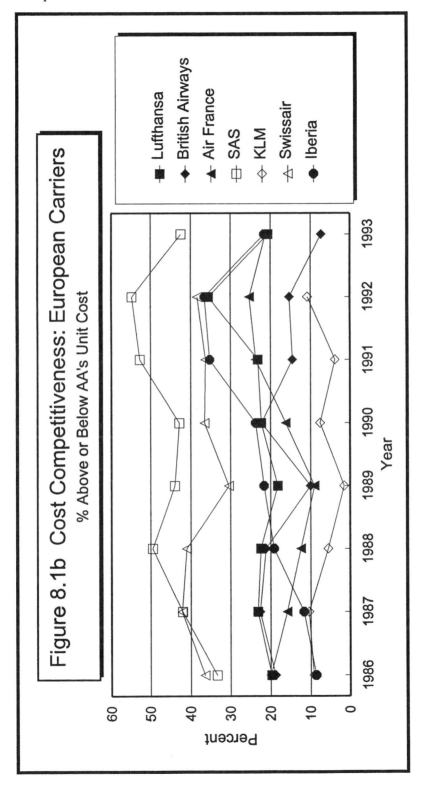

Figure 8.1b Cost Competitiveness: European Carriers
% Above or Below AA's Unit Cost

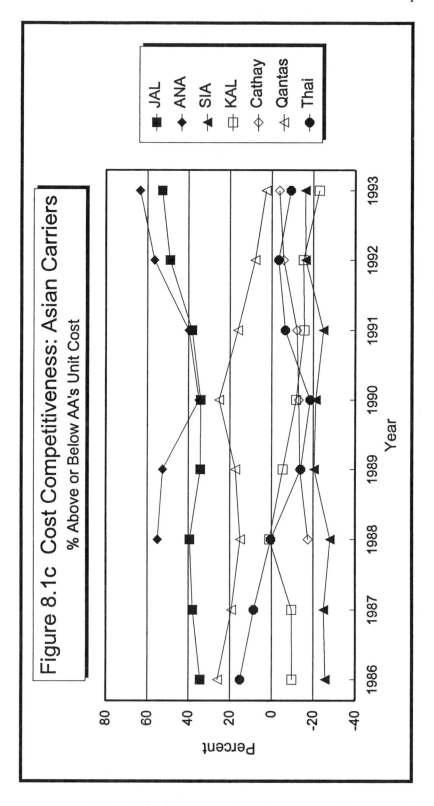

Figure 8.1c Cost Competitiveness: Asian Carriers
% Above or Below AA's Unit Cost

Figures 8.2a-8.2c and 8.3a-8.3c show effects of input price and efficiency on airline cost competitiveness. It is clearly evident that Continental's strong cost competitive position during the period was attributable to its consistently low input prices. Air Canada and Canadian enjoyed substantial input price advantages relative to US carriers, even though the strong Canadian dollar during 1990-1991 almost eliminated their price advantages. However, their inefficiency worked to weaken any cost advantages. As a result, Air Canada and Canadian remained as weak cost competitors during the period. Delta's cost competitive position continued to suffer from relatively higher input prices, but it was able to keep up with the competition from American and United by being relatively more efficient.

The European carriers exhibited a general trend of rising input prices with improving efficiency. The effects of these two opposing forces appeared to counteract against each other. For example, Swissair and KLM's efficiency levels significantly improved during the period, but their input prices also rose significantly. Thus, their cost competitive positions did not show any significant change. When the effect of one factor is stronger than the other, one would expect to see improvement or deterioration in an airline's cost competitive position. For example, BA was able to enhance its relative cost competitive position during the period because its cost savings from efficiency improvements more than offset cost increases caused by rising input prices. On the other hand, Air France's cost competitive position somewhat deteriorated from 1989 because it was not able to improve its efficiency to compensate for increasing costs caused by rising input prices.

A similar trend of rising input prices and improving efficiency was also observed among most Asian carriers. Qantas and KAL were able to improve their cost competitive positions through significant efficiency improvements despite rising input prices. Thai's substantial efficiency improvements prior to 1990, coupled with relatively stable input prices, strengthened its cost competitive position. Since then, slight efficiency deterioration together with rising input prices have considerably weakened its cost competitive position.

8.6 Exchange Rate Effects on Cost Competitiveness

In Chapter 7, the unit cost index is plotted against exchange rates for selected airlines in order to examine exchange rate effects on unit cost. Similarly, Figures 8.4 to 8.8 plot the cost competitiveness indicator against exchange rates for the same airlines. Recall that the cost competitiveness indicator is the portion of unit cost differences attributable to efficiency and input prices, after removing the effects of stage length and output mix. Changes in airline stage length and output mix, over time, are relatively small compared to differences across airlines, unless a certain major event, such as a merger, occurs at that airline. Therefore, changes in the cost competitiveness indicator follow a similar pattern as observed unit cost changes for most airlines. This is evident from comparisons of Figures 8.4-8.8 and Figures 7.11-7.15. These two sets of graphs are almost identical, except for Air France. A significant difference in the changing pattern between Air France's observed unit cost and cost competitiveness indicator is observed after 1991, the year Air France merged with UTA, which resulted in significant changes in network and output characteristics.

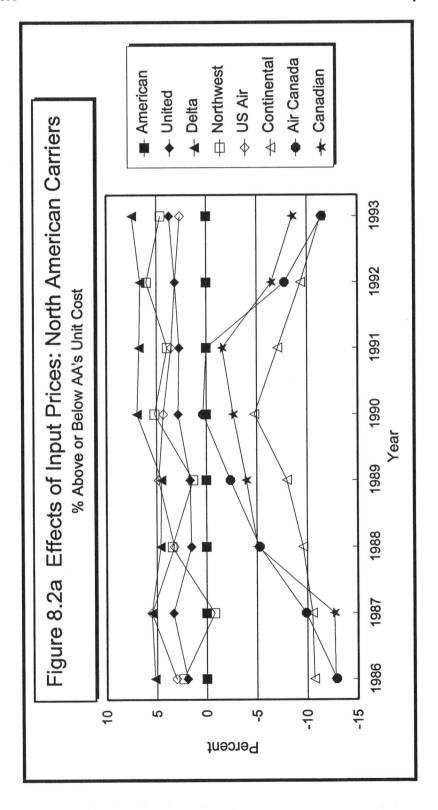

Figure 8.2a Effects of Input Prices: North American Carriers

% Above or Below AA's Unit Cost

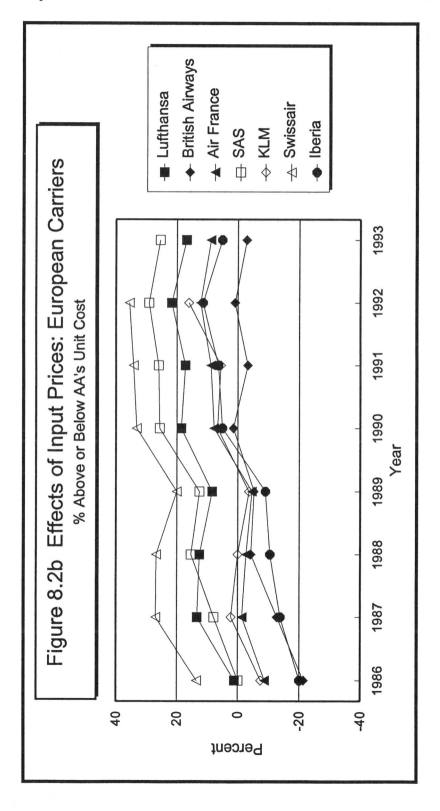

Figure 8.2b Effects of Input Prices: European Carriers
% Above or Below AA's Unit Cost

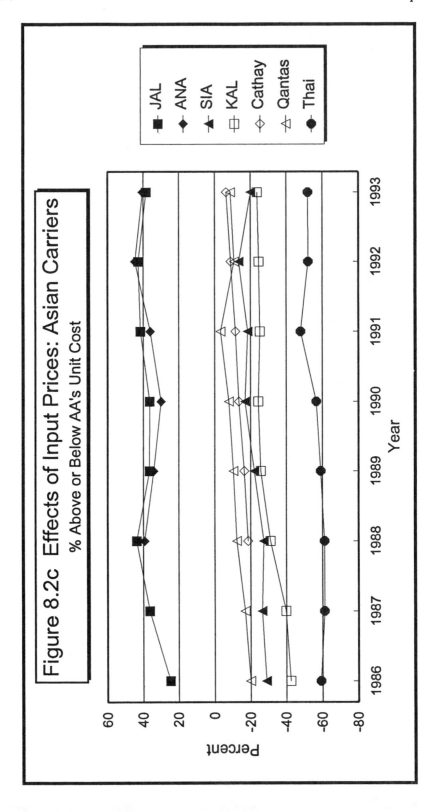

Figure 8.2c Effects of Input Prices: Asian Carriers
% Above or Below AA's Unit Cost

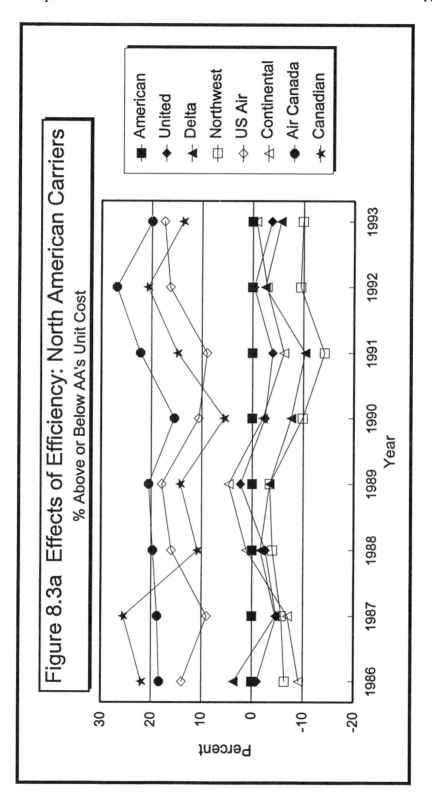

Figure 8.3a Effects of Efficiency: North American Carriers
% Above or Below AA's Unit Cost

172

Chapter 8

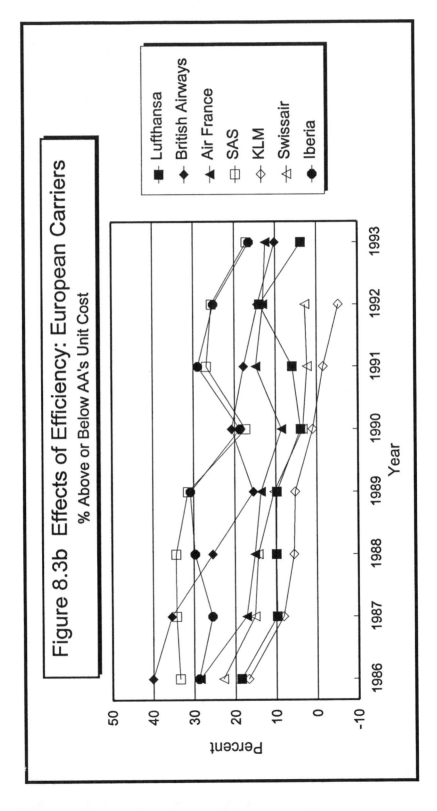

Figure 8.3b Effects of Efficiency: European Carriers

% Above or Below AA's Unit Cost

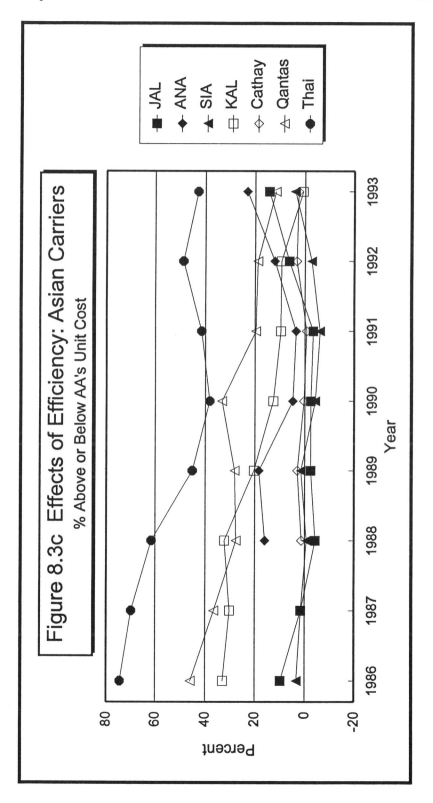

Figure 8.3c Effects of Efficiency: Asian Carriers
% Above or Below AA's Unit Cost

Figures 8.4-8.8 demonstrate that currency appreciation weakens the cost competitive position of a country's home carriers. On the other hand, currency depreciation brings at least temporary relief to home carriers from the pressures of remaining cost competitive. In 1993, JAL would have only had an 8 percent cost disadvantage relative to AA, rather than a 53 percent disadvantage, if the Japanese Yen exchange rate had remained at its 1986 level. Likewise, in 1990, Air Canada would have had a 1 percent cost advantage over AA, instead of a 16 percent cost disadvantage, had there not been a 15 percent appreciation of the Canadian dollar. Between 1990-1993, Air France (AF) was over 20 percent less cost competitive than AA. However, AF would have been fairly cost competitive if the French Franc had remained at its 1986 level. Similarly, Lufthansa would have had an 8 percent cost advantage over AA in 1993, and have been able to remain cost competitive from 1987, had the Deutsche Mark not appreciated 24 percent against the US dollar during the period. On the contrary, due to depreciation of Swedish Krona, SAS suffered a 42 percent cost disadvantage instead of a possible 53 percent. Currency appreciation increases competitive pressures for airlines to improve. However, currency depreciation brings possible negative consequences to airlines by inducing them to be less efficient. Airlines should take advantage of the opportunity, instead of being misled by currency illusions.

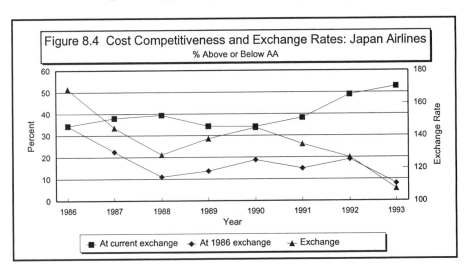

Figure 8.4 Cost Competitiveness and Exchange Rates: Japan Airlines
% Above or Below AA

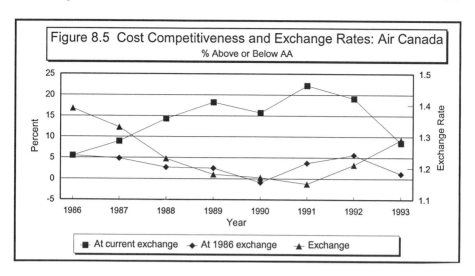

Figure 8.5 Cost Competitiveness and Exchange Rates: Air Canada
% Above or Below AA

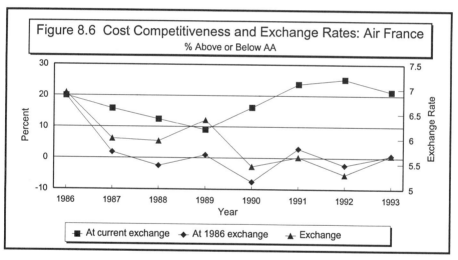

Figure 8.6 Cost Competitiveness and Exchange Rates: Air France
% Above or Below AA

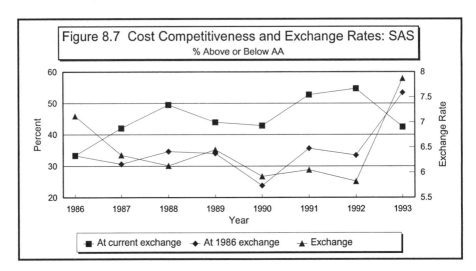

Figure 8.7 Cost Competitiveness and Exchange Rates: SAS
% Above or Below AA

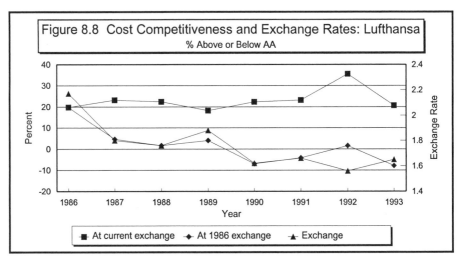

Figure 8.8 Cost Competitiveness and Exchange Rates: Lufthansa
% Above or Below AA

8.7 Summary

This chapter measures and compares the sample airlines' cost competitiveness, which depends on input factor prices and productive efficiency. Observed (system-wide) unit cost differentials between airlines, however, are also influenced by effects of network and output attributes, which must be removed in order to make meaningful comparisons across firms and/or over time within a firm. Therefore, a translog variable cost function is estimated and used to decompose total unit cost differentials into potential sources: stage length, output mix, input prices, and efficiency. Cost decomposition results are then used to develop a cost competitiveness (CC) indicator, after removing effects of stage length and output mix. The main results are summarized as follows:

(a) Carriers in Asia (except JAL and ANA) are generally more cost competitive than major US carriers, though Northwest and Continental are as cost competitive as some Asian carriers. Lower input prices is the dominating reason for their cost competitiveness. And their cost competitiveness relative to AA has decreased over time (except Qantas and KAL).

(b) JAL and ANA are significantly less cost competitive than AA, mainly because of their higher input prices.

(c) Major European carriers were 7% (BA) - 42% (SAS) less cost competitive than AA in 1993, because of the combined effects of higher input prices and lower efficiency. However, European carriers' productive efficiency improved relative to AA during the 1986-93 period;

(d) In 1993, AA, United, and Delta were similar in cost competitiveness, while Northwest and Continental, respectively, enjoyed 5% and 12% cost competitiveness over AA. US Air was least cost competitive among North American carriers, due to its lower efficiency and slightly higher labour prices.

(e) Air Canada was about 8.5% less cost competitive relative to AA, due to its lower productive efficiency. CAI was about 5% less cost competitive relative to AA, also due to its lower efficiency level. Their cost advantages from lower labor prices were overpowered by effects of lower efficiency.

(f) Exchange rate fluctuations have had significant impacts on some carriers' cost competitive positions. For example, in 1993, JAL would have only had an 8 percent cost disadvantage relative to AA, rather than 53 percent, if the Japanese Yen had remained at its 1986 level.

Overall, in the past, input prices together (including exchange rates) have been more important than productive efficiency in determining a carrier's unit cost competitive position. However, the importance of input prices is likely to diminish over time as airlines increase global sourcing of labour, materials, services and other inputs, and as input prices in developing and Newly Industrialized Countries (NICs) continue to rise faster than in developed countries. Furthermore, airlines could actively make efforts to improve performance, while input prices in a country are mostly beyond airlines' control. As liberalization of the airline industry continues, therefore, efficiency will become progressively more important in determining airline cost competitiveness.

Chapter 9
Yields, Costs and Financial Performance

Cost competitiveness is an important determinant of carrier profitability. However, airline profitability also depends on the ability to price above costs. And the ability to set prices above cost depends on market power and the firm's ability to make use of innovative (demand-responsive) pricing techniques and market information. Although cost advantages may confer carriers a basis to exercise market power and price leadership, market power in the airline industry, for most part, has been created by regulatory protection of carriers. Most international airline markets are regulated by bilateral air agreements which restrict competition. As a result, duopolies and oligopolies are the norm rather than exception in many international air transport markets. In such regulated markets, carriers tend to charge high markups over costs. In the past therefore, some carriers have been profitable without being cost competitive because they were able to charge exorbitant prices to consumers. However, as explained in Chapter 3, even the international airline market has become increasingly competitive as a result of a series of liberalization and open skies measures undertaken by the U.S. and other governments, and also as a result of the collapse of IATA as a price cartel. This trend will continue to accelerate and put increasing pressure on high cost carriers.

On the other hand, even in fairly competitive markets such as those in North America, airlines practice time-based dynamic pricing called yield management (or equivalently, revenue maximization). Through revenue management practices, airlines exercise price discrimination using fences around various discount levels. Clever yield management can contribute significantly to airlines' bottom-line profitability, even in fairly competitive markets.

The above discussion indicates that although cost competitiveness is very important for an airline's future success and prosperity, financial profitability also depends on the airline's ability to generate high yields for its traffic. In this chapter, a brief account is made to explain carriers' financial performance by examining both average cost and average yield per unit of output. It is noted that since our output measure is an index created by aggregating five heterogeneous outputs, our discussion will focus on comparing changes in yield and unit cost indices per unit of aggregate output.

Figures 9.1- 9.22 show the average yield and unit cost indices in terms of current U.S. dollars and average yield in constant domestic currency terms. All indices are normalized at the base period, the first year of the sample period, such that they show relative changes for each airline. These indices are not intended to compare airlines operating in different market, network and geographical conditions. Rather, average yield and unit cost indices, in current U.S. dollars, are intended to show changes in relative profitability of each carrier over time, and the average U.S. dollar price consumers pay for to travel with the airline. Average yield, measured in the constant domestic currency terms, intends to show the extent of adjustment and cost control each carrier has been subjected to during the sample period. Due to the repetitive nature of explanation, only the results of selected carriers are described below.

9.1   North American Carriers

Figures 9.1-9.8 show average yield and unit cost indices for the eight North American carriers included in our study. In current U.S. dollar terms, between 1986 and 1995, average yields of Continental (CO), AA, Northwest and UA increased by 39%, 20%, 19%, and 15%, respectively. In contrast, Delta's yield decreased by 2% and US Air's yield increased by only 5%. Meanwhile, US Air's unit cost increased by 11%. Of course, this explains USAir's difficult financial conditions. Since Delta was a high cost-high yield carrier, it had to make the most difficult adjustments. Delta's nominal unit cost index decreased from a 1990 high of 1.11, to about 0.93, about 7% lower than the 1986 unit cost level. As a result, Delta became a profit-making airline. CO's yield had to increase 40% to meet increases in unit cost, which also increased by 39% from 1986. CO suffered losses during most of the 1986-95 sample period because its unit costs increased faster than yield. It is also noted that CO started with very low unit costs in 1986. AA and UA were profitable for most years because they were able to check unit cost increases lower than yield increases. Northwest is an interesting airline in that it managed to raise average yield by 20% while allowing unit cost to increase by 6% between 1986 and 1995. This is despite financial difficulties suffered in the early 1990s, when average yield fell soon after rapid unit cost increases during the late 1980s.

In terms of constant US dollars, with exception of CO, yields of all other U.S. carriers decreased substantially between 1986 and 1995. Decreases ranged from 28% for Delta to 12% for AA. CO's 1995 average yield, in constant U.S. dollars, was virtually the same as that of 1986.

Both average yield and unit costs for Air Canada (AC) and Canadian Airlines International (Canadian), in current U.S. dollars, increased rapidly until 1991, then decreased fairly rapidly. Since yields declined faster than unit costs, AC suffered financial losses during the early 1990s. From 1988 to 1991, Canadian's unit cost increased faster than average yield, after which the average yield decreased faster than unit cost. Canadian thus suffered continuous financial losses from 1988. It is noteworthy that Air Canada's average yield has been about 10% higher than that of Canadian. Also, Canadian's average yield decreased in 1995 while AC's was rising. Obviously, Canadian's offensive strategy against Air Canada was responsible for its continuous financial losses. In constant Canadian dollar terms, Air Canada's average yield has decreased by about 13% since 1986, while Canadian's yield has decreased significantly more, by about 19% since 1986. Notice that AA's average yield in constant U.S. dollars decreased by about 12% from 1986.

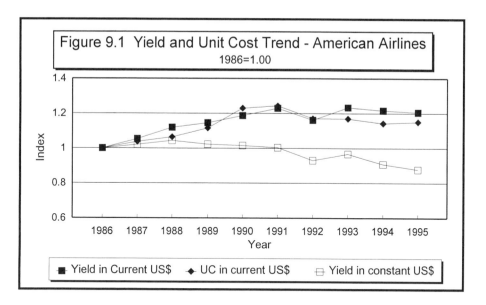

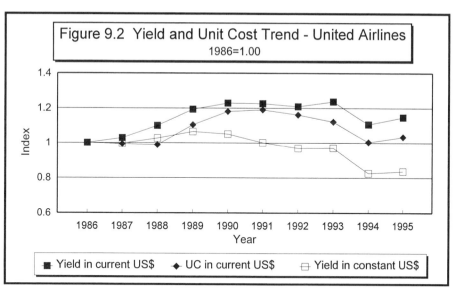

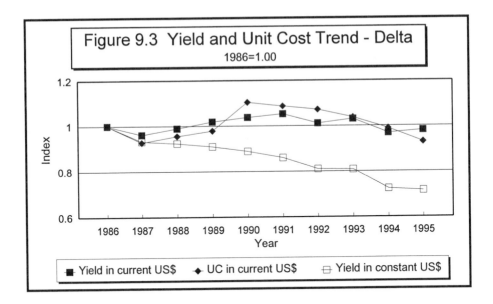

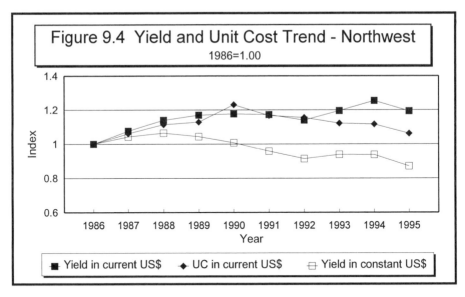

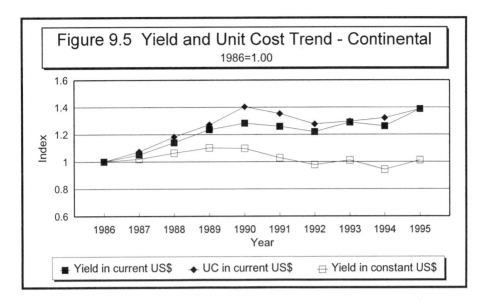

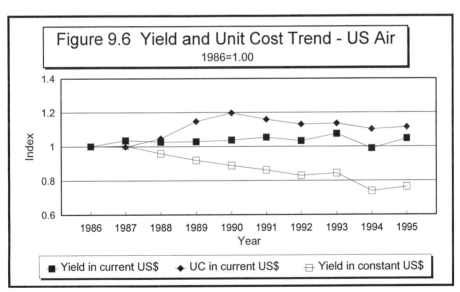

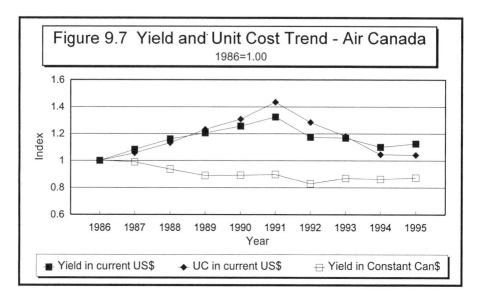

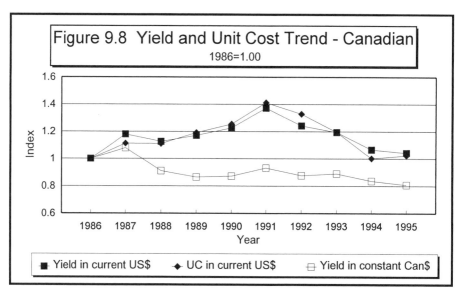

9.2   European Carriers

Figures 9.9-9.15 show average yield and unit cost indices (in current U.S. dollar terms) and the real yield index (measured in constant domestic currency) for the seven European carriers included in our study. In current U.S. dollar terms, between 1986 and 1995, average yields of British Airways (BA), SAS, KLM, Swissair and Iberia increased by 30%, 50%, 20%, 25%, and 51%, respectively. Lufthansa's yield increased by 20% between 1986 and 1994. In contrast, Air France's yield decreased by 3%. In terms of constant domestic currency, the real average yields of BA, Air France, SAS, KLM, Swissair and Iberia decreased by 20%, 45%, 4%, 32%, 37% and 20%, respectively. Lufthansa's real yield in Deutsche Marks decreased by 28% between 1986 and 1994.

BA, KLM and Swissair carefully managed changes in average yield and unit costs in order to secure profits. In fact, all three airlines managed to widen the gap between average yield and unit costs from 1990, ensuring increased profitability. It is remarkable that KLM and Swissair remain profitable despite the fact that their average yields, in real domestic currency terms, decreased by 32% and 38%, respectively, between 1986 and 1995. Lufthansa experienced difficulty during the early 1990s because of higher increases in unit costs than average yield, until it embarked on major restructuring in 1993. Lufthansa's fortune returned in 1994 when its average yield improved and average unit costs decreased. Air France experienced real financial difficulties throughout the sample period, particularly from 1990 when unit costs shot up by more than 20%, in terms of U.S. dollars. Increases in average yield were far short of increased costs. In particular, Air France saw its average yield, in constant French Francs, reduced by 45% between 1986 and 1995. Furthermore, most of this real yield deterioration was due to the 1991 economic recession.

SAS has always been a high cost airline, even after removing the effects of its short-haul route network and other differences (discussed in Chapter 8). Despite financial difficulties caused by higher unit cost increases relative to average yield increases, SAS did not execute any serious down-sizing or restructuring during the study period, 1986-95. In fact, the average yield, in constant Swedish Kronas, decreased by only about 3% between 1986 and 1995. SAS appears to have dealt with its rising unit costs by raising yields (increasing air fares). For example, SAS' average 1995 yield was about 2.5 times KLM's average yield.

Iberia has had financial difficulties, especially after 1989, when unit costs rose faster than average yield. Iberia's 1990 average yield, in constant value Pesetas, was about 20% lower than its 1986 yield.

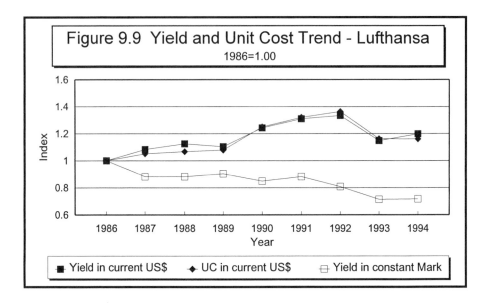

Figure 9.9 Yield and Unit Cost Trend - Lufthansa
1986=1.00

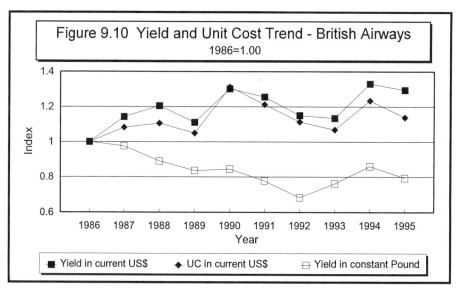

Figure 9.10 Yield and Unit Cost Trend - British Airways
1986=1.00

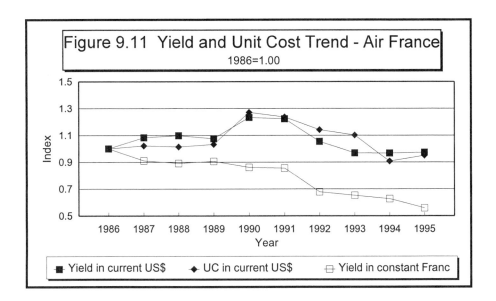

Figure 9.11 Yield and Unit Cost Trend - Air France
1986=1.00

- ■ Yield in current US$
- ◆ UC in current US$
- ⊟ Yield in constant Franc

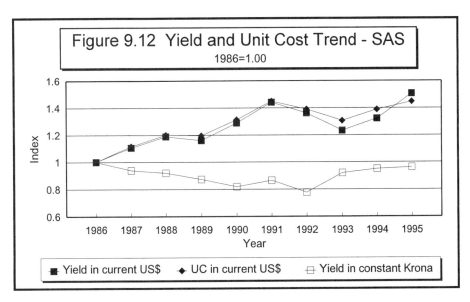

Figure 9.12 Yield and Unit Cost Trend - SAS
1986=1.00

- ■ Yield in current US$
- ◆ UC in current US$
- ⊟ Yield in constant Krona

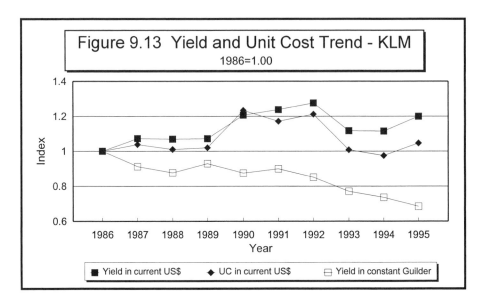

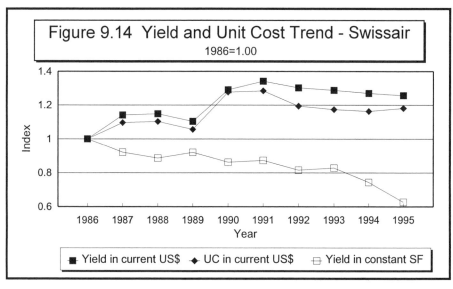

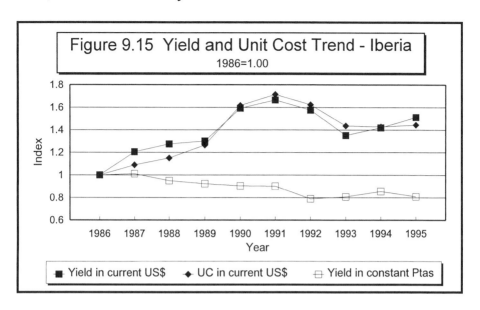

Figure 9.15 Yield and Unit Cost Trend - Iberia
1986=1.00

9.3 Asian and Australian Carriers

Figures 9.16-9.22 show average yield and unit cost indices (in current U.S. dollar terms) and the real yield index (measured in constant domestic currency) for the seven Asian and Australian carriers included in our study. In current U.S. dollar terms, between 1986 and 1995, average yields of Japan Airlines (JAL), Singapore Airlines (SIA), Korean Air (KAL), Cathay Pacific, Qantas and Thai Airways increased by 40%, 33%, 9%, 14%, 39% and 9%, respectively. And between 1988 and 1994, All Nippon Airways'(ANA) yield increased by about 7%.

During the 1986-95 period, Singapore and Thai were the only successful carriers that consistently managed unit cost increases within average yield increases. As a result, both carriers have seen consistent profits. Both SIA and Thai were able to maintain profits despite reduced average yields of 40% and 35%, respectively, in terms of their constant domestic currencies. In contrast, from 1992, JAL had difficulty containing unit cost increases within average yield increases. As a result, JAL incurred a series of substantial financial losses. JAL's average yield, in terms of constant Japanese Yen, decreased by about 35% between 1990 and 1995, indicating unbearable financial pressures on the carrier. ANA's average yield, in constant Japanese Yen, decreased by 35% between 1988 and 1995. This was probably due to two reasons. First, JAL was allowed to enter the Japanese domestic market and compete with ANA and Japan Air System (JAS). And second, ANA's output started to include long-haul international routes. Since 1988, ANA failed to lower its unit costs with decreases in average yield.

In terms of current U.S. dollars, Korean Air's unit cost rose rapidly until 1990, exceeding the rate at which average yield increased. From 1990, unit costs fell faster than decreases in average yield. As a result, Korean Air made profits in 1994 and 1995. As explained in Chapter 6, Korean Air increased productive efficiency over all other world carriers during the 1986-93 period. This efficiency gain allowed Korean Air to successfully deal with a 45% decrease in average yield, measured in constant Korean Wons, between 1986 and 1995. It is noteworthy that in terms of its constant domestic currency, Korean Air's average yield declined more (45%) than that of Japan Airlines (30%) between 1986 and 1995.

During the 1988-95 period, Cathay's unit cost index, measured in current U.S. dollars, increased by 32%, while its average yield increased by 14%. This left Cathay a financial challenge. Cathay's average yield, measured in constant Hong Kong dollars, decreased by over 36% between 1986 and 1995, mainly due to high inflation.

Measured in current U.S. dollars, Qantas was able to contain unit cost increases within average yield increases. As a result, the carrier was able to achieve profitability during most of the sample period. Its average yield, in current US dollars, increased by nearly 39% between 1986 and 1995, while in terms of constant Australian dollars, decreased by 30% between 1986 and 1990, and increased by about 17% between 1990 and 1995. This average yield increase from 1990 was at least partially influenced by the merger with Australian Airlines, which had a relatively short-haul domestic route network. Therefore, necessary unit cost adjustments by Qantas were significantly larger than Figure 9.21 would suggest.

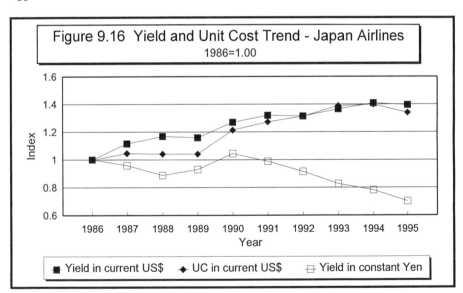

Figure 9.16 Yield and Unit Cost Trend - Japan Airlines
1986=1.00

Legend: ■ Yield in current US$ ◆ UC in current US$ ⊟ Yield in constant Yen

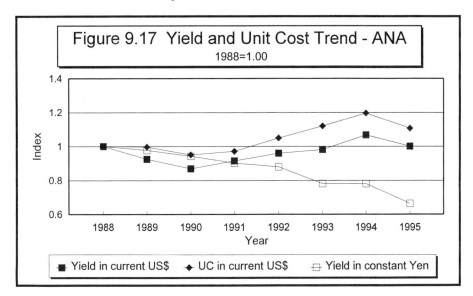

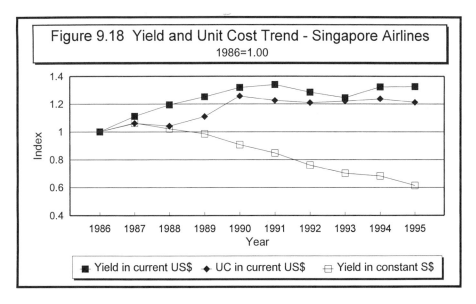

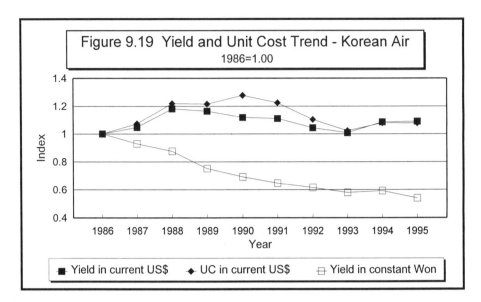

Figure 9.19 Yield and Unit Cost Trend - Korean Air
1986=1.00

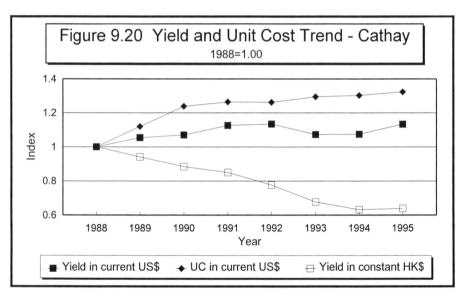

Figure 9.20 Yield and Unit Cost Trend - Cathay
1988=1.00

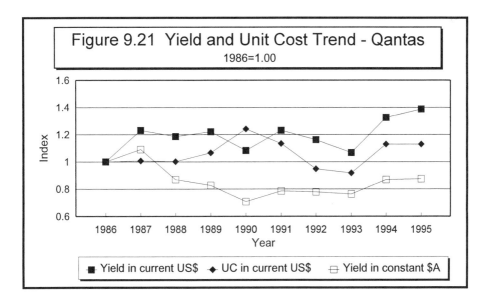

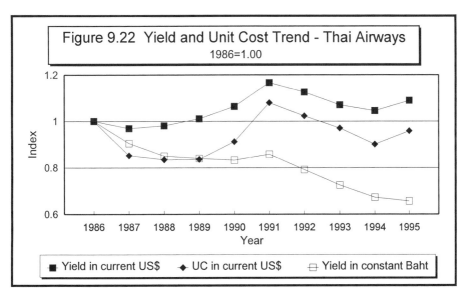

9.4   Comparison Among North American, European, and Asian Carriers

In order to compare across carriers in different continents, average yields and average unit cost indices for North American, European, and Asian carriers are reported in Figures 9.23, 9.24 and 9.25, respectively. These graphs show that between 1986 and 1995, the average yields in terms of the constant value domestic currencies of the North American, European, and Asian carriers decreased by 24%, 26% and 35%, respectively. This means that on average, the Asian carriers had to reduce unit costs significantly more than North American or European carriers.

Figure 9.23 show that between 1989 and 1992, the North American carriers' average unit cost measured in the current U.S. dollars has increased faster than the average yields. As a result, many North American carriers suffered financial losses during this period. Figure 9.24 show that since 1993, the year in which the Package #3 Liberalization measures were introduced in European Union countries, European carriers' average yield (in current U.S. dollar) has increased more than their average unit cost, implying that their profitability has improved since 1993. The improved economy may have contributed to their profitability as well. Figure 9.25 show that despite the fact that Asian carriers' input prices in current U.S. dollar terms have increased rapidly, on average, Asian carriers were able to contain their unit cost increases lower than the increases in their yields throughout the 1986-95 period.

9.5   Summary

In this chapter, average yields, unit costs, and financial performance were reviewed for each airline, and the airline groups by continent. The overall results are summarized below.

- With the exception of previously high cost carriers (USAir and Delta), the average yield for North American carriers, measured in constant domestic currency terms, decreased less than 20% during the 1986-95 period. USAir and Delta needed to make more painful adjustments than other carriers.
- With the exception of USAir and Canadian Airlines, all North American carriers managed to contain cumulative unit cost increases, in current U.S. dollar terms, within average yield increases by 1995, and thus, became profitable.
- Lufthansa, KLM, Swissair, and Air France were subjected to far greater average yield reductions, measured in constant domestic currencies, than any North American carrier. Despite this difficulty, Lufthansa, KLM, and Swissair were able to reduce unit costs to more than offset declines in real yield, and thus, remained largely profitable.
- British Airways, KLM, and Swissair were able to increase profitability due to their ability to maintain unit cost increases less than yield increases, in current U.S. dollar terms. In contrast, SAS, Iberia, and Air France needed further adjustment in order to deal with increasingly competitive markets.

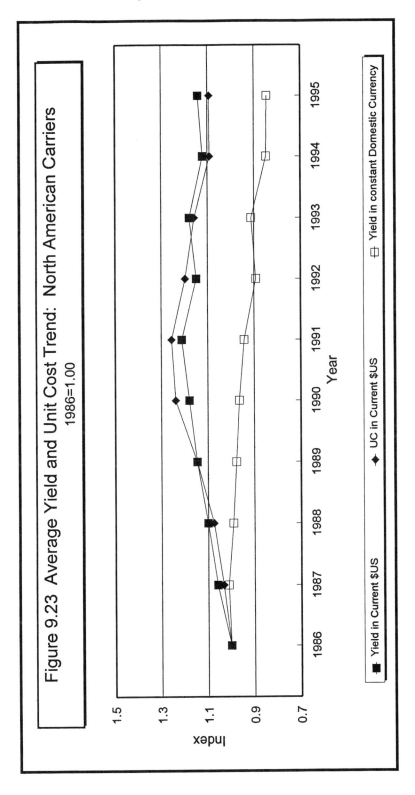

Figure 9.23 Average Yield and Unit Cost Trend: North American Carriers
1986=1.00

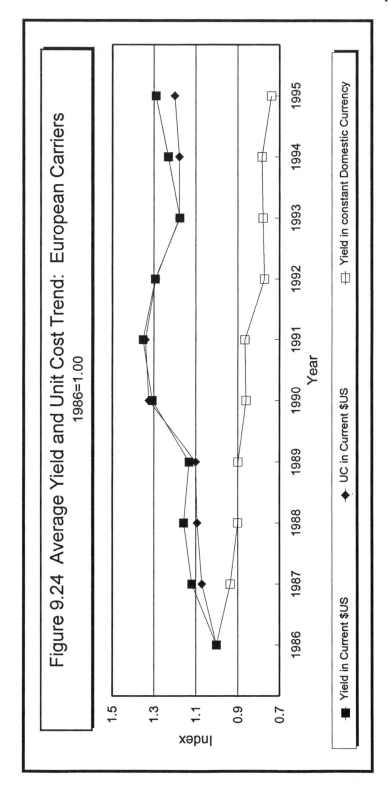

Figure 9.24 Average Yield and Unit Cost Trend: European Carriers
1986=1.00

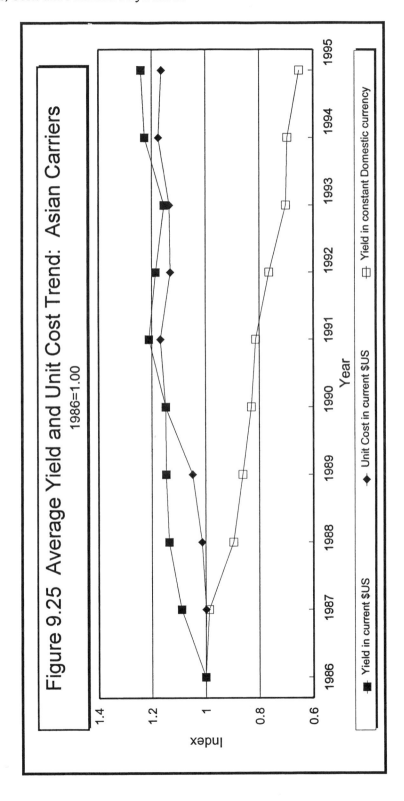

Figure 9.25 Average Yield and Unit Cost Trend: Asian Carriers
1986=1.00

- Overall, Asian carriers were subjected to far more reduction in their real yields, measured in domestic currencies, than North American carriers. However, with the exception of JAL and ANA, they managed to show profits soon after recovering from the severe economic recession. Singapore and Thai were consistently profitable during the entire 1986-95 period. Given that Cathay's unit costs, measured in current U.S. dollars, increased far more than average yield from 1988, Cathay's ability to maintain profitability in the future is questionable especially when it is excluded from serving markets to and from China.

- Despite the fact that Asian carriers' input prices in current U.S. dollar terms have increased rapidly, on average, Asian carriers were able to contain their unit cost increases lower than the increases in their yields throughout the 1986-95 period. As a result, although their real yields measured in domestic currency have declined far more than those of North American or European carriers, Asian carriers as an aggregate showed consistent profitability for most of the 1986-95 period.

- Since 1993, average carriers in North America, Europe, and Asia have improved their yields relative to changes in their unit costs.

Chapter 10
Summary and Conclusions

The focus of this book was to investigate cost competitiveness of the world's airlines. Cost competitiveness (or equivalently, cost advantage) is determined by productive efficiencies and input prices. Initially, we attempted to include nearly 50 airlines in our analysis, but it was impossible to compile complete and consistent time series data on many of these airlines. As a result, our analysis was confined to 22 major world airlines. It is regrettable that we could not compile reliable and systematic data for any of the South American carriers.

10.1 Summary of Findings

Since it is not possible to accurately summarize in a short chapter what we have reported in the past nine, below is an attempt to highlight what we have done in this book and what we found during the course of our study.

Chapter 2 set out to describe the relationship between world economic growth and air traffic growth by region. It highlighted the a strong pro-cyclical relationship between air passenger and freight traffic and the world economy. For example, air passenger traffic (measured in RPK) increased throughout the 1980s at an average rate of six percent per year, while world GDP growth averaged about 3 percent during the same period. This implies an income elasticity value of 2 for air travel demand. The economic recession and Gulf War caused a decline in air traffic in 1991, the first time in over forty years. The cyclical nature of air transport demand indicates that future traffic growth will occur in cycles. The strong correlation between economic growth and air traffic growth implies that at least until the year 2010, air traffic will grow faster in high growth Asia-Pacific economies than in any other region in the world. According to IATA's forecast of the Asia-Pacific region, its share of world total international scheduled passenger traffic will increase from 35.3% in 1993 to 51% in 2010. This implies that overall, airlines based in Asia-Pacific economies are likely to exhibit faster growths than airlines in other continents. Given a forecasted average of 7.2% annual growth, Asian carriers on average will double in size in 10 years. This compares with 50% growth expected for an average North American carrier in 10 years.

Average yields (revenue per unit of output) for airlines have decreased over time in real terms, and this trend is expected to continue in the future. Airlines that could not make sufficient unit cost reductions in response to deteriorating yields, for an extended period of time, either went bankrupt or are operating with state subsidies. Also, the very cyclical nature of air transport demand tends to lead many airlines to over-expand capacities during favorable economic times. As a result, some 70 carriers, including three large US carriers (Pan Am, Eastern, and Midway), went out of business since the mid-1980s. Several major carriers are still having financial difficulties, even after four years of economic growth.

It is clear that codeshare alliances between air carriers will continue to increase to set up and strengthen domestic (or continental) feeder networks and inter-continental service networks. Although most alliances have formed between two airlines, there has been a recent emergence of several multiple alliance groups (alliance families among several carriers). Examples of such groups are the recently announced 'Star' alliance group (United-Air Canada-Thai- Lufthansa-SAS) and American-British Airways alliance group

(AA-BA-Canadian-Qantas-TAT European-Deutsche BA). These groups started as bilateral alliances and later developed into multilateral alliance families.

On the other hand, by acquiring a minority share of partner airlines residing in foreign territories, several major airlines have encountered difficulties and risks in their attempts to form truly global service networks. A unidirectional investment in a foreign airline is like a double-edged sword. When the investment recipient does not perform well in its business, the investor airline is likely to lose most of their invested money. On the other hand, when the investment recipient succeeds and becomes financially competent, it may not want to be constrained by its investor partner's interference. Although memberships in alliance families are likely to undergo many changes in the future, alliance families are expected to form successful global service networks.

Chapter 3 reviewed historical developments and the current status of regulatory environments in the international air transport industry. In North America, particularly in the United States and Canada, domestic deregulation is firmly in place. The US government is actively seeking to create a more liberal aviation regime in international markets through its open skies initiatives. So far, it has reached open skies agreements with 12 European countries, Canada, six central American countries, and 4 Asian countries.

The single European aviation market came into existence on April 1, 1997. Any EU-registered carrier now has the right to run transborder and domestic services within any of the 15 EU member countries, as well as Norway and Iceland. National ownership rules of airlines have been replaced by EC ownership criteria. However, these changes have not been made to extra-EU agreements. Recently, the European Commission obtained the mandate to negotiate with the United States on behalf of the EU member states.

In the Asia-Pacific region, air transport deregulation has been much slower than in North America and Europe. One reason for the slow progress is that some Asian countries feel strongly that their bilateral air service agreements with the U.S. favor American carriers. Without renegotiating fairer agreements, it is pointless to talk about open skies agreements with the U.S. They feel that U.S. carriers enjoy benefits of *de facto* open skies because of a large number of fifth freedom rights enjoyed by some U.S. carriers (United, Northwest and Federal Express) in Asia. As a result, liberalization is almost entirely confined to domestic skies, and multilateralism, where it exists, remains within Asia-Pacific's borders. Protectionist attitudes still prevail among some governments in their policies towards aviation regulation. However, as Asia sees the benefits of open-skies blocs in Europe and North America, with global alliance service networks luring away their traditional passengers, and the U.S. increasing its role as an open skies hub nation, progress will be made in liberalizing Asian skies with the rest of the world.

Chapter 4 provided a preliminary analysis of operating and network characteristics, and input factor prices for airlines included in our study. It also examined the relationship between exchange rate fluctuations and input prices, and the growing global sourcing of input factors.

Asian carriers, with the exception of JAL and ANA, generally enjoy lower input prices than their North American and European counterparts in almost all input categories. European carriers, on average, pay higher input prices, particularly for non-labour inputs. Labour and materials input prices illustrated a clear upward trend over the sample period, while fuel and aircraft prices showed considerable fluctuations. Exchange rate changes have had significant impacts on input prices for some carriers. In the future, global sourcing will reduce some variations in input prices among airlines, and thus, increase competitive pressures on airlines.

Chapter 5 examined efficiency with which airlines use production inputs. This was done after removing the effects of variables which are beyond managerial control. In general, Asian carriers enjoyed higher efficiency of labor inputs than North American and European counterparts. European carriers, however, had higher fuel and aircraft efficiencies while North American carriers achieved higher efficiencies in purchasing and using materials and services. It was noted that productivity or efficiency of a certain input (e.g., labor) may depend on the degree to which other inputs are used, such as labor-saving investment on aircraft and automation. For a complete picture of airline efficiency, we thus stressed the need to look at productive efficiencies of all inputs together.

In Chapter 6, overall productive efficiencies of the sample airlines were measured and compared using two common approaches. First, total factor productivity (TFP) is computed, and then, effects of the variables beyond managerial control are removed from 'gross' TFP measures. The remainder, 'residual TFP' index, is comparable across airlines and over time within an airline. The second alternative approach is to derive an overall efficiency index directly from stochastic frontier production functions, estimated from the data econometrically.

Major U.S. carriers were found to be generally more efficient than Asian carriers, which in turn, were more efficient than European carriers. However, major European and Asian carriers achieved considerably higher productivity growth than their North American counterparts during our sample period. As a result, the productivity gap between North American carriers and other carriers diminished significantly. In 1993, U.S. carriers, on average, were 12% more efficient than European carriers and 4% more efficient than Asian carriers. However, average productive efficiency levels of three aggressive Asian carriers (SIA, KAL and Cathay) reached the same level as the three U.S. mega carriers (United, American and Delta).

For airlines competing in common markets, competition tends to lead to convergence of productive efficiencies. For example, in 1993, there was little difference between residual TFP levels of American, United, and Delta in North America. And in Asia, similar observations were evident for Singapore, Korean Air, and Cathay. Our results also show that European aviation liberalization, which began in 1987, appears to have produced substantial productivity gains for European carriers, and on average, government ownership has significant negative impacts on airline productive efficiencies.

Chapter 7 provided a preliminary analysis of airline cost structures and the effects exogenous factors on airline costs. In 1995, average shares of labor, fuel, capital, and purchased materials and services input, as a portion of total airline costs, were as follows:

Input	*N. America*	*Europe*	*Asia*
Labor	32.5%	32.5%	20.0%
Fuel	11.2%	9.2%	12.6%
Capital	17.1%	13.1%	15.3%
Materials	39.2%	45.2%	52.1%

With a few exceptions, fuel cost shares generally declined during the sample period.

Capital cost shares showed a general downward trend for North American and European carriers, but remained mostly unchanged for Asian carriers. Materials cost shares generally increased over time, probably due to the growing practice of out-sourcing in the airline industry. The cost of all outsourced inputs are counted as the materials input .There was no discernable pattern for direction of labor cost shares.

Asian carriers, excluding JAL and ANA, generally had considerably lower unit costs than North American carriers, which in turn had substantially lower unit costs than European carriers. For most airlines, unit costs peaked around 1990-1991 recession, and declined thereafter.

Chapter 8 measured and compared airline cost competitiveness, which depends on input prices and productive efficiencies. Observed unit cost differentials across airlines and over time within an airline, were decomposed into the effects of differences in input prices, productive efficiencies, and variables beyond managerial control (stage length and size and mix of output). Unit cost differentials attributable to differences in input price and productive efficiencies were used as indicators of cost competitiveness (CC). American Airlines (AA) was used as the benchmark carrier to compare all other airlines.

Asian carriers (except JAL and ANA) are generally more cost competitive than U.S. mega carriers, while Northwest and Continental are on par with some Asian carriers. Lower input prices are the dominant reason for Asian carriers' cost competitiveness. However, because their input prices have increased faster than those in the US, over time, their cost advantage, relative to AA, has decreased (except KAL and Qantas). Korean Air and Qantas improved cost competitiveness relative to AA despite rising input prices by significantly improving productive efficiencies. JAL and ANA are significantly less cost competitive than AA, due mainly to their higher input prices. In 1993, major European carriers had 7% (BA) - 42% (SAS) cost disadvantages compared to AA because of combined effects of higher input prices and lower productive efficiencies. However, on average, growth rates of European carriers' productive efficiency were higher than AA during the 1986-93 period. Exchange rate has had significant impacts on some carriers' cost competitiveness. For example, had the Japanese Yen exchange rate remained at its 1986 level, in 1993, JAL would have had only an 8 percent cost disadvantage relative to AA, instead of an actual 53 percent disadvantage.

In 1993, AA, United, and Delta were similar in cost competitiveness, while Northwest and Continental enjoyed substantial cost advantages over AA. USAir was the least cost competitive among the North American carriers, due primarily to its lower productive efficiency and slightly higher labour prices. Air Canada and Canadian had about 8.5% and 5% cost disadvantages relative to AA, respectively, due to lower productive efficiencies. Their cost advantages from lower labour prices was overwhelmed by lower efficiencies.

In the past, input prices have generally been more important than productive efficiencies in determining carrier cost competitiveness. However, the importance of input prices is likely to diminish over time as airlines increase global sourcing of labour, materials, services and other inputs, and as input prices in developing and Newly Industrialized Countries (NICs) continue to rise faster than in developed economies. Also, increasing global sourcing of inputs and services tends to equalize some input prices between airlines. Therefore, productive efficiencies will become progressively more important in determining airline cost competitiveness.

In Chapter 9, average yields, unit costs, and financial performance were reviewed for each airline individually, and as a group for each geographic region. With the exception of previous high cost carriers (USAir and Delta), the average real yield for North American carriers, measured in constant domestic currency terms, decreased less than 20% during the 1986-95 period. USAir and Delta needed to make more painful adjustments than other carriers because their yields fell more sharply. With the exception of USAir and Canadian Airlines, all other major North American carriers managed to contain their cumulative unit cost increases, in current U.S. dollar terms, to less than yield increases between 1986 and 1995, and thus, became profitable.

Measured in constant domestic currencies, Lufthansa, KLM, Swissair, and Air France were subjected to far greater yield reductions, than any North American carriers. Despite this difficulty, Lufthansa, KLM, and Swissair were able to reduce real unit costs to more than offset drastic declines in real yields, and thus, became profitable. British Airways, KLM, and Swissair have seen consistent profits due to their ability to contain unit cost increases (in current U.S. dollars) within yield increases. In contrast, SAS, Iberia, and Air France needed further restructuring for cost reduction.

Overall, Asian carriers were subjected to far more reduction in real yields (measured in constant value domestic currencies) than North American or European carriers. However, with the exception of JAL and ANA, they managed to show profits soon after recovering from the severe economic recession. Singapore and Thai were consistently profitable during the entire 1986-95 period. Despite the fact that Asian carriers' input prices, in current U.S. dollars, have increased rapidly, Asian carriers, on average, were able to contain unit cost increases to a lower level than yield increases throughout the 1986-95 period.

10.2   Conclusions

The findings of this study lead us to conclude the following:
●   Given forecasted rapid growths, within 10 years, Asian carriers, on average, are likely to double in size if they and their regulators adopt proper strategies so as not not lose market shares to powerful, newly emerged global alliance groups. In contrast, within 10 years, North American carriers, on average, are expected to grow by about 50%. Therefore, the relative power within the air transport industry will shift to Asian carriers.

●   Overall, North American carriers did not achieve any significant productive efficiency improvements during the 1986-93 period. The three U.S. mega carriers were very similar in productive efficiencies and unit cost competitiveness. Among North American carriers in our sample, Northwest and Canadian improved productive efficiency the most. Northwest was also the most productively efficient carrier in North America. Continental still enjoys over 10% cost advantage over U.S. mega carriers, but the gap has been narrowing over time. Both Air Canada and Canadian have significantly lower productive efficiencies as compared to U.S. mega carriers. At least in 1993, USAir was the highest cost carrier in North America (20% higher than U.S. mega carriers). And Air Canada and Canadian had significant unit cost disadvantages relative to U.S. mega carriers. Although Canadian shows up as having a cost advantage relative to Air Canada, part of the gap occurs because we were unable to include Canadian's extraordinary financing costs. Still, we believe that Canadian has some cost advantage over Air Canada due to higher productive efficiencies.

• Productive efficiencies of aggressive Asia-Pacific carriers (SIA, Korean Air, and Cathay) and Qantas reached the level of U.S. mega carriers (United, American and Delta) in 1993. In particular, Singapore and Korean Air enjoyed substantial unit cost advantages relative to U.S. mega carriers. These carriers are expected to gain market shares in the future. Qantas rapidly and consistently improved its productive efficiency, and as a result, improved cost competitiveness, to nearly reach the level of U.S mega carriers in 1993. On the other hand, Cathay Pacific has not improved its productive efficiency by any significant measure since 1988. Although Cathay is still cost competitive relative to U.S. mega carriers, its nearly 20% cost advantage enjoyed in 1988 has steadily eroded over time. Needless to say, Cathay's future depends greatly on China's future aviation policy towards Hong Kong.

→ • The series of liberalization measures undertaken by the European Commission since 1987 has had significant positive effects on European airlines' productive efficiencies. All seven European carriers included in our sample improved productive efficiencies to varying degrees. British Airways improved productive efficiency the most during the 1986-93 period. KLM, Swissair, Lufthansa and British Airways are among the group approaching U.S. mega carriers' productive efficiency levels. But, some distance (5-15%) still exists before they reach the efficiency levels of the U.S. mega carriers. In terms of cost competitiveness, BA and KLM are top among European carriers. But even these two carriers have some cost disadvantage (5-10%) relative to the U.S. mega carriers. Lufthansa, Iberia and Air France have about 20% cost disadvantage relative to U.S. mega carriers. Swissair and SAS have about a 40% cost disadvantage relative to U.S. mega carriers while Iberia and SAS are the least efficient European carriers in our sample. Air France will need to improve yields.

• Although international airline markets have been liberalizing for some time, there has been room for inefficient and high-cost airlines to survive or even see profits. However, as air transport liberalization continues, such room is being closed. Therefore, it is becoming increasingly important for airlines to improve productive efficiencies and control costs.

→ • Some carriers lose money even though they are more efficient and have lower costs than competitors. This occurs mainly because they fail to properly manage yields. That is, they fail to properly price their airline seats. An example appears to be Canadian Airlines International who competes with Air Canada in Canada's domestic market, Canada-U.S. transborder markets, and other international markets. Both carriers have essentially similar markets and serve similar route networks (similar domestic-international mix and similar average stage length, etc.). Canadian enjoys higher productive efficiencies and has lower unit costs than Air Canada. But Canadian has been continuously losing money since 1989 while Air Canada has recovered profitability from 1994. Evidence presented in Chapter 9 indicates that Air Canada has managed to keep yields about 10% higher than Canadian. Even in very competitive markets, clever pricing and yield management can improve a carrier's average yield significantly higher than its competitors.

This highlights the importance for carriers to price intelligently as well as improve productivity and cost competitiveness. Canadian needs to improve the seat pricing. On the other hand, Air Canada needs to further improve productive efficiencies.

● In North America, the three U.S. mega carriers and Northwest have overall managed productivities and unit costs well. Continental, on the other hand, has experienced declining productivity and seen its huge cost advantages diminish. But Continental still has about a 12% cost advantage over the mega carriers. In Europe, KLM, British Airways, and Lufthansa have well managed their productivities and unit costs. Although Swissair has well managed its productivity, it continues to be a high cost carrier because of its home currency appreciation. And in Asia and Oceania, Singapore, Korean Air, and Qantas have well managed productivity and unit costs. They are poised to grow and gain market shares.

10.3 Further Research

As noted in several places in the text, unfortunately we were not able to account for service quality differences between airlines or service quality changes over time. As long as consumers are willing to pay more for higher quality of service, quality should be reflected in productivity and unit cost measurements. One way of accomplishing this is to inflate output quantity for high quality service providers. If there is consistent objective data on service quality for all carriers and all years in our sample, this can be accomplished. Unfortunately, we were unable to collect such quality of service data, and thus could not reflect it in our productivity and unit cost measures. Therefore, efficiency results reported in Chapter 6 and cost competitiveness measures reported in Chapter 8, are likely to be biased against airlines that produce consistently higher quality of service than 'average' carriers, and biased in favor of airlines that produce consistently inferior quality of services. In order to avoid such biases, consistent and objective data on service quality should be compiled in the future.

In measuring productive efficiencies and unit cost competitiveness, we attempted to remove effects of differences in network and market characteristics, which are largely beyond managerial control. Although we believe that average flight stage length, output size and mix, and average load factor which are taken into account in our study are important variables, there could be other variables that need controlling. For example, a knowledgeable and respected airline executive suggested that the intensity of airport congestion experienced by an airline is also an important factor to be considered. We agree . But, we would be able to account for this factor only if consistent data on the percentage of each carrier's flights or traffic originating from, destined to and transiting via severely congested airports, was available. Again, we were not able to collect such data. Therefore, our productivity and unit cost results should be again viewed with some caution.

In measuring productive efficiency, we used two alternative methods: a regression analysis on TFP indices, and estimation of stochastic frontier production functions. We also attempted to conduct some limited experiments to estimate stochastic frontier cost functions, but were unable to obtain reasonable empirical results using this approach. This approach would have allowed us to decompose unit costs into sources, and also, measure productive efficiency in one step. It is worth further exploring this approach in future research.

A new study accounting for all of the above shortcomings of the current one would undoubtedly improve empirical results. However, it is our view that our current results, in totality, have made significant contributions in evaluating and comparing productive efficiencies and cost competitiveness of the world's major airlines. For a few airlines, it was difficult for us to reconcile numbers we obtained from our analysis with what we believe *a priori* about productive efficiencies and unit cost competitiveness. We felt somewhat uneasy to rank airlines based on numbers obtained from econometric analysis of the data. It is a similar uneasy feeling of having to rank students in a class solely on the basis of a final examination score without a teacher's supplementary subjective evaluation. We only hope that airlines ranked low in productive efficiency and/or cost competitiveness scale will understand and forgive us, or even better, encourage us to improve our results by providing us with additional insight and information we may have carelessly neglected.

References

Aigner, D. C.A.K. Lovell, and P. Schmidt (1977), "Formulation and Estimation of Stochastic Frontier Production Function Models", *Journal of Econometrics*, 6, pp.21-37

Air Transport Association of America (1995), *International Affairs Memoranda*, April 13, July 27, and December 8, Washington, D.C.

Airline Business (1996), "A Clearer Direction", June, pp.22-51

AVMARK, Inc. *AVMARK Newsletter*, Lolo, Montana, various issues.

Ballantyne, T. (1996), "Asia's Liberal Minority in the Process to Open Up the Asia-Pacific Market to US and Other Airlines", *Airlines Business*, September 1996, Vol. 12, No.9, 96-97

Baltagi, Badi .H., J. M. Griffin, and D. P. Rich (1995), "Airline Deregulation: the Cost Pieces of the Puzzle", *International Economic Review*, Vol. 36, No.1, February, 245-258

Barla, P. and S. Perelman (1989), "Technical Efficiency in Airlines under Regulated and Deregulated Environments", *Annals and Public and Cooperative Economics*, 60, No. 1, pp.103-124.

Barnard, B. (1996), "EU Wins the Right to Cut Air Deals with the US", *Journal of Commerce*, June 18, 1996, 1A

Battese, G.E. and T.J. Coelli (1988), "Prediction of Firm-level Technical Efficiencies with a Generalized Frontier Production Function and Panel Data", *Journal of Econometrics*, 38, 387-399

Battese, G. E. and T.J.Coelli (1992), "Frontier Production Functions, Technical Efficiency and Panel Data, with Application to Paddy Farmers in India", *The Journal of Productivity Analysis*, 3, pp.153-169.

Battese, G.E. and T. J. Coelli (1995), "A Model for Technical Inefficiency Effects in a Stochastic Frontier Production Function for Panel Data", *Empirical Economics*, 20, pp.325-332

Bauer, P. W.(1990), "Recent Develoments in the Econometric Estimation of Frontiers", *Journal of Econometrics*, 46(1/2), pp.39-56.

Boeing Commercial Airplane Group (1997), *Current Market Outlook: world air travel demand and airplane supply requirements*, Seattle, Washington, USA

Bruning, E.R. (1991), "Market Liberalization and Operating Efficiency in the International Aviation Industry", *International Journal of Transport Economics*, Vol.XVIII, No.3, October, pp259-274

Burgess, L. (1996), "US, Thailand Reach Agreement on Bilateral Aviation Rights", *Journal of Commerce*, January 22,1996, 2B

Caves, Douglas W. and L.R. Christensen (1988), "The Importance of Economies of Scale, Capacity Utilization, and Density in Explaining Interindustry Differences in Productivity Growth", *The Logistics and Transportation Review*, Vol. 24, No. 1, March, 3-32.

Caves, D.W., L.R. Christensen, and W.E. Diewert (1982), Multilateral Comparisons of Output, Input, and Productivity Using Superlative Index Numbers, *Economic Journal*, **92**, 73-86.

Caves, D.W., L. R. Christensen, M.W. Tretheway (1981), U.S. Trunk Air Airlines, 1972-

208

1977: A Multilateral Comparison of Total Factor Productivity, In *Productivity Measurement in Regulated Industries* (T. G. Cowing and R.E. Stevenson, ed.), 47-77, Academic Press, New York.

Caves, Douglas W., L.R. Christensen, and M.W. Tretheway (1984), "Economies of Density Versus Economies of Scale: Why Trunk and Local Service Airline Costs Differ", *Rand Journal of Economics*, 15, 471-489.

Caves, D.W., L.R. Christensen, M.W. Tretheway, and R.J Windle (1987), An Assessment of the Efficiency Effects of U.S. Airline Deregulation via an International Comparison, In *Public Regulation: New Perspectives on Institutions and Policies* (E.E. Bailey, ed.), 285-320, MIT Press, Cambridge, Mass.

Christensen, L.R. and D.W. Jorgenson (1969), "The Measurement of U.S. Real Capital Input, 1929-1967", *The Review of Income and Wealth*, Series 15, No. 1, 293-320

Coelli, T., S. Perelman, and E. Romano (1996), "Airlines, Environment and Technical Efficiency: An International Comparative Study", CREPP Discussion paper 96/10, University of Liege, Liege, Belgium

Comité des Sages (1994), *Expanding Horizons: Civil Aviation in Europe, an Action Programme for the Future,* The European Commission, Brussels.

Denny, M. and M., Fuss (1983), "A General Approach to Intertemporal and Interspatial Productivity Comparisons", *Journal of Econometrics*, 23(3), 315-30.

Distexhe, Veronica and S. Perelman (1993), "Technical Efficiency and Productivity Growth in an Era of Deregulation: the Case of Airlines", a paper presented at the *Third European Workshop on Efficiency and Productivity Measurement*, CORE, Belgium, October.

Doganis, R. (1991), *Flying Off Course: the Economics of International Airlines*, 2nd Edition, Harper Collins Academic (London, UK)

Doyle, Peter, J. Saunders, and V. Wong (1992), "Competition in Global Markets: A Case Study of American and Japanese Competition in the British Market", *Journal of International Business Studies*, 23 (3), 419-442

Dresner, M. and T.H. Oum (1997), "The Effect of Liberalized Air Transport Bilaterals on Foreign Visitor Volumne and Traffic Diversion: the case of Canada", *Proceedings of the 32nd Annual Conference of Canadian Transportation Research Forum*, May 25-28, Toronto, Canada, 180-210

Ehrlich, I., G. Gallais-Hamonno, Z. Liu, and R. Lutter (1994), Productivity Growth and Firm Ownership: An Analytical and Empirical Investigation, *Journal of Political Economy*, Vol. 102, No. 5, 1006-1038

Encaoua, D. (1991), Liberalizing European Airlines: Cost and Factor Productivity Evidence, *International Journal of Industrial Organization*, 9, 109-124.

Estrin, S. and V. Pérontin (1991), "Does Ownership Always Matter ?", *International Journal of Industrial Organization*, Vol. 9, No.1, 55-72

European Commission (1979), *Civil Aviation Memorandum No.1 - The Contribution of the European Communities to the Development of Air Transport Services,* European Commission: Brussels

European Commission (1984), *Civil Aviation Memorandum No.2 - Progress towards the Development of a Community Air Transport Policy,* COM (84) 72, Final, European Commission: Brussels

Försund, F.R., C.A.K. Lovell and P. Schmidt (1980), "A Survey of Frontier Production Functions and of Their Relationship to Efficiency Measurement", *Journal of Econometrics*, 13, 5-25.

Fuss, Melvyn A. and L. Waverman (1992), *Cost and Productivity in Automobile Production: the challenge of Japanese Efficiency*, Cambridge University Press, New York, USA

Gillen, D.W., T.H. Oum and M.W. Tretheway (1985), *Airline Cost and Performance: Implications for Public and Industry Policies*, Centre for Transportation Studies, University of British Columbia, Vancouver, B.C., Canada.

Gillen, D. W., T.H. Oum and M.W. Tretheway (1989), "Privatization of Air Canada: Why It is Necessary in a Deregulated Environment", Canadian Public Policy, Vol. XV, No. 3 (September), 285-299.

Gillen, D.W., T.H. Oum and M.W. Tretheway (1990), "Airline Cost Structure and Policy Implications", *Journal of Transport Economics and Policy*, Vol. 24, No.2, May, 9-34.

Gong, B.-H. and R.C. Sickles (1992), "Finite Sample Evidence on the Performance of Stochastic Frontiers and Data Envelopment Analysis Using Panel Data", *Journal of Econometrics*, 51, pp259-284

Good, David H. and E. L. Rhodes (1991), "Productive Efficiency, Technological Change and the Competitiveness of U.S. Airlines in the Pacific Rim", *Journal of the Transportation Research Forum*, Vol. 31, No.2, 347-358

Good, D.H., M.I. Nadiri, L.H. Röller, and R.C. Sickles (1993), Efficiency and Productivity Growth Comparisons of European and U.S. Air Airlines: A First Look at the Data, *The Journal of Productivity Analysis*, 4, 115-125.

Good, D.H., L.H. Röller, and R.C. Sickles (1995), Airline Efficiency Differences between Europe and the US: Implications for the Pace of EC Integration and Domestic Regulation, *European Journal of Operational Research*, 80 (1), January, 508-518.

Greene, W.H. (1990), "A Gamma Distributed Stochastic Frontier Model", *Journal of Econometrics*, 46,141-163.

Greene, W.H. (1993), "The Econometric Approach to Efficiency Analysis", in H.O. Fried, C.A. Knox Lovell, and S.S. Schmidt eds. *The Measurement of Productive Efficiency: Techniques and Applications*, Oxford University Press, pp.68-119.

Grosskopf, S. (1993), "Efficiency and Productivity", in H.O. Fried, C.A. Knox Lovell, and S.S. Schmidt eds. *The Measurement of Productive Efficiency: Techniques and Applications*, Oxford University Press, pp.160-194.

Haanappel, P.P.C. (1983), *Pricing and Capacity Determination in International Air Transport*, Kluwer: Deventer, The Netherlands.

Hendersen, D. (1992), "Searching for Magic in '92", *Air Transport World*, Jan., page 31.

Hill, L. (1997), "Bilateral Ballistics", *Air Transport World*, 2/97, 53-61

Hooper, P. (1997), "Airline Market in Asia - the domestic/international regulatory interface", working paper, Institute of Transport Studies, The University of Sydney.

IATA, (1991), *The Economic Benefits of Air Transport*, Geneva.

Jha, R. and B.S. Sahni (1992), "Towards Measuring Airline Technical Inefficiency: the Case of Canadian Airlines Industry", *International Journal of Transport*

210

Economics, Vol. XIX, No. 1, February, pp45-59

Jondrow, J., C.A.K.Lovell, I. Materov, and P. Schmidt (1982), "On the Estimation of Technical Inefficiency in the Stochastic Frontier Production Function", *Journal of Econometrics*, 19, pp.233-238

Julius,D. (1996) "International Aviation and National Competitiveness," memo,British Airways, June.

Kayal, M. and L. Burgess (1996), "Last Minute Negotiations Keep Flight Plans up in Air", *Journal of Commerce*, July 1, 1996, 4B

Kayal, M. (1997a), "European Airlines Flying in Open Skies", *Journal of Commerce*, March 31 1997, 1B

Kayal, M. (1997b), "US, Japan Aim for a Blueprint in Final Round of Aviation Talks", *Journal of Commerce*, April 9, 1997, 1A

Kayal, M. (1997c), "Italy Promises Air Pact with US", *Journal of Commerce*, April 10, 1997. 2B

Kayal, M. (1997d), "Britain, Japan: Formidable Head Winds to Open Skies", *Journal of Commerce*, April 14, 1997, 1A

Knibb, D. (1993), "Asia's Little Tigers: an Expanding Group of Regional Carriers is Taking a Greater Share of Intra-Asia Passenger Traffic as Markets Matures", *Airline Business*, October, 1993

Kumbhakar, S.C., S. Ghosh, and J. McGuckin (1991), "A Generalized Production Frontier Approach for Estimating Determinants of Inefficiency in US Dairy Farms", *Journal of Business and Economic Statistics*, 9, pp.279-286.

Liu, Z. (1995), "The Comparative Performance of Public and Private Enterprises: the case of British Ports", *Journal of Transport Economic and Policy*, Vol. 29, No. 3 (September), 263-274.

Loeb, S., E. Bruning, and M. Hu (1994), "Government's Role in a Post-Deregulated Environment: the Case of International Aviation", *Proceedings of the 29th Canadian Transportation Research Forum*, Victoria, B.C., May

Lovell, C.A. Knox (1993), "Production Frontiers and Productive Efficiency", in H.O. Fried, C.A. Knox Lovell, and S.S. Schmidt eds. *The Measurement of Productive Efficiency: Techniques and Applications*, Oxford University Press, pp.3-67.

Lovell, C.A. K. and P. Schmidt (1988), "A Comparison of Alternative Approaches to the Measurement of Productive Efficiency", in A. Dogramaci and R. Färe (eds) *Applications of Modern Production Theory: Efficiency and Productivity*, Boston: Kluwer Academic Publishers, pp.3-32.

Mackey, M. (1997), "Goodbye to the Orient", *Air Transport World*, 1/97, 54-55

Madala, G.S. (1979), " A Note on the Form of the Production Function and Productivity", in *Measurement and Interpretation of Productivity*, National Research Council, Washington, D.C., pp. 309-317.

McKenna, E. (1996), "U.S. Shifts Air Accord Efforts to Asia After Big Year in Europe", *Aviation Daily*, Vol. 323, No. 3, January 4, 1996, p. 20.

Meeusen, W. and J. van den Broeck (1977), "Efficiency Estimation from Cobb-Douglas Production Functions with Composed Error", *International Economic Review*, 8, pp.435-444

Mefford, Robert N. (1986), "Determinants of Productivity Differences in International Manufacturing", *Journal of International Business Studies*, 17(1), 63-82

Mitchell, Donna (1991), "Canadian International Air Transport Historical Background and Current Policy", *Ministerial Task Force on International Air Policy: Research Reports*, Transport Canada: Ottawa

Norman, V. and S. Strandenes (1994), " Deregulation of Scandanavian Airlines: A Case Study of the Oslo-Stockholm Route", in Krugman, P. and A. Smith, eds. *Empirical Studies of Strategic Trade Policy*, Chicago: University of Chicago Press, 1994.

Oum,T.H. (1980), *Demand for Freight Transportation with a Special Emphasis on Model Choice in Canada*, Center for Transportation Studies, University of British Columbia, Vancouver, Canada.

Oum, T.H. (1992), "An Analysis of the Division of the World Policy for the Canadian Airline Industry", an unpublished report, Faculty of Commerce and Business, the University of British Columbia, Vancouver, Canada

Oum, T.H., M.W. Tretheway, and Y. Zhang (1991), "Capacity Utilization and Measurement of Scale Economies" *Journal of Business and Economic Statistics*, vol.9, No.1, pp.137-141.

Oum, T. H. and C. Yu (1995), "A Productivity Comparison of the World's Major Airlines", *Journal of Air Transport Management*, Vol. 2, No. 3/4, pp.181-195.

Oum, Tae H., and Y. Zhang (1991), "Utilization of Quasi-Fixed Inputs and Estimation of Cost Functions," *Journal of Transport Economics and Policy*, vol.25, No.2, 121-134.

Oum, Tae H., and Y. Zhang (1995), "Competition and Allocative Efficiency: The Case of Competition in the U.S. Telephone Industry," *Review of Economics and Statistics*, vol. 77, no.1, 82-96.

Porter, Michael E. (1990), *The Competitive Advantage of Nations*, The Free Press, New York, N,Y.

Ray, Subhash C. and X. Hu (1993), "A Nonparametric Decomposition of the Malmquist Productivity Index: A Study of Airlines' Data", a paper presented at the *Third European Workshop on Productivity*, CORE, Belgium, October.

Reed, A. (1996), "The Gains also Rise", *Air Transport World*, October, pp.87-88.

Reifschneider, D. And R. Stevenson (1991), "Systematic Departures from the Frontier: a Framework for the Analysis of Firm Inefficiency", *International Economic Review*, Vol. 32, No.3, pp.715-723

Schmidt, P. (1986), "Frontier Production Functions", *Econometric Reviews*, 4(2), 289-328

Stevenson, R.E. (1980) "Likelihood Functions for Generalized Stochastic Frontier Estimation", *Journal of Econometrics*, 13, pp.57-66

Summers, R. and A. Heston (1991), The Penn World Table (Mark 5): An Expanded Set of International Comparisons, 1950-1988, *Quarterly Journal of Economics*, Vol. 106, Issue 2, May, 327-368.

Toyne, B., J.S. Arpan, A.H. Barnett, D.A. Ricks, T.A. Shimp (1984), "The International Competitiveness of the U.S. Textile Mill Products Industry: Corporate Strategies for the Future", *Journal of International Business Studies*, 15(4), 145-165

Transport Canada (1994), *Canada's International Air Transportation Policy: Statement by the Minister of Transport*, December 20, Ottawa

Transport Canada (1995), *Second Carrier Designation Policy*, March 10, Ottawa

Trepo, G.X. (1997), "Air France: History of a Turnaround", a paper presented at the First

212

Conference of the Air Transport Research Group of the World Conference on Transport Research Society, Vancouver, Canada, June 25-27, 1997.

Tretheway, M. and T. H. Oum (1992), *Airline Economics: Foundations for Strategy and Policy*, Centre for Transportation Studies, University of British Columbia, Vancouver, Canada.

Windle, Robert J. (1991), "The World's Airlines: A Cost and Productivity Comparison", *Journal of Transport Economics and Policy*, Vol.25, No.1, January, 31-49.

Wright, Richard W., and D.A. Ricks (1994), "Trends in International Business Research: Twenty-Five Years Later", *Journal of International Business Studies*, 25 (4), 687-701

Yu, C. (1997), "The Effects of Exogenous Variables in Efficiency Measurement - A Monte Carlo Study", *European Journal of Operational Research*, forthcoming

About the Authors

Tae Hoon (Tae) Oum, MBA, PhD

Dr. Oum is Van Dusen Foundation Professor of Management, Faculty of Commerce and Business Administration, The University of British Columbia, Vancouver, Canada. Prior to joining UBC in 1983, he taught at School of Business, Queen's University at Kingston, Canada. He was also a Visiting Professor at Osaka University, Korea Transport Institute, and Shanghai Jiaotong University.

Dr.Oum specializes in policy analysis, demand modelling, cost and productivity analysis, globalization and competitiveness issues of transportation and telecommunications industry. He has published and edited over 20 books and several major conference proceedings, published over 100 papers in academic and business journals, have written numerous research reports for Canadian and foreign government agencies, major corporations, and the World Bank on the transportation and teleommuncations policy and management issues. He has also advised many Canadian and other government agencies, major airlines, and telecommunications firms in North America, Asia and Europe.

He is the president of the Air Transport Research Group (ATRG) and the chairman of the Publication Committee of the World Conference on Transport Research (WCTR) Society. He serves on Editorial Boards of <u>Journal of Transport Economics and Policy</u>, <u>Transport Policy</u>, <u>Journal of Air Transport Management</u>, <u>Journal of Air Transportation World Wide</u>, and <u>Transportation Research E</u>. He is also a member of International Advisory Group (IAG) of the Pacific Economic Cooperation Council (PECC).

Chunyan Yu, Msc (Business Administration), PhD

Dr. Yu is a post-doctoral research associate at the Faculty of Commerce and Business Administration, The University of British Columbia. She specializes in productivity and efficiency analysis, cost structures and other industrial organization issues, and public policy analysis involving transportation industries. She has published a number of papers in various international journals. She has conducted a number of applied econometric research projects on air and rail transportation industries including a report to The Royal Commission on National Passenger Transportation of Canada. She has written her PhD dissertation entitled, "A Comparative Study of Alternative Methods for Efficiency Measurement with Applications to the Transportation Industry" (University of British Colubmia, Vancouver, Canada: 1995).

Index

Transportation Research, Economics and Policy

1. I. Salomon, P. Bovy and J-P. Orfeuil (eds.):
   A Billion Trips a Day. Tradition and Transition
   in European Travel Patterns. 1993   ISBN 0-7923-2297-5
2. P. Nijkamp and E. Blaas: *Impact Assessment and*
   Evaluation in Transportation Planning. 1994   ISBN 0-7923-2648-2
3. B. Johansson and L.-G. Mattson (eds.):
   Road Pricing: Theory, Empirical Assessment,
   and Policy. 1995   ISBN 0-7923-3134-6
4. Y. Hayashi and J. Roy:
   Transport, Land-Use and the Environment.
   1996   ISBN 0-7923-3728-X
5. T.F. Golob, R. Kitamura and L. Long:
   Panels for Transportation Planning. Methods
   and Applications. 1997.   ISBN 0-7923-9966-8
6. T.H. Oum and C. Yu:
   Winning Airlines: Productivity and Cost
   Competitiveness of the World's Major Airlines   ISBN 0-7923-8010-X

Kluwer Academic Publishers — Boston / Dordrecht / London